American Casebook Series
Hornbook Series and Basic Legal Texts
Nutshell Series

of

WEST PUBLISHING COMPANY
P.O. Box 64526
St. Paul, Minnesota 55164–0526

ACCOUNTING

Faris' Accounting and Law in a Nutshell, 377 pages, 1984 (Text)

Fiflis, Kripke and Foster's Teaching Materials on Accounting for Business Lawyers, 3rd Ed., 838 pages, 1984 (Casebook)

Siegel and Siegel's Accounting and Financial Disclosure: A Guide to Basic Concepts, 259 pages, 1983 (Text)

ADMINISTRATIVE LAW

Davis' Cases, Text and Problems on Administrative Law, 6th Ed., 683 pages, 1977 (Casebook)

Gellhorn and Boyer's Administrative Law and Process in a Nutshell, 2nd Ed., 445 pages, 1981 (Text)

Mashaw and Merrill's Cases and Materials on Administrative Law–The American Public Law System, 2nd Ed., 976 pages, 1985 (Casebook)

Robinson, Gellhorn and Bruff's The Administrative Process, 3rd Ed., 978 pages, 1986 (Casebook)

ADMIRALTY

Healy and Sharpe's Cases and Materials on Admiralty, 2nd Ed., 876 pages, 1986 (Casebook)

Maraist's Admiralty in a Nutshell, 2nd Ed., 379 pages, 1988 (Text)

Schoenbaum's Hornbook on Admiralty and Maritime Law, Student Ed., 692 pages, 1987 (Text)

Sohn and Gustafson's Law of the Sea in a Nutshell, 264 pages, 1984 (Text)

AGENCY—PARTNERSHIP

Fessler's Alternatives to Incorporation for Persons in Quest of Profit, 2nd Ed., 326 pages, 1986 (Casebook)

AGENCY—PARTNERSHIP—Cont'd

Henn's Cases and Materials on Agency, Partnership and Other Unincorporated Business Enterprises, 2nd Ed., 733 pages, 1985 (Casebook)

Reuschlein and Gregory's Hornbook on the Law of Agency and Partnership, 625 pages, 1979, with 1981 pocket part (Text)

Selected Corporation and Partnership Statutes, Rules and Forms, 621 pages, 1987

Steffen and Kerr's Cases and Materials on Agency-Partnership, 4th Ed., 859 pages, 1980 (Casebook)

Steffen's Agency-Partnership in a Nutshell, 364 pages, 1977 (Text)

AGRICULTURAL LAW

Meyer, Pedersen, Thorson and Davidson's Agricultural Law: Cases and Materials, 931 pages, 1985 (Casebook)

ALTERNATIVE DISPUTE RESOLUTION

Kanowitz' Cases and Materials on Alternative Dispute Resolution, 1024 pages, 1986 (Casebook)

Riskin and Westbrook's Dispute Resolution and Lawyers, 223 pages, 1987 (Coursebook)

Riskin and Westbrook's Dispute Resolution and Lawyers, Abridged Ed., 223 pages, 1987 (Coursebook)

Teple and Moberly's Arbitration and Conflict Resolution, (The Labor Law Group), 614 pages, 1979 (Casebook)

AMERICAN INDIAN LAW

Canby's American Indian Law in a Nutshell, 2nd Ed., about 319 pages, 1988 (Text)

Getches and Wilkinson's Cases on Federal Indian Law, 2nd Ed., 880 pages, 1986 (Casebook)

List current as of July, 1988

T7202—1g

I

ANTITRUST LAW

Gellhorn's Antitrust Law and Economics in a Nutshell, 3rd Ed., 472 pages, 1986 (Text)

Gifford and Raskind's Cases and Materials on Antitrust, 694 pages, 1983 with 1985 Supplement (Casebook)

Hovenkamp's Hornbook on Economics and Federal Antitrust Law, Student Ed., 414 pages, 1985 (Text)

Oppenheim, Weston and McCarthy's Cases and Comments on Federal Antitrust Laws, 4th Ed., 1168 pages, 1981 with 1985 Supplement (Casebook)

Posner and Easterbrook's Cases and Economic Notes on Antitrust, 2nd Ed., 1077 pages, 1981, with 1984–85 Supplement (Casebook)

Sullivan's Hornbook of the Law of Antitrust, 886 pages, 1977 (Text)

See also Regulated Industries, Trade Regulation

ART LAW

DuBoff's Art Law in a Nutshell, 335 pages, 1984 (Text)

BANKING LAW

Lovett's Banking and Financial Institutions in a Nutshell, 2nd Ed., about 455 pages, 1988 (Text)

Symons and White's Teaching Materials on Banking Law, 2nd Ed., 993 pages, 1984, with 1987 Supplement (Casebook)

BUSINESS PLANNING

Painter's Problems and Materials in Business Planning, 2nd Ed., 1008 pages, 1984 with 1987 Supplement (Casebook)

Selected Securities and Business Planning Statutes, Rules and Forms, about 475 pages, 1987

CIVIL PROCEDURE

American Bar Association Section of Litigation—Reading on Adversarial Justice: The American Approach to Adjudication, edited by Landsman, 217 pages, 1988 (Coursebook)

Casad's Res Judicata in a Nutshell, 310 pages, 1976 (text)

Cound, Friedenthal, Miller and Sexton's Cases and Materials on Civil Procedure, 4th Ed., 1202 pages, 1985 with 1987 Supplement (Casebook)

Ehrenzweig, Louisell and Hazard's Jurisdiction in a Nutshell, 4th Ed., 232 pages, 1980 (Text)

Federal Rules of Civil-Appellate Procedure—West Law School Edition, about 600 pages, 1988

Friedenthal, Kane and Miller's Hornbook on Civil Procedure, 876 pages, 1985 (Text)

Kane's Civil Procedure in a Nutshell, 2nd Ed., 306 pages, 1986 (Text)

CIVIL PROCEDURE—Cont'd

Koffler and Reppy's Hornbook on Common Law Pleading, 663 pages, 1969 (Text)

Marcus and Sherman's Complex Litigation–Cases and Materials on Advanced Civil Procedure, 846 pages, 1985 (Casebook)

Park's Computer-Aided Exercises on Civil Procedure, 2nd Ed., 167 pages, 1983 (Coursebook)

Siegel's Hornbook on New York Practice, 1011 pages, 1978 with 1987 Pocket Part (Text)

See also Federal Jurisdiction and Procedure

CIVIL RIGHTS

Abernathy's Cases and Materials on Civil Rights, 660 pages, 1980 (Casebook)

Cohen's Cases on the Law of Deprivation of Liberty: A Study in Social Control, 755 pages, 1980 (Casebook)

Lockhart, Kamisar, Choper and Shiffrin's Cases on Constitutional Rights and Liberties, 6th Ed., 1266 pages, 1986 with 1988 Supplement (Casebook)—reprint from Lockhart, et al. Cases on Constitutional Law, 6th Ed., 1986

Vieira's Civil Rights in a Nutshell, 279 pages, 1978 (Text)

COMMERCIAL LAW

Bailey and Hagedorn's Secured Transactions in a Nutshell, 3rd Ed. about 390 pages, 1988 (Text)

Epstein, Martin, Henning and Nickles' Basic Uniform Commercial Code Teaching Materials, 3rd Ed., 704 pages, 1988 (Casebook)

Henson's Hornbook on Secured Transactions Under the U.C.C., 2nd Ed., 504 pages, 1979 with 1979 P.P. (Text)

Murray's Commercial Law, Problems and Materials, 366 pages, 1975 (Coursebook)

Nickles, Matheson and Dolan's Materials for Understanding Credit and Payment Systems, 923 pages, 1987 (Casebook)

Nordstrom, Murray and Clovis' Problems and Materials on Sales, 515 pages, 1982 (Casebook)

Nordstrom, Murray and Clovis' Problems and Materials on Secured Transactions, 594 pages, 1987 (Casebook)

Selected Commercial Statutes, about 1525 pages, 1988

Speidel, Summers and White's Teaching Materials on Commercial Law, 4th Ed., 1448 pages, 1987 (Casebook)

Speidel, Summers and White's Commercial Paper: Teaching Materials, 4th Ed., 578 pages, 1987 (Casebook)—reprint from Speidel, et al. Commercial Law, 4th Ed.

Speidel, Summers and White's Sales: Teaching Materials, 4th Ed., 804 pages, 1987 (Casebook)—reprint from Speidel, et al. Commercial Law, 4th Ed.

COMMERCIAL LAW—Cont'd

Speidel, Summers and White's Secured Transactions—Teaching Materials, 4th Ed., 485 pages, 1987 (Casebook)—reprint from Speidel, et al. Commercial Law, 4th Ed.

Stockton's Sales in a Nutshell, 2nd Ed., 370 pages, 1981 (Text)

Stone's Uniform Commercial Code in a Nutshell, 2nd Ed., 516 pages, 1984 (Text)

Uniform Commercial Code, Official Text with Comments, 1155 pages, 1987

Weber and Speidel's Commercial Paper in a Nutshell, 3rd Ed., 404 pages, 1982 (Text)

White and Summers' Hornbook on the Uniform Commercial Code, 3rd Ed., Student Ed., about 1200 pages, 1988 (Text)

COMMUNITY PROPERTY

Mennell and Boykoff's Community Property in a Nutshell, 2nd Ed., 432 pages, 1988 (Text)

Verrall and Bird's Cases and Materials on California Community Property, 5th Ed., about 587 pages, 1988 (Casebook)

COMPARATIVE LAW

Barton, Gibbs, Li and Merryman's Law in Radically Different Cultures, 960 pages, 1983 (Casebook)

Glendon, Gordon and Osakive's Comparative Legal Traditions: Text, Materials and Cases on the Civil Law, Common Law, and Socialist Law Traditions, 1091 pages, 1985 (Casebook)

Glendon, Gordon, and Osakwe's Comparative Legal Traditions in a Nutshell, 402 pages, 1982 (Text)

Langbein's Comparative Criminal Procedure: Germany, 172 pages, 1977 (Casebook)

COMPUTERS AND LAW

Maggs and Sprowl's Computer Applications in the Law, 316 pages, 1987 (Coursebook)

Mason's Using Computers in the Law: An Introduction and Practical Guide, 2nd Ed., 288 pages, 1988 (Text)

CONFLICT OF LAWS

Cramton, Currie and Kay's Cases-Comments-Questions on Conflict of Laws, 4th Ed., 876 pages, 1987 (Casebook)

Scoles and Hay's Hornbook on Conflict of Laws, Student Ed., 1085 pages, 1982 with 1986 P.P. (Text)

Scoles and Weintraub's Cases and Materials on Conflict of Laws, 2nd Ed., 966 pages, 1972, with 1978 Supplement (Casebook)

Siegel's Conflicts in a Nutshell, 469 pages, 1982 (Text)

CONSTITUTIONAL LAW

Barron and Dienes' Constitutional Law in a Nutshell, 389 pages, 1986 (Text)

Engdahl's Constitutional Federalism in a Nutshell, 2nd Ed., 411 pages, 1987 (Text)

Lockhart, Kamisar, Choper and Shiffrin's Cases-Comments-Questions on Constitutional Law, 6th Ed., 1601 pages, 1986 with 1988 Supplement (Casebook)

Lockhart, Kamisar, Choper and Shiffrin's Cases-Comments-Questions on the American Constitution, 6th Ed., 1260 pages, 1986 with 1988 Supplement (Casebook)—abridgment of Lockhart, et al. Cases on Constitutional Law, 6th Ed., 1986

Manning's The Law of Church-State Relations in a Nutshell, 305 pages, 1981 (Text)

Marks and Cooper's State Constitutional Law in a Nutshell, about 300 pages, 1988 (Text)

Miller's Presidential Power in a Nutshell, 328 pages, 1977 (Text)

Nowak, Rotunda and Young's Hornbook on Constitutional Law, 3rd Ed., Student Ed., 1191 pages, 1986 with 1988 Pocket Part (Text)

Rotunda's Modern Constitutional Law: Cases and Notes, 2nd Ed., 1004 pages, 1985 with 1988 Supplement (Casebook)

Williams' Constitutional Analysis in a Nutshell, 388 pages, 1979 (Text)

See also Civil Rights, Foreign Relations and National Security Law

CONSUMER LAW

Epstein and Nickles' Consumer Law in a Nutshell, 2nd Ed., 418 pages, 1981 (Text)

Selected Commercial Statutes, about 1525 pages, 1988

Spanogle and Rohner's Cases and Materials on Consumer Law, 693 pages, 1979, with 1982 Supplement (Casebook)

See also Commercial Law

CONTRACTS

Calamari & Perillo's Cases and Problems on Contracts, 1061 pages, 1978 (Casebook)

Calamari and Perillo's Hornbook on Contracts, 3rd Ed., 904 pages, 1987 (Text)

Corbin's Text on Contracts, One Volume Student Edition, 1224 pages, 1952 (Text)

Fessler and Loiseaux's Cases and Materials on Contracts, 837 pages, 1982 (Casebook)

Friedman's Contract Remedies in a Nutshell, 323 pages, 1981 (Text)

Fuller and Eisenberg's Cases on Basic Contract Law, 4th Ed., 1203 pages, 1981 (Casebook)

Hamilton, Rau and Weintraub's Cases and Materials on Contracts, 830 pages, 1984 (Casebook)

LAW SCHOOL PUBLICATIONS—Continued

CONTRACTS—Cont'd

Jackson and Bollinger's Cases on Contract Law in Modern Society, 2nd Ed., 1329 pages, 1980 (Casebook)

Keyes' Government Contracts in a Nutshell, 423 pages, 1979 (Text)

Schaber and Rohwer's Contracts in a Nutshell, 2nd Ed., 425 pages, 1984 (Text)

Summers and Hillman's Contract and Related Obligation: Theory, Doctrine and Practice, 1074 pages, 1987 (Casebook)

COPYRIGHT

See Patent and Copyright Law

CORPORATE FINANCE

Hamilton's Cases and Materials on Corporate Finance, 895 pages, 1984 with 1986 Supplement (Casebook)

CORPORATIONS

Hamilton's Cases on Corporations—Including Partnerships and Limited Partnerships, 3rd Ed., 1213 pages, 1986 with 1986 Statutory Supplement (Casebook)

Hamilton's Law of Corporations in a Nutshell, 2nd Ed., 515 pages, 1987 (Text)

Henn's Teaching Materials on Corporations, 2nd Ed., 1204 pages, 1986 (Casebook)

Henn and Alexander's Hornbook on Corporations, 3rd Ed., Student Ed., 1371 pages, 1983 with 1986 P.P. (Text)

Jennings and Buxbaum's Cases and Materials on Corporations, 5th Ed., 1180 pages, 1979 (Casebook)

Selected Corporation and Partnership Statutes, Rules and Forms, 621 pages, 1987

Solomon, Schwartz' and Bauman's Materials and Problems on Corporations: Law and Policy, 2nd Ed., 1391 pages, 1988 (Casebook)

CORRECTIONS

Krantz's Cases and Materials on the Law of Corrections and Prisoners' Rights, 3rd Ed., 855 pages, 1986 with 1988 Supplement (Casebook)

Krantz's Law of Corrections and Prisoners' Rights in a Nutshell, 2nd Ed., 386 pages, 1983 (Text)

Popper's Post-Conviction Remedies in a Nutshell, 360 pages, 1978 (Text)

Robbins' Cases and Materials on Post Conviction Remedies, 506 pages, 1982 (Casebook)

CREDITOR'S RIGHTS

Bankruptcy Code, Rules and Forms, Law School Ed., 792 pages, 1988

Epstein's Debtor-Creditor Law in a Nutshell, 3rd Ed., 383 pages, 1986 (Text)

Epstein, Landers and Nickles' Debtors and Creditors: Cases and Materials, 3rd Ed., 1059 pages, 1987 (Casebook)

CREDITOR'S RIGHTS—Cont'd

LoPucki's Player's Manual for the Debtor-Creditor Game, 123 pages, 1985 (Coursebook)

Riesenfeld's Cases and Materials on Creditors' Remedies and Debtors' Protection, 4th Ed., 914 pages, 1987 (Casebook)

White's Bankruptcy and Creditor's Rights: Cases and Materials, 812 pages, 1985, with 1987 Supplement (Casebook)

CRIMINAL LAW AND CRIMINAL PROCEDURE

Abrams', Federal Criminal Law and its Enforcement, 882 pages, 1986 (Casebook)

Carlson's Adjudication of Criminal Justice, Problems and References, 130 pages, 1986 (Casebook)

Dix and Sharlot's Cases and Materials on Criminal Law, 3rd Ed., 846 pages, 1987 (Casebook)

Federal Rules of Criminal Procedure—West Law School Edition, about 500 pages, 1988

Grano's Problems in Criminal Procedure, 2nd Ed., 176 pages, 1981 (Problem book)

Israel and LaFave's Criminal Procedure in a Nutshell, 4th Ed., 461 pages, 1988 (Text)

Johnson's Cases, Materials and Text on Criminal Law, 3rd Ed., 783 pages, 1985 (Casebook)

Johnson's Cases on Criminal Procedure, 859 pages, 1987 with 1988 Supplement (Casebook)

Kamisar, LaFave and Israel's Cases, Comments and Questions on Modern Criminal Procedure, 6th Ed., 1558 pages, 1986 with 1988 Supplement (Casebook)

Kamisar, LaFave and Israel's Cases, Comments and Questions on Basic Criminal Procedure, 6th Ed., 860 pages, 1986 with 1988 Supplement (Casebook)—reprint from Kamisar, et al. Modern Criminal Procedure, 6th ed., 1986

LaFave's Modern Criminal Law: Cases, Comments and Questions, 2nd Ed., 903 pages, 1988 (Casebook)

LaFave and Israel's Hornbook on Criminal Procedure, Student Ed., 1142 pages, 1985 with 1987 P.P. (Text)

LaFave and Scott's Hornbook on Criminal Law, 2nd Ed., Student Ed., 918 pages, 1986 (Text)

Langbein's Comparative Criminal Procedure: Germany, 172 pages, 1977 (Casebook)

Loewy's Criminal Law in a Nutshell, 2nd Ed., 321 pages, 1987 (Text)

Saltzburg's American Criminal Procedure, Cases and Commentary, 3rd Ed., 1302 pages, 1988 with 1988 Supplement (Casebook)

LAW SCHOOL PUBLICATIONS—Continued

CRIMINAL LAW AND CRIMINAL PROCEDURE—Cont'd

Uviller's The Processes of Criminal Justice: Investigation and Adjudication, 2nd Ed., 1384 pages, 1979 with 1979 Statutory Supplement and 1986 Update (Casebook)

Uviller's The Processes of Criminal Justice: Adjudication, 2nd Ed., 730 pages, 1979. Soft-cover reprint from Uviller's The Processes of Criminal Justice: Investigation and Adjudication, 2nd Ed. (Casebook)

Uviller's The Processes of Criminal Justice: Investigation, 2nd Ed., 655 pages, 1979. Soft-cover reprint from Uviller's The Processes of Criminal Justice: Investigation and Adjudication, 2nd Ed. (Casebook)

Vorenberg's Cases on Criminal Law and Procedure, 2nd Ed., 1088 pages, 1981 with 1987 Supplement (Casebook)

See also Corrections, Juvenile Justice

DECEDENTS ESTATES

See Trusts and Estates

DOMESTIC RELATIONS

Clark's Cases and Problems on Domestic Relations, 3rd Ed., 1153 pages, 1980 (Casebook)

Clark's Hornbook on Domestic Relations, 2nd Ed., Student Ed., 1050 pages, 1988 (Text)

Krause's Cases and Materials on Family Law, 2nd Ed., 1221 pages, 1983 with 1986 Supplement (Casebook)

Krause's Family Law in a Nutshell, 2nd Ed., 444 pages, 1986 (Text)

Krauskopf's Cases on Property Division at Marriage Dissolution, 250 pages, 1984 (Casebook)

ECONOMICS, LAW AND

Goetz' Cases and Materials on Law and Economics, 547 pages, 1984 (Casebook)

See also Antitrust, Regulated Industries

EDUCATION LAW

Alexander and Alexander's The Law of Schools, Students and Teachers in a Nutshell, 409 pages, 1984 (Text)

Morris' The Constitution and American Education, 2nd Ed., 992 pages, 1980 (Casebook)

EMPLOYMENT DISCRIMINATION

Jones, Murphy and Belton's Cases on Discrimination in Employment, 1116 pages, 1987 (Casebook)

Player's Cases and Materials on Employment Discrimination Law, 2nd Ed., 782 pages, 1984 (Casebook)

EMPLOYMENT DISCRIMINATION—Cont'd

Player's Federal Law of Employment Discrimination in a Nutshell, 2nd Ed., 402 pages, 1981 (Text)

Player's Hornbook on the Law of Employment Discrimination, Student Ed., 708 pages, 1988 (Text)

See also Women and the Law

ENERGY AND NATURAL RESOURCES LAW

Laitos' Cases and Materials on Natural Resources Law, 938 pages, 1985 (Casebook)

Rodgers' Cases and Materials on Energy and Natural Resources Law, 2nd Ed., 877 pages, 1983 (Casebook)

Selected Environmental Law Statutes, about 650 pages, 1988

Tomain's Energy Law in a Nutshell, 338 pages, 1981 (Text)

See also Environmental Law, Oil and Gas, Water Law

ENVIRONMENTAL LAW

Bonine and McGarity's Cases and Materials on the Law of Environment and Pollution, 1076 pages, 1984 (Casebook)

Findley and Farber's Cases and Materials on Environmental Law, 2nd Ed., 813 pages, 1985 with 1988 Supplement (Casebook)

Findley and Farber's Environmental Law in a Nutshell, 2nd Ed., about 348 pages, 1988 (Text)

Rodgers' Hornbook on Environmental Law, 956 pages, 1977 with 1984 pocket part (Text)

Selected Environmental Law Statutes, about 650 pages, 1988

See also Energy Law, Natural Resources Law, Water Law

EQUITY

See Remedies

ESTATES

See Trusts and Estates

ESTATE PLANNING

Lynn's Introduction to Estate Planning, in a Nutshell, 3rd Ed., 370 pages, 1983 (Text)

See also Taxation, Trusts and Estates

EVIDENCE

Broun, Meisenholder, Strong and Mosteller's Problems in Evidence, 3rd Ed., about 420 pages, 1988 (Problem book)

Cleary, Strong, Broun and Mosteller's Cases and Materials on Evidence, 4th Ed., about 1050 pages, 1988 (Casebook)

Federal Rules of Evidence for United States Courts and Magistrates, 370 pages, 1987

LAW SCHOOL PUBLICATIONS—Continued

EVIDENCE—Cont'd

Graham's Federal Rules of Evidence in a Nutshell, 2nd Ed., 473 pages, 1987 (Text)

Kimball's Programmed Materials on Problems in Evidence, 380 pages, 1978 (Problem book)

Lempert and Saltzburg's A Modern Approach to Evidence: Text, Problems, Transcripts and Cases, 2nd Ed., 1232 pages, 1983 (Casebook)

Lilly's Introduction to the Law of Evidence, 2nd Ed., 585 pages, 1987 (Text)

McCormick, Sutton and Wellborn's Cases and Materials on Evidence, 6th Ed., 1067 pages, 1987 (Casebook)

McCormick's Hornbook on Evidence, 3rd Ed., Student Ed., 1156 pages, 1984 with 1987 P.P. (Text)

Rothstein's Evidence, State and Federal Rules in a Nutshell, 2nd Ed., 514 pages, 1981 (Text)

Saltzburg's Evidence Supplement: Rules, Statutes, Commentary, 245 pages, 1980 (Casebook Supplement)

FEDERAL JURISDICTION AND PROCEDURE

Currie's Cases and Materials on Federal Courts, 3rd Ed., 1042 pages, 1982 with 1985 Supplement (Casebook)

Currie's Federal Jurisdiction in a Nutshell, 2nd Ed., 258 pages, 1981 (Text)

Federal Rules of Civil-Appellate Procedure—West Law School Edition, about 600 pages, 1988

Forrester and Moye's Cases and Materials on Federal Jurisdiction and Procedure, 3rd Ed., 917 pages, 1977 with 1985 Supplement (Casebook)

Redish's Cases, Comments and Questions on Federal Courts, 878 pages, 1983 with 1988 Supplement (Casebook)

Vetri and Merrill's Federal Courts, Problems and Materials, 2nd Ed., 232 pages, 1984 (Problem Book)

Wright's Hornbook on Federal Courts, 4th Ed., Student Ed., 870 pages, 1983 (Text)

FOREIGN RELATIONS AND NATIONAL SECURITY LAW

Franck and Glennon's United States Foreign Relations Law: Cases, Materials and Simulations, 941 pages, 1987 (Casebook)

FUTURE INTERESTS

See Trusts and Estates

HEALTH LAW

See Medicine, Law and

IMMIGRATION LAW

Aleinikoff and Martin's Immigration Process and Policy, 1042 pages, 1985 with 1987 Supplement (Casebook)

IMMIGRATION LAW—Cont'd

Weissbrodt's Immigration Law and Procedure in a Nutshell, 345 pages, 1984 (Text)

INDIAN LAW

See American Indian Law

INSURANCE

Dobbyn's Insurance Law in a Nutshell, 281 pages, 1981 (Text)

Keeton's Cases on Basic Insurance Law, 2nd Ed., 1086 pages, 1977

Keeton and Wydiss' Insurance Law, Student Ed., about 1024 pages, 1988 (Text)

Wydiss and Keeton's Course Supplement to Keeton and Wydiss's Insurance Law, 425 pages, 1988 (Casebook)

York and Whelan's Cases, Materials and Problems on General Practice Insurance Law, 2nd Ed., about 811 pages, 1988 (Casebook)

INTERNATIONAL LAW

Buergenthal International Human Rights in a Nutshell, about 275 pages, 1988 (Text)

Buergenthal and Maier's Public International Law in a Nutshell, 262 pages, 1985 (Text)

Folsom, Gordon and Spanogle's International Business Transactions – a Problem-Oriented Coursebook, 1160 pages, 1986, with Documents Supplement (Casebook)

Folsom, Gordon and Spanogle's International Business Transactions in a Nutshell, 3rd Ed., about 484 pages, 1988 (Text)

Henkin, Pugh, Schachter and Smit's Cases and Materials on International Law, 2nd Ed., 1517 pages, 1987 with Documents Supplement (Casebook)

Jackson and Davey's Legal Problems of International Economic Relations, 2nd Ed., 1269 pages, 1986, with Documents Supplement (Casebook)

Kirgis' International Organizations in Their Legal Setting, 1016 pages, 1977, with 1981 Supplement (Casebook)

Weston, Falk and D'Amato's International Law and World Order—A Problem Oriented Coursebook, 1195 pages, 1980, with Documents Supplement (Casebook)

INTERVIEWING AND COUNSELING

Binder and Price's Interviewing and Counseling, 232 pages, 1977 (Text)

Shaffer and Elkins' Interviewing and Counseling in a Nutshell, 2nd Ed., 487 pages, 1987 (Text)

INTRODUCTION TO LAW STUDY

Dobbyn's So You Want to go to Law School, Revised First Edition, 206 pages, 1976 (Text)

LAW SCHOOL PUBLICATIONS—Continued

INTRODUCTION TO LAW STUDY—Cont'd

Hegland's Introduction to the Study and Practice of Law in a Nutshell, 418 pages, 1983 (Text)

Kinyon's Introduction to Law Study and Law Examinations in a Nutshell, 389 pages, 1971 (Text)

See also Legal Method and Legal System

JURISPRUDENCE

Christie's Text and Readings on Jurisprudence—The Philosophy of Law, 1056 pages, 1973 (Casebook)

JUVENILE JUSTICE

Fox's Cases and Materials on Modern Juvenile Justice, 2nd Ed., 960 pages, 1981 (Casebook)

Fox's Juvenile Courts in a Nutshell, 3rd Ed., 291 pages, 1984 (Text)

LABOR LAW

Gorman's Basic Text on Labor Law—Unionization and Collective Bargaining, 914 pages, 1976 (Text)

Grodin, Wollett and Alleyne's Collective Bargaining in Public Employment, 3rd Ed., (The Labor Law Group), 430 pages, 1979 (Casebook)

Leslie's Labor Law in a Nutshell, 2nd Ed., 397 pages, 1986 (Text)

Nolan's Labor Arbitration Law and Practice in a Nutshell, 358 pages, 1979 (Text)

Oberer, Hanslowe, Andersen and Heinsz' Cases and Materials on Labor Law—Collective Bargaining in a Free Society, 3rd Ed., 1163 pages, 1986 with Statutory Supplement (Casebook)

Rabin, Silverstein and Schatzki's Labor and Employment Law: Cases, Materials and Problems in the Law of Work, (The Labor Law Group), about 1000 pages, 1988 with Statutory Supplement (Casebook)

See also Employment Discrimination, Social Legislation

LAND FINANCE

See Real Estate Transactions

LAND USE

Callies and Freilich's Cases and Materials on Land Use, 1233 pages, 1986 (Casebook)

Hagman's Cases on Public Planning and Control of Urban and Land Development, 2nd Ed., 1301 pages, 1980 (Casebook)

Hagman and Juergensmeyer's Hornbook on Urban Planning and Land Development Control Law, 2nd Ed., Student Ed., 680 pages, 1986 (Text)

Wright and Gitelman's Cases and Materials on Land Use, 3rd Ed., 1300 pages, 1982, with 1987 Supplement (Casebook)

LAND USE—Cont'd

Wright and Wright's Land Use in a Nutshell, 2nd Ed., 356 pages, 1985 (Text)

LEGAL HISTORY

Presser and Zainaldin's Cases on Law and American History, 855 pages, 1980 (Casebook)

See also Legal Method and Legal System

LEGAL METHOD AND LEGAL SYSTEM

Aldisert's Readings, Materials and Cases in the Judicial Process, 948 pages, 1976 (Casebook)

Berch and Berch's Introduction to Legal Method and Process, 550 pages, 1985 (Casebook)

Bodenheimer, Oakley and Love's Readings and Cases on an Introduction to the Anglo-American Legal System, 2nd Ed., 166 pages, 1988 (Casebook)

Davies and Lawry's Institutions and Methods of the Law—Introductory Teaching Materials, 547 pages, 1982 (Casebook)

Dvorkin, Himmelstein and Lesnick's Becoming a Lawyer: A Humanistic Perspective on Legal Education and Professionalism, 211 pages, 1981 (Text)

Greenberg's Judicial Process and Social Change, 666 pages, 1977 (Casebook)

Kelso and Kelso's Studying Law: An Introduction, 587 pages, 1984 (Coursebook)

Kempin's Historical Introduction to Anglo-American Law in a Nutshell, 2nd Ed., 280 pages, 1973 (Text)

Murphy's Cases and Materials on Introduction to Law—Legal Process and Procedure, 772 pages, 1977 (Casebook)

Reynolds' Judicial Process in a Nutshell, 292 pages, 1980 (Text)

See also Legal Research and Writing

LEGAL PROFESSION

Aronson, Devine and Fisch's Problems, Cases and Materials on Professional Responsibility, 745 pages, 1985 (Casebook)

Aronson and Weckstein's Professional Responsibility in a Nutshell, 399 pages, 1980 (Text)

Mellinkoff's The Conscience of a Lawyer, 304 pages, 1973 (Text)

Pirsig and Kirwin's Cases and Materials on Professional Responsibility, 4th Ed., 603 pages, 1984 (Casebook)

Schwartz and Wydick's Problems in Legal Ethics, 2nd Ed., 341 pages, 1988 (Casebook)

Selected Statutes, Rules and Standards on the Legal Profession, 449 pages, 1987

Smith's Preventing Legal Malpractice, 142 pages, 1981 (Text)

Wolfram's Hornbook on Modern Legal Ethics, Student Edition, 1120 pages, 1986 (Text)

LAW SCHOOL PUBLICATIONS—Continued

LEGAL RESEARCH AND WRITING

Child's Materials and Problems on Drafting Legal Documents, 286 pages, 1988 (Text)

Cohen's Legal Research in a Nutshell, 4th Ed., 450 pages, 1985 (Text)

Cohen and Berring's How to Find the Law, 8th Ed., 790 pages, 1983. Problem book by Foster, Johnson and Kelly available (Casebook)

Cohen and Berring's Finding the Law, 8th Ed., Abridged Ed., 556 pages, 1984 (Casebook)

Dickerson's Materials on Legal Drafting, 425 pages, 1981 (Casebook)

Felsenfeld and Siegel's Writing Contracts in Plain English, 290 pages, 1981 (Text)

Gopen's Writing From a Legal Perspective, 225 pages, 1981 (Text)

Mellinkoff's Legal Writing—Sense and Nonsense, 242 pages, 1982 (Text)

Ray and Ramsfield's Legal Writing: Getting It Right and Getting It Written, 250 pages, 1987 (Text)

Rombauer's Legal Problem Solving—Analysis, Research and Writing, 4th Ed., 424 pages, 1983 (Coursebook)

Squires and Rombauer's Legal Writing in a Nutshell, 294 pages, 1982 (Text)

Statsky's Legal Research and Writing, 3rd Ed., 257 pages, 1986 (Coursebook)

Statsky and Wernet's Case Analysis and Fundamentals of Legal Writing, 3rd Ed., about 450 pages, 1988 (Text)

Teply's Programmed Materials on Legal Research and Citation, 2nd Ed., 358 pages, 1986. Student Library Exercises available (Coursebook)

Weihofen's Legal Writing Style, 2nd Ed., 332 pages, 1980 (Text)

LEGISLATION

Davies' Legislative Law and Process in a Nutshell, 2nd Ed., 346 pages, 1986 (Text)

Eskridge and Frickey's Cases on Legislation, 937 pages, 1987 (Casebook)

Nutting and Dickerson's Cases and Materials on Legislation, 5th Ed., 744 pages, 1978 (Casebook)

Statsky's Legislative Analysis and Drafting, 2nd Ed., 217 pages, 1984 (Text)

LOCAL GOVERNMENT

Frug's Cases and Materials on Local Government Law, about 1000 pages, 1988 (Casebook)

McCarthy's Local Government Law in a Nutshell, 2nd Ed., 404 pages, 1983 (Text)

Reynolds' Hornbook on Local Government Law, 860 pages, 1982, with 1987 pocket part (Text)

Valente's Cases and Materials on Local Government Law, 3rd Ed., 1010 pages, 1987 (Casebook)

MASS COMMUNICATION LAW

Gillmor and Barron's Cases and Comment on Mass Communication Law, 4th Ed., 1076 pages, 1984 (Casebook)

Ginsburg's Regulation of Broadcasting: Law and Policy Towards Radio, Television and Cable Communications, 741 pages, 1979 with 1983 Supplement (Casebook)

Zuckman, Gaynes, Carter and Dee's Mass Communications Law in a Nutshell, 3rd Ed., 538 pages, 1988 (Text)

MEDICINE, LAW AND

Furrow, Johnson, Jost and Schwartz' Health Law: Cases, Materials and Problems, 1005 pages, 1987 (Casebook)

King's The Law of Medical Malpractice in a Nutshell, 2nd Ed., 342 pages, 1986 (Text)

Shapiro and Spece's Problems, Cases and Materials on Bioethics and Law, 892 pages, 1981 (Casebook)

Sharpe, Fiscina and Head's Cases on Law and Medicine, 882 pages, 1978 (Casebook)

MILITARY LAW

Shanor and Terrell's Military Law in a Nutshell, 378 pages, 1980 (Text)

MORTGAGES

See Real Estate Transactions

NATURAL RESOURCES LAW

See Energy and Natural Resources Law

NEGOTIATION

Edwards and White's Problems, Readings and Materials on the Lawyer as a Negotiator, 484 pages, 1977 (Casebook)

Peck's Cases and Materials on Negotiation, 2nd Ed., (The Labor Law Group), 280 pages, 1980 (Casebook)

Williams' Legal Negotiation and Settlement, 207 pages, 1983 (Coursebook)

OFFICE PRACTICE

Hegland's Trial and Practice Skills in a Nutshell, 346 pages, 1978 (Text)

Strong and Clark's Law Office Management, 424 pages, 1974 (Casebook)

See also Computers and Law, Interviewing and Counseling, Negotiation

OIL AND GAS

Hemingway's Hornbook on Oil and Gas, 2nd Ed., Student Ed., 543 pages, 1983 with 1986 P.P. (Text)

Kuntz, Lowe, Anderson and Smith's Cases and Materials on Oil and Gas Law, 857 pages, 1986, with Forms Manual (Casebook)

Lowe's Oil and Gas Law in a Nutshell, 2nd Ed., about 402 pages, 1988 (Text)

See also Energy and Natural Resources Law

LAW SCHOOL PUBLICATIONS—Continued

PARTNERSHIP

See Agency—Partnership

PATENT AND COPYRIGHT LAW

Choate, Francis and Collins' Cases and Materials on Patent Law, 3rd Ed., 1009 pages, 1987 (Casebook)

Miller and Davis' Intellectual Property—Patents, Trademarks and Copyright in a Nutshell, 428 pages, 1983 (Text)

Nimmer's Cases on Copyright and Other Aspects of Entertainment Litigation, 3rd Ed., 1025 pages, 1985 (Casebook)

PRODUCTS LIABILITY

Fischer and Powers' Cases and Materials on Products Liability, 685 pages, 1988 (Casebook)

Noel and Phillips' Cases on Products Liability, 2nd Ed., 821 pages, 1982 (Casebook)

Phillips' Products Liability in a Nutshell, 3rd Ed., 307 pages, 1988 (Text)

PROPERTY

Bernhardt's Real Property in a Nutshell, 2nd Ed., 448 pages, 1981 (Text)

Boyer's Survey of the Law of Property, 766 pages, 1981 (Text)

Browder, Cunningham and Smith's Cases on Basic Property Law, 4th Ed., 1431 pages, 1984 (Casebook)

Bruce, Ely and Bostick's Cases and Materials on Modern Property Law, 1004 pages, 1984 (Casebook)

Burke's Personal Property in a Nutshell, 322 pages, 1983 (Text)

Cunningham, Stoebuck and Whitman's Hornbook on the Law of Property, Student Ed., 916 pages, 1984 with 1987 P.P. (Text)

Donahue, Kauper and Martin's Cases on Property, 2nd Ed., 1362 pages, 1983 (Casebook)

Hill's Landlord and Tenant Law in a Nutshell, 2nd Ed., 311 pages, 1986 (Text)

Kurtz and Hovenkamp's Cases and Materials on American Property Law, 1296 pages, 1987 with 1988 Supplement (Casebook)

Moynihan's Introduction to Real Property, 2nd Ed., 239 pages, 1988 (Text)

Uniform Land Transactions Act, Uniform Simplification of Land Transfers Act, Uniform Condominium Act, 1977 Official Text with Comments, 462 pages, 1978

See also Real Estate Transactions, Land Use

PSYCHIATRY, LAW AND

Reisner's Law and the Mental Health System, Civil and Criminal Aspects, 696 pages, 1985 with 1987 Supplement (Casebooks)

REAL ESTATE TRANSACTIONS

Bruce's Real Estate Finance in a Nutshell, 2nd Ed., 262 pages, 1985 (Text)

Maxwell, Riesenfeld, Hetland and Warren's Cases on California Security Transactions in Land, 3rd Ed., 728 pages, 1984 (Casebook)

Nelson and Whitman's Cases on Real Estate Transfer, Finance and Development, 3rd Ed., 1184 pages, 1987 (Casebook)

Nelson and Whitman's Hornbook on Real Estate Finance Law, 2nd Ed., Student Ed., 941 pages, 1985 (Text)

Osborne's Cases and Materials on Secured Transactions, 559 pages, 1967 (Casebook)

REGULATED INDUSTRIES

Gellhorn and Pierce's Regulated Industries in a Nutshell, 2nd Ed., 389 pages, 1987 (Text)

Morgan, Harrison and Verkuil's Cases and Materials on Economic Regulation of Business, 2nd Ed., 666 pages, 1985 (Casebook)

See also Mass Communication Law, Banking Law

REMEDIES

Dobbs' Hornbook on Remedies, 1067 pages, 1973 (Text)

Dobbs' Problems in Remedies, 137 pages, 1974 (Problem book)

Dobbyn's Injunctions in a Nutshell, 264 pages, 1974 (Text)

Friedman's Contract Remedies in a Nutshell, 323 pages, 1981 (Text)

Leavell, Love and Nelson's Cases and Materials on Equitable Remedies and Restitution, 4th Ed., 1111 pages, 1986 (Casebook)

McCormick's Hornbook on Damages, 811 pages, 1935 (Text)

O'Connell's Remedies in a Nutshell, 2nd Ed., 320 pages, 1985 (Text)

York, Bauman and Rendleman's Cases and Materials on Remedies, 4th Ed., 1029 pages, 1985 (Casebook)

REVIEW MATERIALS

Ballantine's Problems

Black Letter Series

SECURITIES REGULATION

Hazen's Hornbook on The Law of Securities Regulation, Student Ed., 739 pages, 1985, with 1988 P.P. (Text)

Ratner's Securities Regulation: Materials for a Basic Course, 3rd Ed., 1000 pages, 1986 (Casebook)

Ratner's Securities Regulation in a Nutshell, 3rd Ed., 316 pages, 1988 (Text)

LAW SCHOOL PUBLICATIONS—Continued

SECURITIES REGULATION—Cont'd

Selected Securities and Business Planning Statutes, Rules and Forms, 493 pages, 1987

SOCIAL LEGISLATION

Hood and Hardy's Workers' Compensation and Employee Protection Laws in a Nutshell, 274 pages, 1984 (Text)

LaFrance's Welfare Law: Structure and Entitlement in a Nutshell, 455 pages, 1979 (Text)

Malone, Plant and Little's Cases on Workers' Compensation and Employment Rights, 2nd Ed., 951 pages, 1980 (Casebook)

SPORTS LAW

Schubert, Smith and Trentadue's Sports Law, 395 pages, 1986 (Text)

TAXATION

Dodge's Cases and Materials on Federal Income Taxation, 820 pages, 1985 (Casebook)

Garbis, Struntz and Rubin's Cases and Materials on Tax Procedure and Tax Fraud, 2nd Ed., 687 pages, 1987 (Casebook)

Gelfand and Salsich's State and Local Taxation and Finance in a Nutshell, 309 pages, 1986 (Text)

Gunn and Ward's Cases and Materials on Federal Income Taxation, about 815 pages, 1988 (Casebook)

Hellerstein and Hellerstein's Cases on State and Local Taxation, 5th Ed., about 1060 pages, 1988 (Casebook)

Kahn and Gann's Corporate Taxation and Taxation of Partnerships and Partners, 2nd Ed., 1204 pages, 1985 (Casebook)

Kaplan's Federal Taxation of International Transactions: Principles, Planning and Policy, 635 pages, 1988 (Casebook)

Kragen and McNulty's Cases and Materials on Federal Income Taxation: Individuals, Corporations, Partnerships, 4th Ed., 1287 pages, 1985 (Casebook)

McNulty's Federal Estate and Gift Taxation in a Nutshell, 3rd Ed., 509 pages, 1983 (Text)

McNulty's Federal Income Taxation of Individuals in a Nutshell, 4th Ed., about 500 pages, 1988 (Text)

Pennell's Cases and Materials on Income Taxation of Trusts, Estates, Grantors and Beneficiaries, 460 pages, 1987 (Casebook)

Posin's Hornbook on Federal Income Taxation of Individuals, Student Ed., 491 pages, 1983 with 1987 pocket part (Text)

Rose and Chommie's Hornbook on Federal Income Taxation, 3rd Ed., 923 pages, 1988 (Text)

TAXATION—Cont'd

Selected Federal Taxation Statutes and Regulations, about 1400 pages, 1989

Solomon and Hesch's Cases on Federal Income Taxation of Individuals, 1068 pages, 1987 (Casebook)

TORTS

Christie's Cases and Materials on the Law of Torts, 1264 pages, 1983 (Casebook)

Dobbs' Torts and Compensation—Personal Accountability and Social Responsibility for Injury, 955 pages, 1985 (Casebook)

Keeton, Keeton, Sargentich and Steiner's Cases and Materials on Tort and Accident Law, 1360 pages, 1983 (Casebook)

Kionka's Torts in a Nutshell: Injuries to Persons and Property, 434 pages, 1977 (Text)

Malone's Torts in a Nutshell: Injuries to Family, Social and Trade Relations, 358 pages, 1979 (Text)

Prosser and Keeton's Hornbook on Torts, 5th Ed., Student Ed., 1286 pages, 1984, with 1988 pocket part (Text)

See also Products Liability

TRADE REGULATION

McManis' Unfair Trade Practices in a Nutshell, 2nd Ed., about 430 pages, 1988 (Text)

Oppenheim, Weston, Maggs and Schechter's Cases and Materials on Unfair Trade Practices and Consumer Protection, 4th Ed., 1038 pages, 1983 with 1986 Supplement (Casebook)

See also Antitrust, Regulated Industries

TRIAL AND APPELLATE ADVOCACY

Appellate Advocacy, Handbook of, 2nd Ed., 182 pages, 1986 (Text)

Bergman's Trial Advocacy in a Nutshell, 402 pages, 1979 (Text)

Binder and Bergman's Fact Investigation: From Hypothesis to Proof, 354 pages, 1984 (Coursebook)

Goldberg's The First Trial (Where Do I Sit?, What Do I Say?) in a Nutshell, 396 pages, 1982 (Text)

Haydock, Herr and Stempel's, Fundamentals of Pre-Trial Litigation, 768 pages, 1985 (Casebook)

Hegland's Trial and Practice Skills in a Nutshell, 346 pages, 1978 (Text)

Hornstein's Appellate Advocacy in a Nutshell, 325 pages, 1984 (Text)

Jeans' Handbook on Trial Advocacy, Student Ed., 473 pages, 1975 (Text)

Martineau's Cases and Materials on Appellate Practice and Procedure, 565 pages, 1987 (Casebook)

McElhaney's Effective Litigation, 457 pages, 1974 (Casebook)

Nolan's Cases and Materials on Trial Practice, 518 pages, 1981 (Casebook)

LAW SCHOOL PUBLICATIONS—Continued

Legal Writing: Getting It Right and Getting It Written

By

Mary Barnard Ray
University of Wisconsin Law School

and

Jill J. Ramsfield
Georgetown University Law Center

WEST PUBLISHING CO.
ST. PAUL, MINN., 1987

COPYRIGHT © 1987 By WEST PUBLISHING CO.
                   50 West Kellogg Boulevard
                   P.O. Box 64526
                   St. Paul, Minnesota 55164–0526

Library of Congress Cataloging-in-Publication Data

Ray, Mary B.
  Legal writing.

  (American casebook series)
  1. Legal composition, I. Ramsfield, Jill J. II. Title. III. Series.

KF250.R39 1987 808'.06634 86–28955

ISBN 0-314-32494-1

Ray & Ramsfield Legal Writing

2nd Reprint—1988

To Mother, Dad, Dennis, and Mark;

———

To Mom, Dad, Judy, and Chip;

———

and to our students.

Introduction

This book is a desktop reference for legal writers. As such, it responds to the myriad questions we have received in the course of teaching legal writing over the years. These questions could not be answered by classroom lectures or textbooks alone because they are questions that need immediate answers during the writing process. Until now, those immediate questions could be answered only by referring to a legal writing instructor or to several books, a task that took too much time.

No longer. Here, in a few moments, the answers can be found. This book is designed to be a companion to the Harvard *Uniform System of Citation,* to lie next to it and to do for grammatical and analytical writing problems what the Blue Book is designed to do for citations. This book is your handbook.

As a handbook, it answers the small technical questions peculiar to legal writing, such as whether to use *infer* or *imply,* or what *dangling modifier* means or why there are problems in constructing arguments. It also suggests improvements for large-scale matters, such as organization and tone. It addresses the chronic problems that all writers face now and then, such as getting started and meeting deadlines. And it also answers questions that come up only in legal writing, such as what writing principles are critical when drafting contracts or jury instructions.

This handbook thus provides aids to the mastery of the complex task of legal writing, but it cannot substitute for that mastery. Translating legal analysis into structured legal formats is a complex and sophisticated process that incorporates knowledge of the law, experience, and common sense. This handbook offers the components of good legal writing, but you must synthesize those components to master them.

All the entries are arranged alphabetically. The book, therefore, is one large index with text or cross-references under each entry, so that individual entries are easy to find. For example, to determine how to punctuate a list, you can look under LISTS, STRUCTURE OF or SEMICOLONS or COMMAS. For ideas on Issue Statements, you can look under ISSUE STATEMENTS or BRIEFS. If you do not find the answers you need under the term you check first, think of an idea related to the entry and look there, or check the master list of entries. Thus you should be able to find your answer easily. If, after finding the entry you were looking for, you want more information on related topics, you can find that information by referring to the other entries or outside sources cross-referenced within the entry.

Examples are set off by different typeface, as are words used as words. This makes examples easier to find and avoids a clutter of quotation marks. In longer entries, subsections are set off by numbers and sub-subsections by letters, so that particular subpoints are easier to find. Citations are fictitious. Controversial grammatical points have been resolved in favor of the clearer choice for legal writing. When applicable, we have resolved these points in accordance with *A Uniform System of Citation* (Harvard Law Review Association 14th ed. 1986) and the *U.S. Government Printing Office Style Manual* (rev. ed. 1984) because these sources are the recognized authorities in legal writing.

We wrote this book because our students and colleagues requested it. We hope it meets your needs as well.

Mary Barnard Ray
Jill J. Ramsfield

December, 1986

Acknowledgements

We thank our colleagues who supported this endeavor and our students, who inspired it. It is our students who continue to challenge and encourage us, and we thank them for their enthusiasm and feedback.

Special thanks to Valerie Youngs, our secretary. This book is as much hers as ours. To her, we extend our gratitude for her patience, dedication, selflessness, and untiring energy. Thanks also to Theresa Dougherty, our secretary for the final draft, whose computer expertise and cheerful efficiency were especially welcome at the end of the long task of writing this book.

We especially thank our families and friends, who lived through the writing process with us and who celebrated its completion with us. We also thank Mary Ann Birchler Polewski and Dennis Ray for their advice and support. Thanks also to Kathy Soukup, who provided the quality child care essential to a working mother's peace of mind.

Finally, we thank each other for the humor, honesty, and mutual respect that saw us through this project and kept our friendship thriving.

*

Master List of Entries

A OR AN?

Use **an** before all nouns beginning with a vowel or vowel sound; this includes nouns that begin with **h** where the **h** is not voiced, such as **an hour**. Use **a** before all nouns beginning with a voiced consonant, such as **a hearing**. For related information, see ARTICLES, GRAMMAR.

ABBREVIATIONS OF NAMES IN TEXT

In text, abbreviate the name of a party if the initials are widely recognized, such as **NLRB** or **NBC**; see Blue Book rule 6.1. Also abbreviate words commonly used and abbreviated in company titles, such as **Co., Corp., Inc., Ltd., &,** and **No.**; see Blue Book rule 10.2.1(c). Finally, abbreviate conventional personal titles such as **Mr., Mrs.,** and **Ms.**

ABHORRENCE OF OR ABHORRENCE FOR?

Use **abhorrence of**; **abhorrence for** is incorrect.

ABOVE

Above is equivalent to **supra**. Although you can use **above** to refer the reader to previous text, avoid sending the reader back farther than a few paragraphs. Legal readers like to keep moving. For details about **supra**, see Blue Book rules 3.6 and 4.2. For related information, see LEGALESE.

ABSTRACT NOUNS

Abstract nouns describe ideas or general concepts, in contrast to concrete nouns, which describe tangible items. For example, **justice** and **transportation** are abstract; **courtroom** and **bicycle** are concrete. In general, choose concrete nouns because they are more readable and more effective. Use abstract nouns when you need them to describe ideas accurately or to de-emphasize an unfavorable fact, such as the details of an auto accident caused by your client. In that situation, you might use the abstract phrase, **after the collision**, rather than the concrete phrase, **after Smith's van hit Alexander's motorcycle**. For problems related to abstract nouns, see PRECISION, subsections 3 and 7, and ACCURACY, subsection 1(b). For uses of abstract nouns, see EMPHASIS, subsection 2.

ACCURACY

In legal writing, you must always be accurate. Even when you are revising for READABILITY and eloquence, do not sacrifice accuracy. The following rules should help you maintain accuracy while REVISING.

1. Accuracy in WORD CHOICE.

(a) Use only one term to identify each key person, thing, or idea.

Even though the defendant *admitted* while in custody that he had been using drugs, this *admission* of impropriety is not relevant to the present case.

rather than

Even though the defendant *commented* while in custody that he had been using drugs, this *admission* of impropriety is not relevant to the present case.

The latter version leaves the reader guessing but not knowing the exact relationship between **commented** and **admission of impropriety**. Using synonyms is particularly risky with legal readers because they will wonder if your changed terms mean you changed meaning, when you may have only been trying to add VARIETY. For more examples and discussion of this point, see REPETITION and AMBIGUITY, WAYS TO AVOID.

(b) Use the most specific word you can. Often inaccuracies occur because the writer chose an unnecessarily general term and as a result inadvertently broadened the term's reference. For example, do not say **vehicle** when you mean to refer only to **school bus**. For more on this, see PRECISION.

(c) Make the meaning of your words clear in context.

She released him from employment as soon as she was no longer bedridden.

rather than,

She let him go as soon as she could get out of bed.

Although the first version is not as concise or as interesting, it is accurate. Although you usually need to be specific in legal writing, you may need to be vague on some occasions. For a discussion of these exceptions, see EMPHASIS, subsection 2.

(d) Make sure each pronoun is unambiguous. For example, if only one woman is mentioned in your text, you need not worry about **she** causing inaccuracy. If, however, two or more appear, then **she** is likely to be ambiguous. In this situation, check each **she**.

Ms. Jones did not ask Ms. Wilson to double-check the amount, because Ms. Wilson [not she] routinely checked all the amounts listed.

For more on this, see PRONOUNS and AMBIGUITY, WAYS TO AVOID.

(e) Make sure each **this** is unambiguous. **This** is the pronoun most likely to cause inaccuracies. **This** can refer to an idea or a thing, one word or a whole sentence; as a result, you must make sure that the reader always knows what **this** means. If there is any question, add the appropriate noun after **this**.

The court reasoned that the difference in the age of the fetuses was not the factor determining this issue. *This reasoning* . . . .

For more examples, see THIS; PRONOUNS; and AMBIGUITY, WAYS TO AVOID.

2. Accuracy in sentence structure.

Place all modifiers and modifying phrases immediately next to the word modified.

Our client has arranged *with other subcontractors* to fill the ditches.

rather than

Our client has arranged to fill the ditches *with other subcontractors*.

For related general information, see MODIFIERS and SENTENCE STRUCTURE.

3. Accuracy in citations.

(a) Make sure all the volume and page numbers are correct. Incorrect cites irritate readers. The reader checking the cite gets the volume listed, flips to the page, and finds some case having nothing to do with the point. See CITATIONS and CITATIONS, BASIC FORMATS.

(b) Use a pinpoint cite to refer to a particular rule, holding, quotation, or proposition in a source. PINPOINT CITES pinpoint the exact page. These specific references are greatly appreciated by any reader whose job it is to evaluate the merits of the point being made. For a general discussion of citations, see CITATIONS; CITATIONS, BASIC FORMATS; and CITATIONS, PARALLEL.

(c) Use correct citation form. Especially watch the spacing, a frequent source of error. Judges in particular find citation errors distracting, so use letter-perfect citations to enhance your credibility. For details on proper citation form, see CITATIONS; CITATIONS, BASIC FORMAT; CITATIONS, PARALLEL; and CITATIONS, STRING.

For general accuracy concerns in the earlier stages of the WRITING PROCESS, see ORGANIZATION, LARGE–SCALE and ORGANIZATION, SMALL–SCALE. For accuracy concerns in some specific legal situations, see CONTRACTS, DRAFTING; GENERAL CORRESPONDENCE LETTERS; and BAD NEWS, SOFTENING IT. For related writing concerns, see PRECISION.

ACTIVE VERBS
See ACTIVE VOICE.

ACTIVE VOICE
Active voice is the term for the grammatical structure indicating that the subject of the sentence performs or causes the action expressed

by the verb. Because the subject does the acting and the verb describes that action, active voice moves the reader's eye from the left to right.

The *boy hit* the ball.

Defendant argued that the *court should suppress* the evidence.

The *court decided* that freedom of association was not an issue.

This use of active voice prevents the legal reader from having to double back to understand the point.

The *ball was hit* by the boy.

It was argued by the defendant that the *evidence should be suppressed* by the court.

It was decided that freedom of association was not an issue.

The passive voice can also create a sentence that is less precise, as in the last example, which makes the reader wonder who decided.

Active voice also makes the sentence shorter in most cases.

The *court held* that the *plaintiff could not collect* punitive damages.

rather than

It was held by the court that punitive *damages could not be collected* by the plaintiff.

Therefore, if wordiness is a problem in your writing, read through the draft once when REVISING just for active voice. Check each subject and verb and translate from passive to active whenever active is appropriate. For related information, see CONCISENESS.

Use active voice unless the writing requires the passive for effect. For examples of times when passive is useful, see PASSIVE VOICE.

Additionally, use active voice to eliminate any ambiguity caused by e.g., vague verbs, such as **consists of, concerns,** or **involves.**

The government's actions in this case violated the plaintiff's right to privacy.

rather than

This case involves the right to privacy.

Active voice also can eliminate ambiguity caused by linking verbs, such as **seems, feels,** or **were.**

The court has presented two inconsistent standards of review in jury misconduct cases.

rather than

The court seems unsure about the standard of review in these kinds of cases.

Use linking verbs only when they accurately state the situation.

Awarding custody to the mother is in the best interests of the children.

For related information, see VERBS, LINKING.

ACTUALLY

Actually means **in fact.** Use it as an adverb only to distinguish facts from figurative speech.

The defendant actually hid the knife by sliding it under the cake.

Because legal writers rarely use figurative speech, they also rarely use **actually.** Therefore, for ACCURACY, avoid using it casually.

ADJECTIVES

Adjectives modify nouns or pronouns. Proper adjectives are adjectives derived from proper names. Capitalize most proper adjectives: **American banking system, the Atlantic seaboard, Vietnamese refugees.** Do not capitalize an adjective derived from a proper name when it has been used frequently and for a long time in the general language: **cesarean operation, india ink, italic type, murphy bed,** or **venetian blinds.**

For an extensive list of adjectives derived from proper names, see *U.S. Government Printing Office Style Manual* 41–42 (rev. ed. 1973).

Predicate adjectives are adjectives that follow linking verbs, such as **is** or **seems,** and describe the subject of those verbs.

The case is *relevant.*

Use adjectives only when they are needed or, as Twain said, "As to the adjective: when in doubt, strike it out." If you find yourself writing several adjectives to modify one noun, stop and find the noun that more precisely states your meaning.

Mr. Barnes has frequently testified as an expert witness on bone disease.

rather than

Mr. Barnes is a known, respected, and often-used authority on bone diseases.

For related examples and explanation, see MODIFIERS.

ADVERBS

Adverbs modify verbs, adjectives, or other adverbs.

Mr. Smith *justly* cannot be penalized for acting *very carefully.*

Avoid overusing them; too many adverbs can bog down a sentence while adding a minimum of information. Three adverbs you can omit readily are **clearly, merely,** and **obviously.** Another adverb you can view with suspicion is **very,** because it usually weakens the point rather than strengthening it, as in the example above. For related information, see CLEARLY, OBVIOUSLY, VERY, CONCISENESS, and MODIFIERS.

AFFECT OR EFFECT?

In legal writing you usually want **effect** when using the noun and **affect** when using the verb.

This law had a sweeping effect.

but

This law affected police procedures.

This is because **effect** as a noun means **something that was the result of another action**, while **affect** as a noun means a **feeling**. **Affect** as a verb, however, means **to influence**. Occasionally you will need **effect** as a verb if you mean **to cause to come into being**.

Through persistent lobbying, the group effected a change in the inheritance laws.

AFORESAID

When writing to clients, substitute **mentioned earlier, named earlier,** or some other more explanatory phrase. One of the most virulent complaints coming from the general public is that lawyers use LEGALESE, and **aforesaid** is viewed as legalese.

In a legal document written to be read by other lawyers, such as a pleading, you may use **aforesaid**, but you must use it precisely because lawyers will interpret the term literally. Never toss it in carelessly, thinking that it will in itself add a patina of authenticity to the document. **Aforesaid** means you are referring to something mentioned earlier rather than something mentioned afterward. For example, you would say the **aforesaid defendant** only if another defendant is mentioned later and you mean to exclude that other defendant. Do not use **aforesaid defendant** if you have only one defendant or if you mean to include all defendants.

If you observe this rule, you will find that you have few occasions to use **aforesaid**.

AGREE TO OR AGREE WITH?

The choice between **agree to** and **agree with** is based on IDIOM, which means there is a right or wrong choice in most cases. For example, you would always say, **I agree to help you,** but **I agree with your idea.**

In general, use **agree to** when the subject is concurring with something and will act accordingly. For example, **agree to** is frequently used in contracts.

We agree to represent you in this matter.

or

My client agrees to settle out of court with the following provisions.

Use **agree with** when the subject is voicing agreement but not making any actual commitments.

I agree with you that large settlements are increasing insurance premiums.

or

The State agrees with the court's concern for the preservation of fifth amendment rights, but . . . .

6

AGREEMENT, SUBJECTS AND VERBS

Agreement here means using plural verbs with plural subjects and singular verbs with singular subjects. Problems with agreement most frequently occur when the subject and verb are separated by a long phrase and the writer loses track of the subject along the way. As a result, the verb may agree with some noun in the long phrase rather than with the subject. You can usually avoid this problem by keeping the subject and verb close together. This will also improve the readability of your text.

Since 1979, *section 4* of the Export Administration Act has created much controversy. That section gives the President authority to impose foreign policy and national security controls on exports.

rather than

Since 1979, the *section* of the Export Administration Act giving the President authority to impose foreign policy and national security controls on exports *have created* much controversy.

For a general discussion of related concerns, see READABILITY and SENTENCE STRUCTURE.

AGREEMENTS, WRITTEN

See CONTRACTS, DRAFTING.

ALL AROUND OR ALL ROUND?

Use **all round**, because you mean **well rounded**, not **circling around**.

ALL READY OR ALREADY?

All ready means a group is **prepared for some sort of action**. **Already** means **by this or a specified time or previously**.

ALL RIGHT OR ALRIGHT?

In legal writing, use the space. **Alright** is the informal, less accepted equivalent.

ALL ROUND OR ALL AROUND?

See ALL AROUND or ALL ROUND?

ALL, SINGULAR OR PLURAL?

All is singular when it means **the only thing**.

All that the new law can do is force the courts to resolve the conflict.

All is plural, however, when it means the **whole group**.

All the changes in the contract were made in writing.

ALL TOGETHER OR ALTOGETHER?

All together means that a group of people, things, or events are together. Altogether means entirely and with all included or counted, or on the whole, with everything considered.

ALLITERATION

Alliteration is the repetition of similar consonant sounds, as the f's in fast and furious fighting. Alliteration can be useful in legal writing because it can help the reader remember a phrase or can add drama, but it must be used sparingly and with care.

Having been terrified twice by the defendant's previous assaults, the plaintiff hesitated before she fled.

but not

Two times terrified, Theresa tarried before taking off down the alley.

When using alliteration, first be sure that the content of the phrase is indeed worth remembering. If it is not, the alliteration will be a distraction, no matter how graceful it sounds. Second, make sure that the repeated sound creates an appropriate feeling. For example, a repeated t sound can sound harsh, while a repeated s can sound soothing.

The attorney was known for the smoothness and simplicity of his writing style.

Finally, read the passage aloud to make sure it works, because longer twisters torture tired readers. For a discussion of related techniques, see EMPHASIS and REPETITION.

ALREADY OR ALL READY?

See ALL READY OR ALREADY?

ALRIGHT OR ALL RIGHT?

See ALL RIGHT OR ALRIGHT?

ALTERNATIVE

Use alternative only when referring to two choices, not more. Commonly alternative is used when more than two choices exist; however, readers who enjoy the proper use of language will appreciate your precise use of alternative.

ALTHOUGH OR THOUGH?

In many situations you can use either word. Although is more elegant and therefore more appropriate for briefs, law review articles, and all but informal legal writings.

In two situations you can use though only.

1. Use though in such phrases as even though or as though.

2. Use **though** at the end of a sentence or at the end of a phrase.

She promised, though.

or

She promised, though, to come to the hearing.

Though at the end of a sentence is correct but rather informal for legal writing, so try substituting the following.

Nevertheless, she promised.

or

She promised, however, to come to the hearing.

ALTOGETHER OR ALL TOGETHER?
See ALL TOGETHER OR ALTOGETHER?

A.M.
It is written **a.m.** Use the phrase only after an hour.

We will meet at 9:00 a.m.

When **a.m.** appears at the end of a sentence, as in the previous example, use only one period.

AMBIGUITY, WAYS TO AVOID
In legal writing, a word or phrase is ambiguous if, in context, it permits more than one meaning. "Given a choice between a word that can carry the proper meaning and one that must carry it, choose the latter." W. Rivers, *Writing: Craft and Art* 34 (Prentice-Hall 1975). The following rules should help you avoid ambiguity.

1. Avoid misplaced MODIFIERS.

Sometimes a modifying phrase, because of its position, could modify any of several words in a sentence.

The defendant refused to service the car belonging to the man who insulted him *with good reason*.

Here **with good reason** should modify **refused** instead of **insulted**. To avoid ambiguity, place the modifying phrase right next to the word modified.

The defendant, *with good reason*, refused to service the car belonging to the man who had insulted him.

For other problems associated with modifiers, see MODIFIERS, DANGLING and MODIFIERS, SQUINTING.

2. Avoid ambiguous PRONOUNS.

Sometimes pronouns cause ambiguity because they can logically refer to either of several nouns. The pronoun most likely to cause ambiguity is **this**, because **this** can refer to any idea or object.

You must ultimately make a judgment about the weight of the evidence. This will help you decide what the verdict should be.

Does **this** refer to **judgment** or **evidence**? To avoid the problem, add the appropriate noun after **this**.

You must ultimately make a judgment about the weight of the evidence. This judgment will help you decide what the verdict should be.

The pronoun second most likely to cause ambiguity is **it**, again because **it** can refer to any object or idea. Usually **it** becomes ambiguous when some other noun comes between **it** and the antecedent, which is the noun to which **it** refers.

The first will is less ambiguous than the second will because it omits the deceased's spouse.

To solve this problem, you may replace **it** with the noun.

The first will is less ambiguous than the second because the first will omits the decedent's spouse.

Or you may rephrase the sentence, so that no other noun comes between **it** and its antecedent.

The second will created some confusion by referring to the decedent's spouse; as a result, the first will is less ambiguous because it omits the decedent's spouse.

Although **this** and **it** are the most likely offenders, all pronouns should be watched for potential ambiguity. In general, check **he** or **she** whenever the content of your writing involves two people of the same sex. Check **they** to make sure there is no question about who is included in the group. **We** is a special problem in legal writing because you may, by using **we**, inadvertently speak for your whole law firm or organization. Never use **we** when you really mean **I**; use **we** only when you are speaking officially for the organization of which you are a part, as one judge may do when drafting an opinion for the whole bench. For related information, see PRONOUNS and ANTECEDENTS.

AMONG OR BETWEEN?

Use **between** when discussing two options and **among** when discussing more than two.

Conferences were held between the plaintiff's and the defendant's attorneys, the plaintiff's attorney and estate's trustees, and the defendant's attorney and the estate's trustees.

rather than

Conferences were held between the plaintiff's attorney, the defendant's attorney, and the estate's trustees.

Although the former version is less concise, it leaves no question about who met with whom.

Use **among** to indicate that more than two parties are meeting.

A Conference was held among the plaintiff's attorney, the defendant's attorney, and the estate's trustee.

ANALOGOUS CASES

An analogous case is a case whose facts are similar to the factual situation being analyzed; thus the details of the analogous case are essential to the analysis. When writing your analysis in MEMOS or BRIEFS, describe those essential details, which may include the rule, the rationale, the holding, the LEGALLY SIGNIFICANT FACTS, or DICTA central to understanding the case's significance. Make sure that, if the comparison is essential to the analysis, you include enough information to allow the reader to compare or distinguish the analogous case from the subject of the memo or brief. Avoid including unnecessary detail. For related information, see ARGUMENT SECTION, DISCUSSION SECTION, RULES, HOLDINGS, and PARALLEL STRUCTURE.

AND

There are three points to remember about this conjunction. First, although it is not wrong to start a sentence with **and**, doing so draws attention to the word. Therefore, before starting a sentence with **and** ask yourself if that word is really what you want to emphasize. Often it is not.

Second, use **and** to join sentences only when the sentence logically should be joined with the verbal equivalent of a plus sign.

Finally, avoid overusing **and** to join sentences, because it can lead to long, lackluster sentences.

For related general information, see CONJUNCTIONS.

AND/OR

Avoid this construction because it creates ambiguity. Decide whether the logical connection between the two phrases, words, or clauses is disjunctive, which requires **or**, or conjunctive, which requires **and**.

The court may, in its discretion, meet with the child *or* parents *or both* to determine *any of* the following factors affecting the best interests of the child: (1) the child's own preferences, (2) the parents' ability *and* willingness to provide consistent, adequate care, *and* (3) the parents' willingness to cooperate with each other if joint custody is awarded.

rather than

The court may, in its discretion meet with the child *and/or* parents to determine factors affecting the best interests of the child, such as (1) the child's own preferences *and/or* desires, (2) the parents' ability *and/or* willingness to provide consistent *and/or* adequate care, *and/or* (3) the parents' willingness to cooperate with each other if joint custody is awarded.

If the items can be disjunctive, conjunctive, or both, state that explicitly.

Either the Company or its agents, or both, may . . . .

rather than

The Company and/or its agents may . . . .

For related information, see OR and AND.

ANIMALS, ARE THEY HE, SHE, OR IT?
Use it.

ANTE–OR ANTI–?
Ante- means in front of or before, as in antebellum.

Anti- means against, or opposite, as in anti-intellectual and antibody.

ANTECEDENTS
An antecedent is the noun to which a pronoun refers.

Ms. Williams' *aunt* willed her estate to charity.

Here aunt is the antecedent of her. For problems related to this, see AMBIGUITY, WAYS TO AVOID, subsection 2. For related information, see NOUNS and PRONOUNS.

ANTI- OR ANTE-?
See ANTE– OR ANTI–?

ANYBODY, SINGULAR OR PLURAL?
Anybody uses singular verbs.

Anybody who believes in justice believes in a fair trial.

Anybody is rather informal, so use anyone in formal legal writing, such as briefs or articles.

ANYONE, SINGULAR OR PLURAL?
Anyone uses singular verbs.

Anyone is entitled to a fair trial.

APOSTROPHES
Apostrophes, like decimal points, belong in specific places.

1. Use an apostrophe to create the possessive form of a noun.
   plaintiff's = belonging to one plaintiff.
   plaintiffs' = belonging to more than one plaintiff.
   Pettuses' = belonging to the Pettuses.

Do not use an apostrophe, however, to form possessives of PRO-NOUNS.

its	=	belonging to it.
yours	=	belonging to you.
theirs	=	belonging to them.
whose	=	belonging to whom.
ours	=	belonging to us.
hers	=	belonging to her.

For more explanation, see POSSESSIVES.

2. Use an apostrophe to form plurals of letters, figures, symbols, and words used as words.

7's
C's
¶'s
two *that's* in a sentence

3. Use an apostrophe as a substitution for a letter or letters.

it's	=	it is.
you're	=	you are.
don't	=	do not.

In most legal writing, however, do not use contractions. For more explanation, see CONTRACTIONS.

APPEAL

Use **appeal** as a term of art only, referring to the appeal of a case. Avoid using **appeal** informally in legal writing.

The appeal will be decided next week.

rather than

The defendant's counsel appealed to the court to deny the motion.

For related information, see TERMS OF ART.

APPELLATE BRIEFS

Appellate courts have specific rules about the FORMAT and content of appellate briefs. Read your local rules carefully, because most appellate courts will reject briefs that do not conform to their rules. For example, most courts require certain colors for covers; certain typesets, margins, and page lengths; and certain organization and content. Be aware of these rules before you begin writing your appellate brief, so that you know the confines within which you must work. Similarly, check the number of days you have for writing the brief and know how your jurisdiction counts those days. Then mark the deadline on that calendar and count backwards to schedule your WRITING PROCESS.

In your schedule, make sure you allow a lot of time at the end for refining the format. Most jurisdictions require a table of contents that includes the POINT HEADINGS and a table of authorities that includes references to specific pages where each authority is used; these tables take time to assemble. Also make sure that the typist has plenty of time to finish this process before filing the brief, so that you will be sure to meet your deadline. For related information, see DEADLINES, MEETING THEM.

Generally, an appellate brief contains a STATEMENT OF THE CASE with specific references to the record, ISSUE STATEMENTS, an ARGUMENT SECTION, POINT HEADINGS and subheadings, and a conclusion. Use PERSUASIVE WRITING when writing your appellate brief. For more information on format, see BRIEFS.

APPENDIX

Appendices can be used in any kind of legal writing to assist the reader but not to replace important material that should be included in the text. Legal readers prefer appendices to refer to statutes, cases, excerpts from the record, and similar documents that are not needed in their entirety in the text but are helpful for reference. Therefore, use appendices in MEMOS to include applicable statutes; in PRETRIAL BRIEFS to include affidavits, references to any pretrial documents, or applicable statutes; in TRIAL BRIEFS to include references to the record or to applicable statutes; and in APPELLATE BRIEFS to include references to the pretrial record, trial record, JURY INSTRUC- TIONS, or statutes.

Label each appendix as Appendix A, B, C, and so forth. Refer to each separately by surrounding this phrase with PARENTHESES. (See Appendix A).

Check your local appellate rules for any specific requirements for appendices to appellate briefs.

APPLICATION

In MEMOS or BRIEFS, application refers to the process by which the relevant RULES of law are applied to the factual situation being analyzed. In a memo, the application is part of the DISCUSSION SECTION. In a brief, it is part of the ARGUMENT SECTION. While a comprehensive approach to application is beyond the scope of this book, the following may get you started.

1. Apply the law according to its own structure. For example, if there are three subsections of a statute, apply all three in the statute's order or in the order used by courts in interpreting the statute.

2. Make sure your application reflects step-by-step logic. Just as a court reasons from RULES to a holding, so you must reason from rules to your prediction or conclusion. For some hints on reasoning, see SYLLOGISMS. For a more detailed approach to reasoning see P. Schlag and D. Skover, *Tactics of Legal Reasoning* (Carolina Academic Press 1986).

3. When appropriate, explain the connection between the facts and reasoning of this situation, and the facts and reasoning of analogous cases. Either compare to or distinguish from ANALOGOUS CASES.

4. Examine both the strengths and weaknesses of your client's case and balance them against each other. The reader should know how the RULES, POLICY, and EQUITY can be used to build or challenge your arguments. Then the reader should know how and why these factors tip the balance in one direction.

Do not, however, include this information as four separate items on a list. Instead, weave these parts together as dictated by the law and facts themselves. A mechanical listing will defeat the analytical purpose, while a careful consideration and building of the subparts will result in a thorough analysis.

APPOSITIVE

An appositive is a noun or phrase that comes right after a noun and describes that noun.

The defendant, *Great West Power*, settled before the trial began.

It is useful for inserting extra information into a sentence. Keep the appositive short, however, to avoid creating sentences that are hard to read. For related problems, see READABILITY and AGREEMENT, SUBJECTS AND VERBS. For a discussion of other uses of appositives, see UNOBTRUSIVE DEFINITIONS.

ARGUMENT HEADINGS

See POINT HEADINGS.

ARGUMENT SECTION

The Argument is that section in a pretrial, trial, or appellate brief presenting the legal argument from the client's point of view.

The Argument should contain the following information:

(1) all the RULES applicable to this fact situation, whether from statutory or common law;

(2) an APPLICATION of the rules to these facts, which argues the strengths of the client's position and rebuts the weaknesses; and

(3) an analysis of the POLICY and EQUITY questions, if useful to client's position or essential to complete analysis.

Write the Argument in a persuasive style and from the client's point of view. The Argument should include POINT HEADINGS and subheadings, which outline the argument's main legal points and give the reasons behind those points.

Organize the Argument either inductively or deductively. Deductive organization, which is usually best, begins with a rule, uses analogous cases where appropriate, and then applies the law to these facts to reach a specific conclusion based on that rule. Inductive organization begins with the particulars of the case being analyzed and works through each rule to reach a general conclusion. For more help with organization, see ORGANIZATION, LARGE–SCALE and ORGANIZATION, SMALL–SCALE.

The Argument should include LEGALLY SIGNIFICANT FACTS, or those facts of the case being analyzed that are necessary to the analysis. All facts used in the argument section should also appear in the STATEMENT OF FACTS or STATEMENT OF THE CASE; no new facts should appear in the argument section.

ARTICLES, GRAMMAR

Articles is the grammatical term for a, an, and the. For a discussion of their use, see A OR AN? and THE. For law review articles, see ARTICLES, PUBLISHED.

ARTICLES, PUBLISHED

Articles differ from other forms of legal writing because their AUDIENCE is scholarly as well as practical and because they reflect the writer's opinion more openly than do other forms. Consider the following in writing an article.

1. Tell the reader your point at the beginning of the article rather than building up to it at the end. Most legal readers like to know what they are reading about and then see the explanation because they can then follow and evaluate the writer's reasoning that leads to that point. This point can be stated at the end of your introduction or in the very first sentence of the article. For related information, see ORGANIZATION; ORGANIZATION, LARGE–SCALE; ORGANIZATION, SMALL–SCALE; and PARAGRAPHS.

2. Make sure that your FORMAT reflects the substance of your piece. As in a brief, any HEADINGS or subheadings should be helpful signals, not merely a parroting of traditional format. Try using sentences or phrases that communicate your argument, rather than just depending on words like Introduction, or Historical Background.

3. Use FOOTNOTES to substantiate points and to provide valuable historical or background information. Avoid using footnotes just to use them; instead make sure they are sensible and useful to the reader.

4. Allow yourself more leverage in using FIGURATIVE MEANING, EMOTIONAL LANGUAGE, and your own PERSUASIVE STYLE than you would in briefs or memos. Because the article is your commentary on a given subject, also allow your STYLE and TONE wider range. Do not, however, range so far that you lessen your credibility.

5. In articles, honor the same fundamental of legal writing that you do in briefs; make every word count. It is tempting to say more than is necessary in articles, but giving into that temptation can lose readers.

For related information, see CONCISENESS, PRECISION, and READABILITY.

AS

To avoid ambiguity, avoid using **as** in place of **because** or **since**.

The trial was delayed because the plaintiff fell ill.

rather than

The trial was delayed as the plaintiff fell ill.

For related information, see TRANSITIONS and PRECISION.

AS A MATTER OF FACT

You probably do not need this phrase. Try marking it out and revising what is left into a more concise, forceful statement. See CONCISENESS.

AS IF OR AS THOUGH?

Either one means **in the same way that it would be if**.

They can be used interchangeably.

AS OR LIKE?

In a comparison, use **as** to connect CLAUSES.

She argues as a good lawyer should argue.

rather than

She argues like a good lawyer should.

Use **like** only to introduce a noun phrase.

She argues like Justice Cardozo.

AS THOUGH OR AS IF?

See AS IF OR AS THOUGH?

AS TO

As to can be used as a preposition, in which case it takes an object.

As to the adjective: when in doubt strike it out.—Mark Twain

As to jury trials, our system compares with few others in the world.

Use **as to** rarely and with care to avoid two problems. First, do not use **as to** if it is stuffy in context. For example, in a letter to a client, write the following.

Regarding your request for . . . .

rather than

As to your request for . . . .

Second, avoid overusing **as to**. If you use it once a page, you are probably overusing it. To find a different but equally accurate connecting phrase, see TRANSITIONS.

ASTERISKS

Asterisks are sometimes used for acknowledgements in law review articles or for a single footnote. In typeset print, asterisks are also sometimes used interchangeably with ELLIPSES. In typewritten, formal legal writing, asterisks are distracting, so use periods for ellipses. In informal writing, asterisks are used to mark a single footnote; the only occasion you are likely to find to do this in legal writing, however, is to add a small point in an informal memo to a coworker.

For related information, see PUNCTUATING QUOTES.

AT THE TIME THAT

Try using **when** instead. See CONCISENESS.

AT THIS POINT IN TIME

Try using **now** or **currently** for a clearer, more concise sentence. See CONCISENESS.

ATTORNEY OR LAWYER?

Generally, **attorney** refers to the specific person representing a party to a suit.

Attorney Schwartz moved for a new trial.

or

The attorney for the defense objected to the question.

The term **lawyer** refers to the general category of people qualified to practice law.

Several hundred lawyers attended last year's ABA convention.

AUDIENCE

To maximize the effectiveness of your writing, define your audience, or reader, before you begin to write. This will help you organize and present your information in a way that communicates to your reader. For example, your audience may be a judge, another attorney, or a community of practicing attorneys and legal scholars; each of these audiences might have different questions about the same content. As a result, you need to be versatile enough to answer that audience's questions. The following questions can help you define your audience.

1. Is the audience a lawyer or a lay person? If a lawyer, use TERMS OF ART and KEY TERMS precisely. If a lay person, avoid legal terms that do not have clear definitions in lay persons' terms. For related information, see LEGALESE and JARGON.

18

2. Is your audience an experienced attorney or an inexperienced one? If experienced, address the legal issues with sophisticated, precise terms that respect that experience. If inexperienced, give longer explanations in simpler terms.

3. Is your audience particular about FORMAT or STYLE requirements? If so, meet them. Even if you disagree personally with these requirements, it is wiser to follow them because your job as a writer is to communicate your point to this particular audience, not to change that audience's writing quirks. If there is no way of knowing the requirements, use a conventional, comprehensive format familiar to all legal readers.

4. Are you writing for more than one audience, such as for both attorneys and professors? If so, list separately the requirements of each, then fuse them at each stage of the WRITING PROCESS. For example, if one audience wants a great deal more technical information than the other, you may put non-essential technical information in FOOTNOTES or an APPENDIX.

5. Is your audience friendly or hostile? Use TONE appropriately.

6. Are you persuading or informing your audience? If the former, use PERSUASIVE WRITING; if the latter, use OBJECTIVE WRITING.

7. What are the objectives and interests of your audience? Make sure your paper is useful to that audience; for example, make sure you have answered the questions asked, given adequate explanations, persuaded properly, or asked for specific relief. Add nothing that is of no use to your audience.

AUXILIARY VERB
See VERBS, AUXILIARY.

BACKGROUND FACTS
These facts fill in the gaps between LEGALLY SIGNIFICANT FACTS. Although they are not essential in the issues, they are essential to the reader's understanding of the general situation. Thus the STATEMENT OF FACTS contains enough background to complete the context. Background facts should be minimized, however, to avoid making the Statement of Facts too long. For related information, see ISSUE STATEMENTS and QUESTIONS PRESENTED.

BAD NEWS, GIVING IT
For any lawyer, being the bearer of bad news is as unavoidable as it is distasteful. Unlike a fortune teller, who can base predictions solely on the client's desires, the lawyer must base his or her prediction on sound analysis of law and fact.

A lawyer can, however, use an understanding of readers and of writing to make that bad news more palatable. The following techniques can be helpful for presenting bad news in a letter, memo, or brief.

1. In a letter.

When you must write a bad news letter, try organizing the letter into three parts that do the following: (a) set the TONE of the letter, (b) deliver the bad news, and (c) re-establish the tone. Think of this as a sandwich organization; place your meat between two slices of bread to make it more palatable.

(a) The first slice of bread: set the tone.

In the first paragraph, establish the TONE you want to take with the reader. For example, you might want to be kind.

Mr. Alexander has asked us to help straighten out some apparent confusion regarding your bill to him for equipment repairs made in June 1985. As I understand it, ...

Or you might want to be tough.

You stated in your letter of March 14, that our client, Mr. Alexander, owes you $480 for equipment repairs you made in June 1985. This is incorrect. As Mr. Alexander has explained previously, ...

You might choose to be warm and personal.

Thank you for inviting me to speak at the Society's annual awards banquet. Regrettably, ...

You might choose to be distant.

This letter concerns a bill for $480 from Efficient Equipment Repair Service to Alexander Associates, which states that the charges are for equipment repairs completed in June 1985. . . .

If answering a request, you may want to restate that request, so that the reader knows you paid attention to the request before saying no.

In your letter to Mr. Alexander dated March 14, you asked him to pay $480 for "equipment repairs made to three typewriters in June 1985." You stated that this payment was long overdue and you threatened to bring suit if you did not receive payment by May 1, 1986.

(b) The meat: deliver the bad news.

At the beginning of paragraph two, state the bad news plainly so that the reader cannot misinterpret what you are saying.

In your letter to Mr. Alexander dated March 14, you asked Mr. Alexander to pay $480 for "equipment repairs made to three typewriters in June 1985." You stated that this payment was long overdue and you threatened to bring suit if you did not receive payment by May 1, 1986.

> *Mr. Alexander, however, does not believe he owes you this*
> *money because he has no record of these repairs being made*
> *. . . .*

Follow this statement with your reasons, if appropriate. This paragraph will be unemotional and matter-of-fact, regardless of the tone of the other paragraphs.

> Mr. Alexander, however, does not believe he owes you this money because he has no record of these repairs being made. Instead, his records show only that Efficient Equipment Repair Service repaired one typewriter on June 12, 1985. Alexander Associates received a statement charging $40 for this work from the repairman before he left. On July 1, 1985, Alexander Associates mailed a check for $40 to Efficient Equipment Repair Service . . . .

This section may also extend for several paragraphs if needed.

(c) The other piece of bread: re-establish the tone.

In the final paragraph, re-establish your tone while you state some closing technicalities. For example, you may suggest that the reader call if he or she has questions.

> If you have any further questions concerning this matter, you may call me at (505) 555–1234.

If you are being kind, you may wish the reader some sort of relevant good fortune.

> I enjoyed our conversation at the convention and look forward to reading your article on . . . .

If you are being tough, you may close with a final declarative statement.

> I trust that this explains the matter to your satisfaction.

For related information see BAD NEWS, SOFTENING IT; GENERAL CORRESPONDENCE LETTERS; and TONE IN LETTERS.

2. In a memo.

Sometimes you must tell a senior partner that a client does not have a case. When this happens, state your conclusion in specific, matter-of-fact language.

> Mr. Allen will probably not convince a jury to award damages under the theory of strict liability because he cannot show that . . . .

Then lay out your reasoning thoroughly. Answer all possible questions your reader will likely ask, one by one.

If at all possible, offer viable alternatives. Maybe some other theory is possible. Maybe some other approach, such as negotiation, is desirable. These alternatives greatly reduce the sting of a negative answer.

3. In a brief.

Sometimes you must deal with precedent, policy, or facts that go against your client's position. For help here, see BAD NEWS, SOFTENING IT.

BAD NEWS, SOFTENING IT

Soften bad news when you do indeed have to communicate the bad news to the reader but you want to keep the reader from reacting to the news in some way undesirable to your position.

Be careful about softening bad news too much, however, because it is possible to state the bad news so abstractly that the reader misses the point altogether. For example, if in an opinion letter you needed to tell your client that he or she would lose a suit, you might state the following.

Although you may bring suit, your chance of recovering your investment is slim. The company at fault has declared bankruptcy, and thus . . . .

rather than

Although the results might not be exactly what you desire, you may nevertheless choose to bring suit.

With that caveat in mind, use the following techniques to soften the blow. For related information, see BAD NEWS, GIVING IT; GENERAL CORRESPONDENCE LETTERS; and TONE IN LETTERS.

1. Use a dependent clause.

You can put the bad news in a dependent clause (see PARTS OF A SENTENCE) and then put that clause in a sentence based on a more favorable fact.

Although he was exceeding the speed limit, Mr. Jones was driving no faster than other cars on that road at that time. Indeed he was passed by several cars just a few minutes before the accident.

This technique is particularly useful in PERSUASIVE WRITING.

To determine what word to use at the first of your dependent clause, see TRANSITIONS. For a general discussion of the technique, see SENTENCE STRUCTURE, Subsection 3.

2. Use more abstract terms.

A second way to soften bad news is to state it in abstract, rather than concrete terms. This technique is most likely to be useful when you have an unfavorable fact that cannot be logically set in a more favorable context. Thus if your client hit a parked car, you might refer to the event this way.

Both cars were damaged in the collision.

If, however, the other party hit your client's parked car, you might refer to the same event this way.

When the defendant's car smashed into the rear left fender of the plaintiff's car, the impact crumpled the fender and shoved it into the back seat, so that the folded metal came within three inches of the driver's seat.

The limitations of this method are obvious in this example; even if you offer the court your abstract version, your adversary will probably offer the concrete one. It may be, however, that your adversary will overdo it, or underdo it, and you can take advantage of that mistake.

3. Use a less emphatic sentence structure.

You can use sentence structure to de-emphasize one point at the same time you are using it to emphasize another, more favorable point.

Although defendant violated his parole on one occasion three months ago, he has shown exemplary behavior ever since.

For a more detailed discussion of this technique, see SENTENCE STRUCTURE.

BAD OR BADLY?

Use **bad** when modifying a noun and **badly** when modifying a verb. The main problem writers have here is exemplified in the following sentence.

I feel bad about . . . .

rather than

I feel badly about . . . .

Use **bad** because you are describing your emotions, not your ability to physically feel things. You will probably find few occasions to use this phrase in legal writing.

BASED ON

Watch this phrase at the beginning of a sentence, because it can create a dangling modifier.

Based on the plain meaning of this word, this interpretation of the clause is valid.

rather than

Based on the plain meaning of this word, my client should not have to honor this contract.

The interpretation, not the client, is based on the plain meaning. For related general information, see AMBIGUITY, WAYS TO AVOID.

BASICALLY

This word often has no specific meaning in a sentence; if it does not, omit it. Use **basically** if you are in fact contrasting the basis of something to some other aspect of that same thing.

Basically, this is a good theory, but in practice . . . .

It would be better to state your point more precisely.

This theory is based on precedent, but its application of that precedent is flawed in three ways.

BECAUSE OR SINCE?

Use **because** if you mean **because**. **Because** is a precise term; it means only that one event or thing is the cause of something else. Use **since** if you mean to show a relationship in time.

Since the restraining order was issued, the defendant has approached the plaintiff four times.

If you are worried about overusing **because**, you can do three things. First, check to see how frequently **because** appears. As a general rule, you need not worry about overusing **because** until it appears once in every paragraph and more than once in many paragraphs. Second, even if you are using **because** frequently, consider whether that use is needed to make your text clear. For example, you may decide that using **because** more frequently is appropriate because you are explaining the reasoning for a particular conclusion. Finally, if you decide some **because's** must be omitted, you may restructure the sentence to use as a **result, therefore,** or some other accurate transition. For help here, see TRANSITIONS. For a discussion of general, related writing problems, see PARAGRAPHS; LOGICAL LINKS; and CONNECTIONS, MAKING THEM.

BEGINNING

For help beginning the WRITING PROCESS, see GETTING STARTED. For help beginning letters, see OPENINGS FOR LETTERS.

BENDING THE RULES

This can be done with law, with grammar, or with general writing principles. With the law, bend as far as POLICY, EQUITY, canons of construction, and custom will dictate.

With grammar, bend less. Bending grammatical rules often results in ambiguity, which is costly in legal writing. (See AMBIGUITY, WAYS TO AVOID.) Further, many legal readers pride themselves on their knowledge of grammatical rules and are easily distracted by any bending. Your goal in writing is that any reader can understand your content; if readers have to pause to decipher grammatical variations as well as legal ones, they may get lost.

Undaunted, Attorney Jones proceeded with the cross-examination, ignoring the defense's objections.

rather than

Attorney Jones proceeded undauntedly with the cross-examination, irregardless of the defense's objections.

With general writing principles, bend only with good reason. Although concrete rules are useful to help any writer make decisions quickly, at some time or another some rules just do not make sense. For example, you may need to split an infinitive to make your point clear.

The mayor agreed to only suggest the alternative.

rather than

The mayor agreed only to suggest the alternative.

Here, leaving the infinitive unsplit creates a SQUINTING MODIFIER. The safer route, however, is to avoid bending the rule by REVISING.

The mayor agreed that she would only suggest the alternative.

If you cannot revise to avoid the problem, ask yourself, "What will be clear to my reader?" "What most accurately states my point?" Then, using the answers to these questions and your own common sense, bend the rules if need be. For more detail on this point, see COMMON SENSE. For some related concerns, see ACCURACY; PRECISION; READABILITY; and AMBIGUITY, WAYS TO AVOID.

BETWEEN OR AMONG?
See AMONG OR BETWEEN?

BETWEEN YOU AND ME OR BETWEEN YOU AND I?
Use **between you and me**, always; me, the objective case, is the object of the preposition **between**.

BILLS, WRITING THEM
See LEGISLATION or REQUESTS FOR PAYMENT.

BLACK
This term is preferable to **Negro**. It is not capitalized.

For blacks, the Act was particularly significant.

BLUE BOOK
This term refers to *The Uniform System of Citation* (Harvard Law Review Association 14th ed. 1986), the recognized authority for CITATIONS across the country. Most users of the book refer to it now as the Blue Book, as the authors do here. Become familiar with each section of the Blue Book, especially with the inside cover, where short forms appear for BRIEFS and MEMOS, and FOOTNOTES. Another helpful section is H, where tables appear for standard cites in every state.

Unless your state has rules to the contrary, Blue Book rules govern citation form. For details on citation forms derived from the Blue

Book, see CITATIONS; CITATIONS, BASIC FORMATS; CITATIONS, PARALLEL; and CITATIONS, STRING.

BOTH

Use **both** when you are joining two people or things logically in a sentence.

Both courts used this reasoning.

but

The cases are similar.

rather than

Both cases are similar.

In the latter example, the writer is not saying that both cases are similar to something else and therefore should not join the two logically in the sentence.

BOTH . . . AND

Use **both** . . . **and** to emphasize an upcoming pair of entities or concepts.

Both the mayor and the city council approved this action.

rather than

The mayor as well as the city council approved this action.

For related information, see CONJUNCTIONS and TRANSITIONS.

BRACKETS

In general, brackets indicate changes made in a quote. Use brackets around SIC to indicate any significant mistakes occurring in an original quote. See Blue Book rule 5.2.

"The court hold [sic] the evidence admissible."

Also use brackets to change a letter from upper case to lower case or vice versa and to substitute words or letters or other material into the text.

"[E]xcellence in [administrative] procedures is indispensable to carrying out the statute's intent."

Brackets have a few other specialized uses, such as marking shortened forms of case names within footnote CITATIONS. See Blue Book rules 4.2, 20.2, 20.3(c), and 20.5.2.

For more specific information on how to use brackets in quotes, see PUNCTUATING QUOTES.

BREAKING THE RULES
See BENDING THE RULES.

BRIEF ANSWERS

This may be the first section the reader looks at in a memo, so it should give the answer to the QUESTION PRESENTED as definitively as possible, such as Yes, No, or Probably yes. Then give the specific reason for that answer. This should be done in one concise sentence, if possible; in any case, it should be brief. Avoid simply restating the Question Presented in sentence form or leaving the terms too vague. These techniques defeat the purpose of the Brief Answer, which is to inform the reader at a glance whether the answer is yes or no, and why. Together with the Question Presented, the Brief Answer provides the concise thesis of your memo.

For example, if the Question Presented is Under Fed. R. Civ. P. 4(d)(1), Summons: Personal Service, was notice effective when it was delivered to the defendant's wife at her home? then the Brief Answer could be as follows.

Yes; notice was effective because the home of the defendant's wife is his "usual place of abode," that is, the defendant had lived there within the last year, he had moved back there one week after the summons was delivered, and he had received other mail there.

BRIEFS

Briefs are persuasive documents filed with a court to support a client's case. They may take the form of PRETRIAL BRIEFS (sometimes called Memorandum in Support of a Motion or in Opposition to a Motion or MEMORANDUM OF POINTS AND AUTHORITIES), TRIAL BRIEFS, post-trial briefs, or APPELLATE BRIEFS.

Briefs use PERSUASIVE WRITING to predispose the reader to the client's point of view by informing the reader of the applicable law and persuading the reader to decide the issue in favor of the writer's client.

The FORMAT of briefs varies with jurisdiction, so check your local rules for any variation from the following standard format.

[CAPTION]

Check your jurisdiction for the formalities of the caption. This should include (1) the name of the court in which the memorandum is filed; (2) the names of the parties; (3) their status, such as plaintiff or defendant; (4) the case file number; and (5) the title of the memorandum of points and authorities and a description of the motion the memo supports or opposes. For related information, see CAPTIONS.

ISSUE[S]

ISSUE STATEMENTS state the legal questions that, when answered, will determine the outcome of the case. An issue should include the rule of law applicable in this case, the legal question, and the legally significant facts. It should, however, be worded so the reader will be predisposed to decide in favor of the writer's client, while still being accurate enough to be acceptable to the writer's opponent. Many courts like to have the issue presented first, although some prefer this section to follow the Statement of the Case. For related information, see QUESTION PRESENTED.

STATEMENT OF THE CASE

The STATEMENT OF THE CASE should contain the LEGALLY SIG-NIFICANT FACTS, the BACKGROUND FACTS, and the significant EMOTIONAL FACTS. It should also include all applicable procedural history. The facts should be organized logically: by chronology, by topic, or by a combination of both. Facts should be cited to the record or to the pretrial documents as they exist at the time of filing the brief. For related information, see PARENTHETICALS.

ARGUMENT

The ARGUMENT SECTION, like the DISCUSSION SECTION of a memo, presents the general rules of law and any exceptions, and examples of previous applications of that law. The argument then applies that law to the facts of this case, usually using some form of a syllogism, and reaches a specific conclusion. The general ORGANIZA-TION should follow the structure of the law itself, using POINT HEADINGS and subheadings to outline salient legal points and reasoning. The ARGUMENT SECTION should present the law from the perspective most favorable to the client. For more help here, see SYLLOGISMS; ORGANIZATION, LARGE–SCALE and ORGANIZA-TION, SMALL–SCALE. For more suggestions on how to build reasoning, see P. Schlag and D. Skover, *Tactics of Legal Reasoning* (Carolina Academic Press 1986).

CONCLUSION

The conclusion should summarize briefly the reasoning presented in the argument and should request specific relief. The court should know at a glance what result the writer asks for and why. Avoid the traditional **For the foregoing reasons**. This forces the reader to either reread the entire Argument Section or skip the point. Instead, use this last opportunity for a focused summary that delivers the final punch.

BUSINESS LETTERS
See GENERAL CORRESPONDENCE LETTERS.

BUT

But is a powerful conjunction that can mean any of the following: (1) **on the contrary**, (2) **however**, (3) **except that**, or (4) **other than**. Use it in legal writing to make a strong distinction between ideas. Because **but** is so strong, be careful not to overuse it.

He has a strong case for an appeal, but he failed to file the notice of appeal on time.

They should have objected, but neither they nor the court noticed the objectionable grounds in time.

But can also be effective at the first of a sentence, one of the POSITIONS OF EMPHASIS, if you want to emphasize that logical connection between two sentences.

No moral right as such exists in America. But Congress has made several attempts to add the moral right to Title 17.

For related general information, see CONJUNCTIONS; TRANSITIONS; and CONNECTIONS, MAKING THEM.

CAN HARDLY OR CAN'T HARDLY?

Can hardly is always correct. **Can't hardly** never is. In legal writing, it is often better to replace **can hardly** with some other phrase, like **can scarcely** or **can barely**. **Can hardly** is used loosely and frequently in speech, and as a result sounds rather informal.

CAN OR COULD?

See VERB TENSES.

CAN OR MAY?

Use **can** when you mean that the subject is able to do something.

The plaintiff can still lift packages weighing up to thirty pounds.

Use **may** when you mean that the subject has the permission to do something.

The police may search the glove compartment without first obtaining a search warrant if . . . .

CANNOT OR CAN NOT?

Cannot is the correct form in almost all cases.

I cannot represent you in this case.

Can not only appears when **not** is part of another phrase.

He can *not only* request a new hearing but also require a change of venue.

CAPITALIZATION

Legal writers have trouble with capitalization in five places: (1) with proper adjectives, (2) with titles of officials, (3) with the first word after a colon, (4) with common nouns used to refer to specific people or groups, and (5) with subheadings.

1. Proper adjectives.

Capitalize most proper adjectives, which are adjectives formed from proper nouns, such as **American banking system, the Atlantic seaboard,** or **Vietnamese refugees.** Do not capitalize an adjective when it has been used frequently and for a long time in the general language, such as **cesarean operation, india ink, italic type, murphy bed,** or **venetian blinds.** For an extensive list of adjectives derived from proper names, see the *U.S. Government Printing Office Style Manual* 41–42 (rev. ed. 1973).

2. Titles of officials.

Capitalize a title, such as **judge** or **justice**, only when it precedes the judge's or justice's name or when it replaces the name.

Justice Brennan wrote the concurring opinion.

Thank you, Judge, for your advice.

but

The judge signed the search warrant at 3:00 a.m.

For related information, see JUDGES, HOW TO ADDRESS.

3. The first word after a colon.

In general, do not capitalize the first word after the colon, because doing so usually makes the sentence self-consciously ornate, like a person wearing a tiara to a picnic. Capitalize the first word after the colon only to emphasize that word or phrase.

Plaintiff asks the court to deny the motion: This identification evidence should not be suppressed.

For an explanation of when to use colons, see COLONS.

4. Common nouns used to refer to specific people or groups.

Capitalize **Elk** in **He was an Elk**, because the word refers to a specific person and organization, rather than to generic elk grazing on the ranges of Montana. Similarly, write **The Representative spoke at length to us**, because the term **Representative** replaces the person's name, and thus refers to a specific person.

Capitalize **Constitution** only when naming any constitution in full, as in **Constitution of the State of Iowa**, or when referring to the **United States Constitution**. Do not capitalize parts of the constitution, such as **fourth amendment**, **article one**, **section 8**, or **preamble**. Do, however, capitalize **Bill of Rights**. See Blue Book rule 8.

5. Subheadings.

In subheadings, capitalize the initial word and all other substantive words; do not, however, capitalize CONJUNCTIONS or PREPOSITIONS of four or fewer letters. Also do not capitalize **a**, **an**, or **the**. See Blue Book rule 8.

CAPTIONS

Captions appear at the beginning of interoffice memos and all legal documents filed with the court. Captions identify the parties to the dispute, the type of document, and the purpose of the document. Each document has its own specific format and requirements for the caption.

1. Interoffice memos.

In interoffice MEMOS, captions should identify to whom the memo is addressed, who wrote the memo, what the subject matter of the memo is, and what the date is. Check the specific requirements of your office for captions. A typical memo caption follows.

MEMO

To: Fred P. Jones

From: Emily Barnett

Re: Krugman, file no. 48–6709; possible motion to suppress identification evidence

Date: March 27, 1996

2. Pretrial and trial documents.

The caption for a pretrial or trial document filed with a court usually identifies the court; the parties; the status of the parties, such as **plaintiffs, defendants, respondents,** or **appellants**; the file number of the case; and the title of the brief. Check your jurisdiction for its conventions in doing a pretrial brief caption. A typical one follows.

IN THE SUPERIOR COURT OF THE STATE OF WASHINGTON
FOR KING COUNTY

STATE OF WASHINGTON,
                   Plaintiffs,
      vs.
SIDNEY KRUGMAN,
              Defendant.
	NO. 85–3–11658–6
	BRIEF IN SUPPORT OF THE MOTION TO SUPPRESS IDENTIFICATION EVIDENCE

3. Appellate briefs.

Check your jurisdiction for your specific requirements for the caption of an appellate brief. A typical one follows on page 32.

CASE

To avoid confusion, use case only as a term of art, when literally referring to a case. For example, instead of in case of, use if; instead of in many cases, use often; instead of that is not the case, use that is not so. For related, general information, see TERMS OF ART.

CASE BRIEFS

When briefing cases, consider first the reason for which you are briefing, whether it is for class, for research, or for some other purpose. Then tailor your format to that purpose. A number of possibilities exist, ranging from full, formal briefs that find a place for every detail of the case to book briefing, where comments are made in the margins of your book. Whatever your system, make sure it works for you. From the following list and other sources, collect the suggestions that you like to create your own system. Using someone else's system, no matter how comprehensive, will not work unless it makes sense to you.

1. Case briefs for class.

Brief for classes according to the topic outlined by your professor or according to the relevant topic from your table of contents. Then make sure that the issue and HOLDINGS focus on that topic. For example, if the topic is intentional torts, make sure the issue considers the question of intent and the holding answers that question with a specific finding regarding the reason for intent or lack of intent. For related information, see QUESTION PRESENTED.

2. Case briefing for research.

Tailor your case briefs in research to the questions presented, outlined in Step 3 of the RESEARCH STRATEGY CHART. Then brief the case for its purpose in that context and ignore anything irrelevant to that purpose. For example, if you are researching the question of mistake in formation of the contract, brief the case for what it says about mistake; do not go into the details of any irrelevant procedural questions.

There is one exception to this. You may include some other details, such as reversal based on a procedural issue, when the result of the case being briefed differs from the result you want in your factual situation but you still want to use the case to support your client's position.

3. Format.

Whatever your format, make sure it is thorough enough to fulfill your purpose. Consider the following checklist in creating a case brief format that works for you.

SAMPLE FORMAT FOR CASE BRIEFS

CITATION: Make sure you put down the complete citation of the case in proper form here; this will save you time later.

PARTIES: Include all parties to the suit and their status, such as **plaintiff-respondent-victim** or **defendant-appellant-tortfeasor**.

PRIOR PROCEEDINGS: Include any relevant procedural history here, such as **trial court found for the defendant; defendant appealed, court of appeals reversed the trial court's decision; and now this appeal is before the supreme court.**

THEORIES OF THE PARTIES: Include here the theory under which the plaintiff or appellant is bringing the case, such as **false imprisonment** or **breach of contract**. Include here also any defenses the defendant might be raising, such as **consent** or **lack of consideration**.

OBJECTIVES: Consider here the objectives of the parties and write them in your own words, such as **getting specific performance—he wants the goods themselves** or **getting damages—all $55,000** or **getting acquitted.**

FACTS: List here all LEGALLY SIGNIFICANT FACTS and any BACKGROUND FACTS necessary to your own understanding of the case.

ISSUE: State the issue in terms of your purpose in reading the brief. Be as specific as you can with respect to that issue. See QUESTION PRESENTED and ISSUE STATEMENTS.

Did defendant Curtis falsely imprison plaintiff Butterworth when he drove around in the car for seven hours without stopping to let her out?

HOLDING: Answer the issue and give a reason here. See HOLDINGS.

Yes; Curtis falsely imprisoned Butterworth because he used words or acts intended to confine Butterworth, he actually confined her in the car, and Butterworth was aware that she was confined.

REASONING: This is probably the most important part of the case brief. It should include relevant RULES, the APPLICATION of those rules, and the conclusion the court reached. If possible, state this reasoning in terms of a syllogism: the rule is the major premise, the application is the minor premise, and the conclusion is the conclusion. For example, you might first state the entire rule of false imprisonment in your jurisdiction. Then you might show how the court applied that rule to the specific facts of this case; take it step by step so that any holes in the reasoning become clear. Finally, show how the court reached its conclusion. For related information, see SYLLOGISMS.

DICTA: In an opinion, **dicta**, which means **words**, is anything a court says that does not have a direct effect on the outcome of the case. Dicta differs from a holding in that dicta is not binding on courts in subsequent opinions. Dicta can be significant, however, in your use of a case in research or in class. Use dicta to predict a trend in the law, to illuminate the reasoning in this case, or to understand future cases.

COMMENTS: Write here any reaction you have to the case. This may become important when you continue your research or when you are asked in class to give your opinion of the case. Include your gut reaction and any other response you have that synthesizes this case with other cases in the chapter, with other cases in your research project, or with your own understanding of the trend of the law in this particular area. When briefing for class, ask yourself, "Why did the textbook author choose this case? Why is it here?" Answer those questions here.

For a detailed approach to case briefing, see W. Statsky and R. Wernet, *Case Analysis and Fundamentals of Legal Writing* (West 1977).

CASUAL LANGUAGE
　　See COLLOQUIALISMS.

CERTAIN
　　Use **certain** only if your point is literally certain. Because few points you make in legal writing are indeed certain, beware frequent use of the word. For a discussion of related concerns, see MODIFIERS and LITERAL MEANING.

CERTAINLY
See CERTAIN.

CHRONOLOGICAL ORGANIZATON

Use chronological organization in a STATEMENT OF FACTS or STATEMENT OF THE CASE to allow the reader to follow the events in order of occurrence.

Use this organizational scheme when the chronology itself is important to the analysis or when a chronological arrangement would be easiest for the reader to follow. Avoid using this scheme only if TOPICAL ORGANIZATION would be more beneficial to the analysis because the facts separate into categories for each issue. Sometimes combining both works best, such as separating the facts into substantive and procedural categories and then giving the chronological order of events under each category. For related concerns, see ORGANIZATION; ORGANIZATION, LARGE–SCALE; and TOPIC SENTENCES.

CIRCUMLOCUTION
See CONCISENESS, subsection 3.

CITATIONS

The BLUE BOOK, officially called *The Uniform System of Citation* (Harvard Law Review Association 14th ed. 1986), is the universally accepted standard for citations, and thus its rules should be followed in all legal writing. Most states, however, make some adjustments to these rules; if your state has its own style manual or has otherwise established exceptions to Blue Book rules, follow those exceptions in all documents filed to courts in that state.

Citations serve two functions: (1) to provide the reader with a specific authority within the text and (2) to replace long explanations of how that authority is used, for example as a quotation, as a rule, as a related authority, or as an authority that states the contrary of the proposition. Correct use of citations both establishes your credibility as a careful analyst and streamlines your legal writing STYLE. To make citations work for you in these capacities, consider the following.

1. Use citations and SIGNALS to make the reader aware of your precise use of authority. For example, using no signal automatically indicates that the cited authority states the proposition, identifies the source of a quotation, or identifies an authority referred to in the text. For further reference, see Blue Book rule 2.2(d).

2. Use citations as separate sentences following a proposition; avoid using a citation at the beginning of a sentence. A citation stops the reader's eye before the substance of the statement is clear. You may also use citations as clauses in the middle of sentences.

While contracts can provide some protection for an artist's moral rights, Youngs v. Taylor, 999 F.2d 999 (9th Cir. 1999), no single contract can cover the entire scope of those rights.

For related information, see INTRUSIVE PHRASES.

3. Eliminate text that repeats information given in the citation, such as **The court stated that . . . or The court went on to say that . . . or Another case stated the opposing view . . . .**

4. Use short citation forms when citing to immediately preceding authority. If the previous citation is a page or two back, use the full citation, so the reader does not have to backtrack too far. See CITATIONS, BASIC FORMATS. For further reference, see Blue Book rule 4.

5. Include the publisher and the date for all unofficial versions of statutes.

17 U.S.C.A. § 20 (West 1993).

Wash. Rev. Code Ann. § 29.09.040 (West 1984).

6. Give a **PARALLEL CITATION** to all state cases that have them.

Shaw v. Snyder, 101 Wis. 2d 348, 345 N.W.2d 3 (1996).

but

Sandvold v. Twombly, 345 P.2d 534 (Alaska 1996).

7. Give **PINPOINT CITES** when referring to any rules, holdings, quotations, specific propositions, or particulars of a case.

Reason v. Pearson, 33 Wis. 2d 987, 989, 201 N.W.2d 73, 76 (1973).

8. Put spaces after abbreviations that include more than a capital letter.

33 Wis. 2d 987.

or

222 Wash. 2d 346.

Do not insert spaces when the abbreviation is only a capital letter.

345 N.W.2d 31.

or

486 P.2d 692.

9. Check your jurisdiction for its variations on Blue Book rules. For example, the following table shows how cases would be cited under the Blue Book rules and then how the same cases would be cited under Washington's variations as provided in the *Washington Style Manual.*

For related information, see CITATIONS, BASIC FORMATS; CITATIONS, PARALLEL; CITATIONS, PINPOINT; and CITATIONS, STRING. For comprehensive directions on citation form, see E. Maier, *How To Prepare a Legal Citation* (Barron's 1986).

RULE	CATEGORY	BLUEBOOK CITE	WASHINGTON CITE (if different)
	FEDERAL STATUTES:	17 U.S.C. § 106 (1983) 17 U.S.C.A. § 106 (West 1983) 17 U.S.C.A. § 106 (Law. Co-op. 1983)	
	FEDERAL CASES: a. Supreme Court:	Powers v. Lloyd, 45 U.S. 238 (1989).	Powers v. Lloyd, 45 U.S. 238, 436 S. Ct. 733, 42 L. Ed. 2d 36 (1983).
	b. Circuit Court: c. District Court:	O'Sullivan v. Pernitz, 337 F.2d 498 (9th Cir. 1989). Orth v. Ostrander, 167 F. Supp 553 (W.D. Wash. 1989).	
	STATE STATUTES:	Wash. Rev. Code § 2.06.10 (1983). Wash. Rev. Code Ann. § 2.06.10 (West 1984).	RCW 2.06.10.
	STATE CASES: a. Supreme Court:	Fischer v. Mundt, 54 Wash. 2d 632, 45 P.2d 877 (1989).	Fischer v. Mundt, 54 Wn. 2d 632, 45 P.2d 877 (1989).
	b. Court of Appeals:	McDonald v. Noel, 237 Wash. App. 699, 473 P.2d 89 (1989).	McDonald v. Noel, 237 Wn. App. 699, 473 P.2d 89 (1989).
	TO CITE SPECIFIC PAGE: a. First time cited:	Keating v. Cutts, 233 Wash. 2d 56, 58, 77 P.2d 321, 324 (1995).	Keating v. Cutts, 233 Wn. 2d 56, 58, 77 P.2d 321, 324 (1995).
	b. Subsequently:	Keating, 233 Wash. 2d at 58, 77 P.2d at 324.	Keating v. Cutts, supra at 58. OR Keating, 233 Wn. 2d at 58. OR Keating, at 58.
	c. If no intervening cite or if there is not too much distance:	Id. at 58, 77 P.2d at 324.	

TO GIVE SUBSEQUENT HISTORY:
Koutnik v. Landon, 234 F. Supp. 583 (N.D. Pa. 1976), aff'd, 292 F.2d 37 (3d Cir. 1977), cert. denied, 458 U.S. 334 (1988).

CITATIONS, BASIC FORMATS

Case citations should include (1) the name of the case; (2) the volume, standard abbreviation for the book, and page number of the case; (3) the parallel citation, where appropriate; and (4) the year in which the decision was made. The reader should also be able to determine from the citation what court made the decision. Thus if the name of the court is not evident from the abbreviation of the book, as in **Wash. 2d** which indicates the Washington Supreme Court, then indicate (5) who the court is by putting its abbreviation before the date inside the parentheses.

Leraas v. Martin, 894 Wash. 2d 723, 468 P.2d 387 (1989).

but

Johnson v. Strus, 499 P.2d 387 (Alaska 1997).

Because the Alaska Supreme Court does not have an official reporter, the official reporter for that state's decisions is the Pacific Reporter. But the reader would not know what court had made the decision unless **Alaska** was put in the parentheses with the date. Similarly, for federal district court decisions and federal circuit court decisions, the court must be indicated in the parentheses with the date.

Knight v. Skover, 999 F. Supp. 287 (S.D. Iowa 1992).

What follows are examples of basic citation formats for the most-often-used jurisdictions.

1. State cases.

When citing state cases, give the name of the case; the volume of the official reporter, the abbreviation of the official reporter, and the page number on which the case begins; the volume of the parallel citation, the abbreviation for the book in which the parallel citation is found, the page on which the case starts in that book, and the year of the case in parentheses.

Birchler v. Polewski, 978 Wash. 2d 496, 901 P.2d 444 (1991).

Leraas v. Martin, 894 Wash. 2d 723, 468 P.2d 387 (1989).

If the state's official reporter is a regional reporter, include the state in parentheses with the date.

Hansen v. Wark, 946 P.2d 27 (Alaska 1993).

2. Federal district court cases.

When citing federal district court cases, include the name of the case, the volume of the **Federal Supplement** in which the case is found, the abbreviation **F.Supp.**, and the page on which the case begins. Then, in parentheses, put the abbreviation for the court making the decision and the year in which the decision was made. Federal district court decisions after 1932 are cited as follows. See the Blue Book for pre-1932 citation forms becase the formats differ.

Knight v. Skover, 987 F. Supp. 287 (S.D. Iowa 1992).

Mahr v. Huston, 908 F. Supp. 486 (D.D.C. 1997).

For a list of the abbreviations of the district courts see D. Bieber, *Current American Legal Citations With 2100 Examples* 297–330 (Hein 1983).

3. Federal circuit court cases.

When citing federal circuit court decisions, include the name of the case; the volume of the **Federal Reporter** in which the case is found; the abbreviation **F.** or **F.2d** and the page on which the case begins. Then in parentheses include the name of the circuit and the year in which the decision was made. Federal circuit court decisions are cited as follows.

Armstrong v. Williams, 977 F.2d 124 (D.C. Cir. 1991).

For a list of citations of all the circuit courts, see Bieber, *Current American Legal Citations*, 293–296 (1983).

4. U.S. Supreme Court cases.

For U.S. Supreme Court cases, the Blue Book requires that only the *United States Reporter* be cited. Thus give the name of the case, the volume in the United States Reporter in which the case is found, the abbreviation *U.S.*, the page on which the case begins, and, in parentheses, the year of the decision.

Engber v. Koutnik, 959 U.S. 123 (1989).

Always check your jurisdiction for variations on this standard format; for example, some states require that all three reporters be cited, and prefer them in a certain order. The usual order is as follows.

Engber v. Koutnik, 980 U.S. 123, 999 S. Ct. 234, 965 L. Ed. 325 (1989).

For examples of specialty courts, see D. Bieber, *Current American Legal Citations With 2100 Examples* (Hein 1983) and E. Maier, *How to Prepare A Legal Citation*, (Barron's 1986).

CITATIONS, PARALLEL

All United States Supreme Court cases, most state cases, and some federal cases appear in more than one book. Thus a case may have more than one citation, and those are called parallel citations.

The United States Supreme Court and most other courts have one official reporter, which is that jurisdiction's authoritative text. For example, the United States Supreme Court's official reporter is labeled U.S. The Blue Book requires the author to cite to that official text but does not require parellel citations for United States Supreme Court cases. For state cases, however, the Blue Book does require parallel citations to unofficial reporters. Parallel citations are useful because they refer to sources accessible to most legal readers.

Fischer v. Doerr, 437 U.S. 893 (1999).

but

Lamb v. Laffon, 145 Ariz. 212, 700 P.2d 1312 (1989).

Check the tables in section H of the Blue Book for specific directions regarding which reporters to cite in parallel citations for each state. When using PINPOINT CITES, include the specific page number for the parallel cite as well.

CITATIONS, STRING

String cites are citations of two or more cases for the same point. Semicolons separate the individual cites in a string cite, and cases are cited in reverse chronological order.

This rule has been applied uniformly in Arkansas. Lorey v. Jacobi, 99 Ark. 111, 222 S.W.2d 22 (1994); Zuckerman v. Kidwell, 100 Ark. 841, 224 S.W.2d 444 (1993); Arthur v. Christopoulos, 101 Ark. 502, 226 S.W.2d 321 (1992).

String cites can be used to convey the message to the reader that not just one authority stands for a point, but two, three, or four do. If that message is essential to your analysis, then use the string cite. Do not, however, use a string cite just to show that you found more than one case. If one case is sufficient to make the point, omit the other citations. Remember that the doubting legal reader will check most authorities and will be annoyed if each is not pertinent. For format and order of string cites, see Blue Book rules 2.1 and 2.4.

CLARITY

Clarity means writing so the reader can follow the writing step by step, without wondering what a phrase means or what the point of the paper is. When the writing is clear, the reader can forget about the writing itself and focus instead on the merit of the content. The main tools of clarity are (1) using straightforward and logical ORGANIZATION, (2) using precise and familiar words, and (3) using readable and effective SENTENCE STRUCTURE. For related information, see ORGANIZATION, LARGE–SCALE; ORGANIZATION, SMALL–SCALE; PRECISION; and READABILITY.

CLAUSES

A clause is a group of words that includes a subject and a predicate. Several clauses may be combined to form a compound or complex sentence.

Even if the court remands the case [dependent clause], the Plaintiff will not appreciably increase his reward [independent clause].

An independent clause can stand alone as a logical sentence.

The plaintiff will not appreciably increase his reward.

A dependent clause cannot, because it begins with a word or phrase that makes the clause depend logically on another point.

Even if the court remands the case

Not knowing the difference between dependent and independent clauses can lead a writer to misuse COMMAS. This occurs most often with the word **however.**

The court remanded the case; however, the plaintiff did not receive an appreciably higher reward.

rather than

40

The court remanded the case, however, the plaintiff did not receive an appreciably higher reward.

Because **however** joins two independent clauses, those clauses must be separated with a semicolon. For a discussion of clauses in the context of sentences, see SENTENCE STRUCTURE.

CLEARLY

Is the point really clear? If not, omit **clearly**. Similarly, whenever you read the word **clearly** in a text, look for a hole in the writer's logic. In most situations, **clearly** will remind you of the orator who pounds on the podium in the hope that his ardor will obscure his argument's weakness. For a discussion of related concerns, see MODIFIERS, CONCISENESS, and LITERAL MEANING.

CLEAR WRITING

See READABILITY and CLARITY.

CLIENT LETTERS

Client letters may be formal or informal OPINION LETTERS or GENERAL CORRESPONDENCE LETTERS. See those entries or, if appropriate, BAD NEWS, GIVING IT or BAD NEWS, SOFTENING IT.

CLOSINGS FOR LETTERS

Choose the standard closing that suits your writing STYLE and the TONE of your letter. If the tone of your letter is businesslike yet friendly, try **Sincerely** or **Sincerely yours**. If your tone is more formal, try **Yours truly** or **Very truly yours**. Do not worry about seeming insincere; these closings are not taken literally.

Using innovative alternatives only creates undesirable responses, rather than underscoring your sincerity. If you use something more accurate, like **Don't bother me anymore**, you only seem unprofessional or petulant. If you omit the closing, you create an abrupt, impersonal tone that is usually not appropriate, even in a tough collection letter. For more detail on related issues, see TONE IN LETTERS and GENERAL CORRESPONDENCE LETTERS.

COHERENCE

Coherence in writing means writing so that any reader can see easily how all the content fits together. Your first tool for achieving coherence is organization, your second is consistent and unambiguous wording, and your third is clear and adequate transitions. For detail on how to accomplish this, see ORGANIZATION, SMALL–SCALE; PARAGRAPHS; PRECISION; REPETITION; AMBIGUITY, WAYS TO AVOID; CONNECTIONS, MAKING THEM; and TRANSITIONS.

COLLECTIVE NOUNS

A collective noun represents a collection of persons or things regarded as a unit. As such, a collective noun takes a singular verb when it refers to the collection as a whole.

The E.P.A. is determined to press its [not their] claim.

The American Bar Association meets at least once a year.

A collective noun takes a plural verb, however, when it refers to the collection as separate persons or things.

The Student Bar Association have all gone home.

Make sure you do not treat a collective noun as both singular and plural in the same construction.

For a general discussion, see NOUNS.

COLLOQUIALISMS

Colloquialism refers to informal or regional phrases, or words or phrases used in conversation but not in formal writing, such as **ripped off** or **got into**. Rarely will you use colloquialisms in legal writing, not only because they are informal but also because they are usually not precise enough for legal writing. Colloquialisms may appear, however, as a part of a quote. Never resort to colloquialisms only because you cannot think of another word for the idea. There always is another word, so using the colloquialism would be admitting that your vocabulary is inadequate. For related information, see ACCURACY, LITERAL MEANING, and QUOTATION MARKS.

COLONS

The most common use of a colon in legal writing is to introduce a list.

In justifying the exclusion of expert psychiatric evidence, the court listed three concerns: maintaining the integrity of the bifurcated trial procedure, avoiding allowing the guilty to go free, and preserving the defendant's right against self-incrimination.

or

The Company's liability does not include any of the following:

(1) any damage occurring in connection with the use of the equipment in any nuclear facility;

(2) any consequential or incidental damages, including but not limited to loss of profit, damage to associated equipment, cost of capital, and cost of substitute products;

(3) any costs beyond the price of the product and service that gives rise to the claim; or

(4) any claims arising from advice or assistance given by the Company without separate compensation for that advice.

Do not, however, use a colon if each item listed is punctuated as a complete sentence. In that situation, write the introduction to the list as a complete sentence and end it with a period, not a colon.

During the period of this maintenance agreement, if the Company determines that it cannot maintain the equipment in good working order, then the Company must replace the equipment with another unit in good working order. This requirement is subject to the following provisions.

1. If the Company replaces the equipment within two years of the warranty expiration date, then the replacement unit must be one that is newly manufactured, remanufactured, or reconditioned.

2. If the Company replaces the equipment more than two years after the warranty expiration date, then the replacement unit will be one that is refurbished in accordance with the process used to refurbish rental units.

3. If the Company cannot replace the equipment with another unit of the same model, then the replacement unit will be substantially similar or will have greater capabilities.

4. . . . .

You may use a colon instead of a period between two sentences if one sentence sets up an expectation in the reader's mind that the next sentence fulfills.

The intent was clear: he pointed the gun directly at the victim's chest.

You may also use a colon, for emphasis, to introduce a phrase that is not a complete sentence.

The plaintiff has only one motive: recovery for his loss.

Avoid overusing the colon; it creates a dramatic sentence structure that will become too noticeable if overused. For related information, see EMPHASIS.

In general, do not capitalize the first word after the colon, because doing so usually makes the sentence self-consciously ornate. If you want, however, you may capitalize the first word after the colon to emphasize that word.

Plaintiff asks the court to deny the motion: This identification evidence should not be suppressed.

COMBINING WORDS
See HYPHENS.

COMMAS
In general, commas coordinate one part of a sentence with another. A comma may (1) set off an introductory phrase, (2) set off an interrupting phrase, (3) indicate that more information follows in a phrase at the end of the sentence, or (4) signal that a new subject and verb follow a

conjunction. Commas also (5) coordinate dates and (6) set off quotes and items in a list.

Generally, (7) do not use a comma after a conjunction if a verb, but no subject, follows the conjunction. Also do not use a comma between two subjects if both subjects share the same verb.

1.   Comma setting off an introductory phrase.

Use a comma when you place a phrase before the subject, unless that phrase is short and closely related to the subject.

In negligence actions, the theory is that the person being sued had a duty to act and failed to fulfill that duty.

If the consumer disagrees with the information in the report, the agency must investigate again.

First, it assumes that creditors have a definite criteria for creditworthiness.

In contrast, a father who once attempted to retain physical possession of his son by the use of a gun was later determined by the supreme court to be a fit parent for custody.   In <u>Edwards v. Edwards</u>, the father obtained a divorce from his wife .   .   .   .

2.   Comma setting off an interrupting phrase.

Use commas before and after a phrase inserted in the middle of a sentence.

Most economists agree that, in terms of equity, this income should be taxed.

The case is, however, a sample from that system.

The plaintiff, despite warnings from his friends, jumped off the embankment.

Willard Evans, Louise's father, testified at the hearing on the post-conviction motion.

Do not, however, put commas around a restrictive phrase, which comes after the subject but is necessary to describe the subject accurately.

The defendant's belief that the man was reaching for a gun supports instructions about both self-defense and manslaughter.

The standards adopted by the court reflect a prudent lawyer's conduct with his or her client.

For more explanation of restrictive phrases, see THAT OR WHICH?

3.   Comma indicating that more information follows.

Use a comma before extra information added to the end of a sentence.

The holding was poorly reasoned, filled with vague terms and illogical statements.

Privileges fall into the category of exceptions to a general rule, the rule of disclosure.

This court announced its decision in <u>Sherman v. Freedman</u>, which abolished the locality rule.

4. Comma before a conjunction introducing a new subject and verb.

Use a comma before a conjunction that joins two independent CLAUSES.

The defendant expressed a desire to change his plea, but his attorney advised him not to do this.

Some proposals advocate continued use of the family as the basic unit of taxation, but others urge a return to the individual as the taxable unit.

5. Commas coordinating dates.

Use a comma between a specific date and the year (July 4, 1986) but not between a month and the year (July 1986). Also do not use a comma when the date is written before the name of the month (4 July 1986).

6. Commas setting off quotes and items in a list.

For use of commas with quotes, see PUNCTUATING QUOTES. For use of commas in lists, see LISTS, STRUCTURE OF.

7. Situations where commas are not needed.

If two verbs share a common subject, do not put a comma before the conjunction between the verbs.

The driver lost control of his car while moving to the passing lane [ ] and slammed into the rear left fender of the defendant's truck.

Both the defendant and the plaintiff agree that the defendant had the obligation to post appropriate warnings [ ] and was within his rights when he posted the "no trespassing" signs.

The defendant had a duty to act [ ] and failed to fulfill that duty.

Do add a comma, however, if omitting it can cause a misreading of a sentence.

The defendant did see that an ambulance was called, and notified the proper authorities.

Also, do not use a comma between two subjects that share one verb.

Both custodial spouses seeking back payments of child support [ ] and divorcing parents seeking an order for child support will benefit from this rule.

If two phrases are joined by a conjunction but both phrases are short, you may omit the comma if you wish.

The attorney recommended this action [ ] and the client did not object.

COMMON NOUN
See NOUNS.

COMMON SENSE
You must use common sense in legal writing because few rules are absolute. But proceed cautiously when common sense hints at breaking a rule; do so only if the answer to all of the following questions is **yes.**

1. Can I break the rule without sacrificing one shred of ACCURACY?

2. Can I break the rule without sacrificing CLARITY?

3. Can I break the rule without sounding cute, trendy, or overly dramatic?

4. Am I breaking this rule only to meet the requirements of some higher rule? For example, you might choose a less concise phrase because it is more accurate and is easily read, or you might break a rule because the court has broken the rule in stating a proposition and you must for some reason quote the court directly, rather than using a PARAPHRASE. For related information, see BENDING THE RULES.

COMPARE TO OR COMPARE WITH?

Use **compare to** when you are introducing a similarity.

This harm, losing the ability to continue running competitively, can be compared to losing the ability to continue working.

Use **compare with** when you are introducing two items you will subsequently compare or contrast.

This situation can be compared with the defendant's situation in <u>Wheeler v. Bailey</u> . . . .

COMPARISON

Three factors can be used to clarify comparisons: parallel structure, clear transitions, and effective subjects and verbs.

1. Use PARALLEL STRUCTURE.

One of the best ways to write a graceful, effective comparison is to place the items compared in parallel structures. The framework of the parallel structure highlights the similarity or difference in the substance.

In <u>Sampson</u>, the landlord had been asked by tenants to replace burnt-out light bulbs in a stairwell, but had refused to do so. Similarly, Mr. Tyler had been asked to place higher wattage light bulbs in the stairwell, but had refused to do so.

2. Use clear transitions.

Additionally, you can use TRANSITIONS to let the reader know that a comparison or contrast is coming.

In 1919, when the doctrine of the best interest of the child became the controlling consideration in custody disputes, the results of those disputes changed. Until then, custody usually was awarded to fathers. After 1919, *however*, custody usually was awarded to mothers.

3. Use effective subjects and verbs.

Another way to make a comparison shine is to make sure that you have placed the items compared in the main parts of the sentence, the subject and verb. For example, the following passage emphasizes the point that both fetuses were viable.

In Kwaterski, the court found that the unborn infant, in its eighth month of gestation, was viable before the car accident causing its death. Similarly, Dr. Bernhardt found that the Jones infant, in its seventh month of gestation, was viable before the accident causing its death.

The main parts of the sentences are **the court found that the unborn infant was viable** and **Dr. Bernhardt found that the Jones infant was viable**. Making these points the main parts of the sentences emphasizes the similarity, while the difference (**eighth month of gestation** instead of **seventh month**) is stated but downplayed in PREPOSITIONAL PHRASES. For a general discussion of this technique, see SENTENCE STRUCTURE.

COMPLETELY
If it is not really **complete**, do not use **completely**.

COMPLEX SENTENCES
A complex sentence has two or more CLAUSES, or groups of words that each has its own subject and verb; however, unlike in a compound sentence, a complex sentence contains a dependent clause.

Although John was in the room while his father was reading and discussing the will with the attorneys, John sat on the opposite side of the room and did not participate in the discussion.

A dependent clause cannot stand on its own as a sentence because it is attached to the other clause with a subordinating conjunction.

although John was in the room

while his father was reading and discussing the will

Complex sentences are useful for downplaying information because the reader views the independent clause as more important than the dependent clause. But use this structure with discretion; if complex sentences are overused, the text becomes hard to read.

If you wanted to read about complicated sentences, rather than about the grammatical category of complex sentences, see READABILITY or SENTENCE STRUCTURE.

COMPOUND SENTENCES
A compound sentence has two or more independent CLAUSES that are joined by a conjunction. Independent clauses are clauses that have a subject and verb and could stand on their own as complete sentences. Although compound sentences are not as frequently useful in legal writing as COMPLEX SENTENCES, they can be helpful for combining two points that are both logically and structurally parallel.

Other doctors in similar situations do disclose some risks to their patients, [independent clause] and [conjunction] thus you may argue that Dr. Walker did not meet the standard of disclosure set by his profession for cases such as yours [independent clause].

Occasionally compound sentences can also be helpful for avoiding undue emphasis of a minor point. Short sentences are emphatic, so putting a minor point in a short sentence confuses the reader by overemphasizing that point.

The supervisor told Mr. Sykes to remove the cartons from the loading dock before the end of the day, and Mr. Sykes did so.

rather than

The supervisor told Mr. Sykes to remove the cartons from the loading dock before the end of the day. Mr. Sykes did so.

For related information, see SENTENCE STRUCTURE.

COMPUTERS

Using computers for research is fast and effective, but expensive. Therefore, use computers to supplement, not to replace, book research. When you decide to use a computer, go through the first five steps of the following Ten-Step Guide before going to the terminal. Additionally, know the vocabulary of the computer system you are using, whether it be Lexis or Westlaw. They do have differences, although the approach is essentially the same, and you need to be familiar with these differences before you start the following steps.

TEN–STEP GUIDE TO COMPUTER RESEARCH

At your desk.

1. Collect the facts. List the who, what, where, when, why, and how.

2. Analyze the facts according to your preferred system.

   (a) *Westlaw*: **parties, places, objects, basis, defense, relief.**

   (b) *Lexis*: **things, acts, persons, places.**

   Brainstorm at this stage; avoid editing. Give each category a page or a column, and then think of every possible synonym and antonym in order to get accurate search words.

3. Formulate the QUESTION PRESENTED. Brainstorm again, thinking of all the possible questions. Write out those questions following this three-step formula.

   (a) **Under** [what you think the general law is]

   (b) **did** [the legal question, such as, **did X assault Y**]

   (c) **when** [LEGALLY SIGNIFICANT FACTS applicable to this legal question]?

Then organize Issues logically, putting threshold issues first, such as **standing,** and substantive issues later such as **whether X assaulted Y.**

4. Formulate your query.

   (a) Choose terms from the list you made in step 2 and identify the search words most important to your issue, concentrating on terms a court might have used, such as **consideration,** rather than more general terms, such as **payment.**

48

(b) Formulate the search words according to your specific computer language system, using *Westlaw* or *Lexis* root expanders.

(c) Use connectors according to your computer language system so that you carefully limit your query. Consider first the scope of the topic. If it is wide, use more restrictive connectors, such as **within the same paragragh** (/P for Westlaw) or **within the same sentence** (/S). If the scope is narrow, use broader connectors, such as **&**.

5. Choose your database, which is the computer equivalent of the set of books to which you would go to research your QUESTION PRESENTED. Each computer system has a list of databases, such as Northwest (NW), which corresponds to the *Northwest Regional Reporter*, or New York (NY-CS), which corresponds to the *New York Reporter*. Make sure you know which jurisdiction's law will apply and therefore which database you wish to search. If the scope is narrow, put terms within the same case.

6. Map out your research strategy, depending on what sources you already have and what databases you would like to search.

At the computer terminal.

7. Sign on to the system according to its rules.

8. Enter your query according to the directions, and when you come up with a list of sources, make sure you have a usable amount; if not, edit your query.

9. Print out only the material essential to your work; take notes on the rest but be aware of your time, so that you can minimize the time actually signed on. One useful shortcut is to print a list of cases, sign off, and then locate the cases in the reporters.

10. Update the law on the computer only insofar as hardcover SHEPARD'S and other sources are incomplete. However you use the computer, remember that it is not a panacea; it cannot solve all research problems. Similarly, the computer is not error-proof. It is literal, so formulate your query carefully.

For related information, see WRITING PROCESS and GETTING STARTED.

CONCISENESS

Conciseness is at a premium in legal writing. Achieve it whenever possible, although never at the expense of substance. Revise for conciseness by doing the following.

1. Eliminate facts or law that do not bear on this particular analysis. Concentrate on the scope of this problem, so the reader can concentrate on that too. For example, if the only legal issue being discussed in a memorandum is **whether or not there has been an intentional tort**, do not include facts in the analysis that do not bear on intentional tort. For related information, see LEGALLY SIGNIFICANT FACTS, BACKGROUND FACTS, and EMOTIONAL FACTS.

2. Move important material to the beginning of paragraphs and sections; this will eliminate long explanations that reach a result. Instead, give the result and explain it. For more detail and related information, see PARAGRAPHS, TOPIC SENTENCES, and POSITIONS OF EMPHASIS.

3. Make sure that each paragraph advances one of the points in your reasoning. This should help you avoid circumlocution, or discussing again a point already established. Similarly, present only one main point in a paragraph. This will help you make sure you support and explain that point adequately, which will lessen the chance that you will repeat the point later to bring in further support. For related information, see PARAGRAPHS and ORGANIZATION, SMALL-SCALE.

4. Use the key words in a sentence for your subjects and verbs.

Exigent circumstances justify the police's failure to obtain a warrant.

rather than

The crucial fact here is that exigent circumstances existed justifying the police's failure to obtain a warrant.

5. Make CITATIONS speak for themselves, rather than using **the court held** or **the court went on to say.**

The doctrine of moral right is not expressly recognized in New York. Hesler v. Alley Book Division, 952 N.Y.S.2d 552, 555, 761 Misc. 2d 104, 105 (1993).

rather than

The New York Court in Hesler v. Alley Book Division, 952 N.Y.S.2d 552, 555, 761 Misc. 2d 104, 105 (1993), has stated that the doctrine of moral right is not expressly recognized in New York.

6. Use ACTIVE VOICE, rather than passive, because passive voice often requires more words.

The defendant argued that the court should suppress the evidence.

rather than

It was argued by the defendant that the evidence should be suppressed by the court.

7. Omit unneeded ADJECTIVES and ADVERBS.

The court in Thomas does not establish a standard for viability that is any more specific than the fetus' ability to exist separately from its mother.

rather than

Obviously, the court in Thomas appears to fail to definitively establish an unambiguous and undebatable determining standard for when a fetus reaches the medical state of viability that seems to be any more clearly specific than ascertaining medically the fetus' ability to exist separately and apart from its biological mother.

8. Delete unneeded prepositional phrases. For example, substitute **legally** for **on a legal basis** or **defendant's** for **of the defendant.**

The defendant's obligation may have existed morally, but not legally.

rather than

The obligation of the defendant may have existed in a moral sense but not on a legal basis.

9. When possible delete **that** constructions, such as **there are . . . that, there is . . . that,** and **it is . . . that.**

You must go through this process to identify any opinion's key facts.

rather than

This is the process that you must go through to identify any opinion's key facts.

10. Delete long empty phrases that add words with no meaning. If sentences were twenty mule teams, these phrases would be weak mules dragging down the rest of the team. For example, remove **it is clear that,** and just state your point. Remove **it is important to state at the outset that** and just say **first.**

CONCLUSIONS

The Conclusion is the final section in a memo or brief. It is also part of an opinion letter. In all three, the Conclusion may be the first section to which the legal reader turns. In briefs, the Conclusion should summarize briefly the reasoning presented in the argument and should request specific relief. The court should know at a glance what result the writer asks for and why. Avoid the traditional **For the foregoing reasons.** This forces the reader to either reread the entire Argument Section or skip the point. Instead, use this last opportunity for a focused summary that delivers the final punch. For related information, see SUMMARY OF THE ARGUMENT.

In MEMOS, the Conclusion summarizes the main points made in the Discussion, giving a capsule of the reasoning that led to the Brief Answer. It may also contain recommendations to the reader. It does not, however, include any information or reasoning not covered in the Discussion.

In OPINION LETTERS, the Conclusion answers the client's question, often in one sentence. Usually place the Conclusion in the opening if the news is good, after the facts if you want to soften the news, or at the end if the conclusion would not make sense without a lengthy explanation.

In your WRITING PROCESS, write your Conclusion when it is most helpful to do so. For example, if you are having trouble seeing how all your points fit together, you may find it helpful to write the Conclusion before finishing the rest of your draft. Conversely, you may find it more helpful to write the conclusion only after you have written the rest of your draft and your REASONING is clarified.

CONCRETE NOUNS
    See ABSTRACT NOUNS.

CONFORM TO, CONFORM WITH, OR CONFORM IN?
    Conform to.

CONJUNCTIONS
    Conjunctions join phrases, words, or sentences.

1. Classifying conjunctions.

    Conjunctions can be coordinating, such as **and, but, for,** or **or.** They are correlating when they include two words working together, such as **both . . . and** or **either . . . or.** Finally, they are subordinating when they introduce DEPENDENT CLAUSES, such as **although, because, unless, despite, until.**

2. Using conjunctions effectively.

    Conjunctions serve as clear and effective transitions only when used accurately, so choose the conjunction that most accurately communicates the logical connection between the two sentences.

Although the project was not finished by the date scheduled for completion, the contract was not breached because the delay was due to a hailstorm.

rather than

The project was not finished by the date scheduled for completion and the contract was not breached because the delay was due to a hailstorm.

    For help in finding the most accurate conjunction, see TRANSITIONS. For related information, see CONNECTIONS, MAKING THEM.

    Two other problems to watch for when using conjunctions are (1) overusing one conjunction, such as **and,** and (2) using a conjunction to join two things not logically and grammatically parallel. For a discussion of the latter, see PARALLEL STRUCTURE. For advice on the use of specific conjunctions, see AND, AND/OR, BOTH . . . AND, BUT, OR, and NOT ONLY . . . BUT ALSO. For related information, see HOWEVER and SENTENCE STRUCTURE, subsection 2.

CONNECTING WORDS
    See TRANSITIONS.

CONNECTIONS, MAKING THEM
    Making the connection clear between phrases or sentences is like using your car's turn signals correctly when leading a convoy. By letting your readers know where you are going, you increase the chance that those readers will be able to follow your logical route. Consider the following techniques in constructing strong connections.

1.   Use parallel structure. This structure can immediately underscore both the similarities and differences. For example, you can compare two items like this.

In Sampson, the landlord had been asked by tenants to replace burnt-out light bulbs in a stairwell, but had refused to do so. Similarly, Mr. Tyler had been asked to place higher wattage light bulbs in the stairwell, but had refused to do so.

For more on this technique, see PARALLEL STRUCTURE.

2.   Repeat key terms. Use repetition when it is needed for ACCURACY. For example, if you mean this **contract**, do not shift to this **document** or this **agreement**. Changing terms confuses legal readers, who will think that you must mean something else if you changed terms. For more on this technique, see REPETITION.

3.   Use a transition, such as **furthermore, because, although,** or **even if.** Keep in mind, however, that this connection is only as good as the accuracy of the transition word.

The Act did not successfully treat the broader problem of marital status discrimination.   Instead, it shifted inequitable tax burdens between taxpaying groups.

rather than

The Act did not successfully treat the broader problem of marital status discrimination; however, it shifted inequitable tax burdens between taxpaying groups.

Because using an inaccurate transition is more confusing than using none, never throw in a transition carelessly. For more help in choosing accurate transitions, see TRANSITIONS.

CONNECTORS
   See TRANSITIONS and CONNECTIONS, MAKING THEM.

CONNOTATION
   Connotation refers to the meaning implied by a word beyond that word's LITERAL MEANING. For example, a person holding the same position could be described as **stalwart, resolute, determined, unwavering, headstrong, stubborn, mulish,** or **pigheaded.** These words do not differ so much in literal meaning as they do in connotation.

   As you can see from these examples, words do not just have a positive or negative connotation, but fall on a continuum stretching from extremely positive to extremely negative. The extremes of the continuum are effective only if the reader or listener already agrees with you. In legal writing, because you are not addressing such an AUDIENCE, you should avoid the extremes on either end of the continuum. For a discussion of this and related concerns, see WORD CHOICE and PERSUASIVE WRITING.

CONTACT

Contact is rather vague; before you use the word, make sure you want to be that vague. For example, contact is not as specific as telephone, write, or meet with. For related concerns, see PRECISION and WORD CHOICE.

CONTEND

Courts do not contend, only counsel does.

CONTINUAL OR CONTINOUS?

Continual means intermittent or repeated at intervals, such as continual requests for advice.

Continuous means uninterrupted or unbroken, such as continuous vigil or continuous preoccupation with the law.

CONTRACTIONS

Do not use contractions, such as don't or isn't, in legal writing. They are too informal for almost all legal situations. The only exceptions would be in a letter or memo where you want to sound casual.

CONTRACTS, DRAFTING

Keep these general writing principles in mind when drafting contracts.

1. Before writing, make sure you are clear about what parts the contract must include and what situations the contract must cover. Know what the parties in fact want. Precisely because this is an obvious point, it is often overlooked. Try outlining the contract to make sure that all the needed pieces are included and are organized logically. For ways to accomplish this, see OUTLINES and ORGANIZATION FOR THOSE WHO CAN'T OUTLINE.

2. Reconcile yourself to writing many DRAFTS of the contract to get it right. If you try to get all the details right in the first draft, you are likely to miss some important larger points. For help in organizing your drafts, see WRITING PROCESS.

3. Use clear, simple, businesslike language. Much progress has been made in this area, particularly in the areas of insurance and finance. Be on guard, however, for slipping back into the mire of LEGALESE. Use only the technical terms you need and define them if necessary. For ways to do this, see UNOBTRUSIVE DEFINITIONS.

4. Make each clause do one thing, not more. OUTLINES can help you here by breaking down the whole contract into a series of small points.

5. When REVISING, check for ambiguities.

   (a) Check to make sure that you have used only one term for one item or person. Referring to the same person, item, or concept by

54

two different terms creates an ambiguity that invites misunderstandings later. If needed, include a definition section to define all your KEY TERMS, so that the reader understands any unusual terms. For related information, see AMBIGUITY, WAYS TO AVOID.

(b) Check also to make sure that you have not used one term for several different items or persons. This can create unwanted ambiguities. For discussion of related ideas, see AMBIGUITY, WAYS TO AVOID; LISTS, STRUCTURE OF; and PUNCTUATING LISTS.

6. After POLISHING each clause in the contract, reread the document as a whole, looking for larger contradictions between parts of the contract, rather than wording problems within one clause. In your concern for the details, you may have overlooked some larger ambiguities.

7. Somewhere along the line, consult others. No one person can imagine all the pitfalls that the parties to any contract are hoping to avoid. No one person can imagine all the ways some reader can misconstrue a point.

CONTRAST
See COMPARISON.

CORRELATING CONJUNCTIONS
See CONJUNCTIONS and READABILITY.

CORRESPOND TO OR CORRESPOND WITH?
Use **correspond with** if you mean that you and another party are writing to each other. Use **correspond to** if you mean that one point is analogous to another.

COULD CARE LESS OR COULDN'T CARE LESS?
Use neither in formal legal writing.

COULD OR CAN?
See VERB TENSES.

COURTS, HOW TO ADDRESS
See JUDGES HOW TO ADDRESS. Also see Blue Book rule 9.

DANGLING MODIFIERS
See MODIFIERS, DANGLING.

DASHES

The dash, the gigolo of the punctuation world, has its uses and its dangers. It intrigues the writer with its drama and its convenient ambiguity. Like a gigolo, however, its effectiveness is determined by the user's *savoir faire* and restraint. If you overuse the dash in legal writing, you run the risk of looking desperate.

1. Danger of the dash.

Beware the ambiguity of the dash. It can replace a colon, a pair of commas or parentheses, or a transition, so you might use it without thinkng too much. As a result, the reader has to do the extra work of determining how the dash is functioning in this particular context. The reader may not appreciate doing this, may decide not to bother, or may come to the wrong conclusion.

Ms. Willard had decided not to pursue the action further because litigation would be too expensive.

rather than

Ms. Willard has decided not to pursue the action further—litigation would be too expensive.

2. Uses of the dash.

First, a dash will make a phrase stand out on the page. If you use dashes for drama, make sure the content within the dashes is indeed dramatic.

The defendant's action—both understandable and humane in this case—cannot be rightly condemned.

There are no spaces before or after the dash. COMMAS would be more formal here, but not as dramatic.

Second, a dash can show a sudden turn of thought with an undercurrent of humor. This is a pleasing and deft touch, but one for which legal writing provides few opportunities.

Mrs. Smith thought the intruder might be a burglar—or her husband.

Again, you must be very sure that the content can sustain the drama and wry humor the dash promises.

Finally, a dash can set off a mid-sentence phrase when commas would confuse the reader and parentheses would trivialize the content of the interruption.

Julia was on a large and complex daily regimen of drugs. Daily she took three kinds of barbituates—Tuinal, Fiornal, and Fiornal with Codeine—one of which included an opium derivative.

Here you are using it out of rude necessity, and you may prefer to revise the sentence.

Julia was also on a large and complex daily regimen of drugs. Daily she took three kinds of barbituates, one of which included an opium derivative. These barbituates included Tuinal, Fiornal, and Fiornal with Codeine.

For alternative punctuation marks, see COMMAS, COLONS, and PA-RENTHESES. For related information, see EMPHASIS.

DATA

Data means information and is now commonly used in both the singular and the plural, as in these data are fascinating or this data is inconclusive.

DEADLINES, MEETING THEM

Meeting deadlines is a skill you must develop to succeed as a legal writer, because failure to meet them can be a source of malpractice suits. The secret to meeting deadlines successfully is becoming familiar with your overall WRITING PROCESS and adjusting it, so that you do not get behind at any stage in the process. Once you have developed your own process, break that process into subsections and set interim deadlines for each subsection. Mark those deadlines on your calendar, moving backwards from the deadline date and making a special effort to meet each of those interim deadlines. Sometimes it helps to tie the deadline to a person, such as to your secretary or a person who will do a read-through of the ideas. The potential embarrassment at missing the interim deadline may motivate you to meet it.

If you find yourself falling behind, examine your list of tasks to be done and determine which tasks are critical to that stage of the process. For example, you may not have updated your cases and are instead spending time reading law review articles. Or you are spending too much time revising and leaving no time for POLISHING or for absorbing unforeseen disasters. Force yourself to shift to completing the critical tasks before you spend time on nice-but-nonessential tasks.

Each writer usually feels uncomfortable or bogged down somewhere in the writing process; pinpointing which part of the process is uncomfortable and then overcoming this discomfort can also help you meet deadlines. For example, you may feel uncomfortable in (1) PREWRITING, when you are doing research, collecting facts, taking NOTES, reading the law, outlining and organizing; (2) WRITING, when you are actually translating ideas to paper by dictating or typing or writing the first draft; (3) REWRITING, when you are checking large-scale organization and ideas, making sure that all parts of your analysis are present and in a logical order (see ORGANIZATION, LARGE–SCALE); (4) REVISING, when you are checking small-scale organization, PARAGRAPHS, SENTENCE STRUCTURE, WORD CHOICE, TRANSITIONS, and HEADINGS; or (5) POLISHING, when you are checking CITATIONS, spelling, punctuation, and typos.

One way to overcome this discomfort is to decide which stage is most uncomfortable for you, divide it into subparts, and attack those subparts directly. For example, if you are uncomfortable in PREWRIT-ING, give yourself a time limit by which to have your prewriting done.

Then divide your prewriting tasks by doing background research, briefing, and outlining separately. This can help you focus on each task so you do it more efficiently. Set a time to translate that prewriting to writing and force yourself to meet that deadline. Forcing yourself to meet these interim deadlines will help you avoid unnecessary procrastination and will allow you adequate time to fix any problems you find throughout the subsequent stages of writing.

Sometimes in prewriting you can let PROCRASTINATION work for you. As you delay writing, however, let the ideas flow by keeping a notebook handy for any new ideas that can occur any time, any place. Develop a system of taking NOTES that allows you to incubate on your ideas, even if you are not actually at your desk or in the library. Thus procrastination becomes creative incubation. For related concerns, see GETTING STARTED.

If you are uncomfortable about WRITING the first draft, clear your calendar and set aside a time just for that. Remember that the goal here is not to get it right, but to get it written. Do not revise as you write. It takes too much time, is too painful, and distracts you from your main task at this stage, which is to get all your ideas down on paper. Let the creative voice work here; let the ideas flow, no matter how strange they seem. Just get your ideas into words somehow and finish the draft within the time period you set. Then do something else. Let the draft sit. For related concerns, see WRITING BLOCK.

REWRITING is often ignored or subsumed within other writing stages, and this causes problems with meeting deadlines. Give rewriting its own time, again by clearing the calendar and setting aside one large block of time or several small blocks only for that. At this stage, do any major shifting of large sections. Check large-scale organization and make sure all the ideas you wish to include have been stated and are placed in a logical order. See also ORGANIZATION, LARGE–SCALE.

After rewriting, shift to the REVISING stage. Check small-scale organization, TOPIC SENTENCES, TRANSITIONS, SENTENCE STRUCTURE, and WORD CHOICE. Give particular attention to your ISSUE STATEMENTS or QUESTIONS PRESENTED and to the specific details of the Conclusion. See also CONCLUSIONS.

Finally, polish. Check cites, punctuation, spelling, grammar, typos, and any problems peculiar to your writing. Allow at least one day to proofread large documents. See POLISHING.

Thus, by focusing on specific goals at each stage of the writing process and by meeting your interim deadlines for each of these stages, you can successfully meet your final deadline. For related concerns, see WHEN TO STOP.

DEFINITELY

Definitely means for certain or assuredly, and therefore should be avoided in legal writing unless the point is literally definite.

DEFINITIONS, WHEN TO INCLUDE

Add a definition when you are using any technical term, legal or otherwise, that may be unfamiliar to your reader and that is central to your point. If you are worried about insulting the reader by defining a term, see UNOBTRUSIVE DEFINITIONS.

DEMAND FOR PAYMENT

See REQUESTS FOR PAYMENT.

DEPENDENT CLAUSES

A clause is a phrase that includes a subject and a verb; a dependent clause is a clause that is inserted into another sentence and cannot stand alone as a sentence. A dependent clause begins with a subordinating conjunction, such as **when**. For example, in the following sentence, **when it refused to submit a jury instruction on manslaughter** is a dependent clause.

The court abused its discretion when it refused to submit a jury instruction on manslaughter.

For more on how these dependent clauses work in sentences, see SENTENCES, PARTS OF and SENTENCE STRUCTURE. For related definitions, see CLAUSES.

DESPERATION

See HELP; GETTING STARTED; DEADLINES, MEETING THEM; WHEN TO STOP; or WRITING BLOCKS.

DICTA

In an opinion, **dicta**, which means **words**, includes anything a court says that does not have a significant effect on the outcome of the case. Dicta differs from a holding in that dicta is not binding on courts in subsequent opinions. Dicta can be significant, however, in your use of a case in research or in class. Use dicta to predict a trend in the law, to illuminate the reasoning in this case, or to understand future cases. For contrast and context, see HOLDINGS and CASE BRIEFS.

DICTATION

Speak to your secretary before you dictate anything. Ask about particular preferences in format, pronunciation, punctuation, and paragraphing. The more specific you are about the details of dictation, the fewer questions you will have to resolve later.

If you have never dictated, begin with small texts, such as a letter or NOTICE OF MOTION. Before dictating, make some notes for your reference; have your large-scale organization in mind and dictate accordingly; make rewriting corrections on the first draft you get back from the secretary.

If you are really uncomfortable about dictating, go ahead and write out what you are going to dictate and then just read it into the dictaphone to get used to the medium. Then, with each task, write less and talk more.

When you get the draft back from the secretary, delete any passages that are too conversational or otherwise inappropriate. In particular, check for wordiness, a common problem in dictated texts. For help here, see CONCISENESS. Also check for clear, coherent ORGANIZATION. For help here, see TRANSITIONS; ORGANIZATION, LARGE–SCALE; ORGANIZATION, SMALL–SCALE; and COHERENCE. As you discover what your dictation habits are, you can work gradually to eliminate the bad habits, so that less rewriting will be necessary.

DIFFERENT FROM OR DIFFERENT THAN?

Different from is always correct. **Different than** is allowable sometimes, according to some sources, but the rule is unsettled here, so to be safe use **different from**.

DIGRESSION

Digression, or straying from the main point, usually occurs when you are not sure of the main line of the analysis. If you feel yourself digressing, stop and reread your QUESTION PRESENTED or ISSUE STATEMENTS and the RULES you are applying. Think about them. Then reanalyze your ORGANIZATION and decide whether or not the point is essential to the analysis.

If you are still uncertain, let the point sit and move to your Brief Answer or Conclusion. Try to see the larger picture and the result, both of which may illuminate the point's relevance. Alternatively, move to another part of the analysis and then come back. If you can sense that a point is digressing, fight the temptation to elaborate on it, or you will have to eliminate a great deal of your text when REVISING.

For related writing problems, see CONCISENESS. See also BRIEF ANSWERS.

DIRECT OBJECTS

See SENTENCE, PARTS OF.

DISCUSSION SECTION

The Discussion is the section in a memo that presents and analyzes the law. As such, it explains to the reader how the law applies to the facts under analysis and predicts the possible outcome of the problem. The Discussion then, should incorporate the following elements into a logical, unified whole:

(1) the RULES relevant to the analysis;

(2) ANALOGOUS CASES, where appropriate, describing cases that are analogous to the facts being analyzed;

(3) an APPLICATION, which presents both sides' arguments about how the law applies to the facts being analyzed and balances those arguments; and

(4) POLICY and EQUITY, which interact with the rules to balance both sides' arguments and predict an outcome.

The Discussion should use an OBJECTIVE STYLE and should consider the specific requests of the AUDIENCE. Organize the Discussion according to the law being used, moving from the rule to be applied through the application to the specific outcome.

Avoid writing as if the law, application, and outcome are discrete subsections. Instead, let the logical organization of the law dictate your organization. For example, if you have a simple rule you might state the rule, give an example of it, apply it to your facts, and then reach a conclusion. If, however, you have a complicated rule with several subparts, you might state the point of law for each subpart and apply it to your facts before explaining the next subpart.

For related information, see MEMOS.

DISINTERESTED OR UNINTERESTED?

Use **disinterested** if you mean that the person is neutral on the point. Use **uninterested** if you mean that the person does not care about the point.

DRAFTING

See the entry for the specific kind of drafting you are doing, such as CONTRACTS, DRAFTING; LEGISLATION; NOTICE OF MOTION; MOTIONS; or WILLS, DRAFTING. For general writing concerns particularly important in drafting, see ACCURACY; ORGANIZATION; LISTS, STRUCTURE OF; PRECISION; and WRITING PROCESS.

DRAFTS

Always try to write more than one draft of any given legal piece. Let the first draft be creative, thorough, and imperfect. Include everything you think necessary to the piece and all things that you think might be useful.

Then use second, third, fourth, and other drafts for REWRITING, REVISING, and POLISHNG. For related information, see WRITING PROCESS.

DUE TO

Use **due to** only after a linking verb, such as **is** or **seemed**, and only where the phrase following **due to** modifies the subject of the sentence.

This omission was due to negligence, not unforeseeable circumstances.

Here **due to** modifies **omission** and **was** is a linking verb. See VERBS, LINKING.

In all other situations, use **because of.**

This omission occurred because of negligence, not unforeseeable circumstances.

Here **because of** modifies **occurred**, and **occurred** is a transitive verb. Using **due to** to modify a verb may become acceptable someday, but is not generally accepted yet. For related information, see MODIFIERS; TRANSITIONS; and VERBS, TRANSITIVE.

DUNNING LETTERS
See REQUESTS FOR PAYMENT.

DURING THE TIME THAT
Try substituting **while** for CONCISENESS.

EACH
Each means **one of two or more persons, objects, or things considered individually.** As such, **each** takes a singular verb when used as a pronoun.

Each lawyer has his or her own manner of presenting an opening argument.

Fourteen exhibits were presented at the trial; each is important to the outcome of the case.

For related general information, see PRONOUNS.

EDITING OTHER PEOPLE'S WRITING
Be gentle, firm, and focused on your objectives. You are helping a writer communicate to his or her readers, but you are not revising the writer's paper to conform to your personal writing style. Try the following list of read-throughs to make the editing task faster, to insure more comprehensive and consistent editing, and to maintain your focus as editor.

1. Read the paper once from the point of view of the writer's AUDIENCE. Mark in the margins those places where you were lost or confused or had to pause, but do not stop to fix them now.

2. Go back to your markings and try to determine why you were lost or confused. Pinpoint which of the following categories caused the confusion.

   (a) CONTENT. Are the legal ideas confusing? Is the law incomplete or incorrectly stated? Is the logic incomplete? Is an explanation missing?

(b) ORGANIZATION. Are the ideas grouped together correctly? Is the organization easy to follow from any reader's perspective? Are the large-scale ideas marked by reader-based clues, such as subheadings, main sentences, and POSITIONS OF EMPHASIS? Is the small-scale organization easy to follow? Does each paragraph focus on one idea? Are there accurate and adequate TRANSITIONS between sentences and PARAGRAPHS? For further help, see TOPIC SENTENCES and ORGANIZATION, SMALL-SCALE.

(c) READABILITY. Are sentences neither too long nor too short? Are wordy phrases omitted? Are the words used either familiar to the readers, understandable in context, or defined in the text? Are the subjects and verbs strong; do they concentrate on KEY TERMS or TERMS OF ART? Is the ACTIVE VOICE used most often? For further help, see CONCISENESS.

(d) STYLE. Is the style consistent throughout? Is it appropriate to the legal context in which the paper is written, such as objective for a memo, persuasive for a brief, or scholarly for an article?

(e) TONE. Is the level of formality consistent and appropriate to the legal context in which the text will be read?

(f) Mechanics. Are the CITATIONS in correct form and FORMAT for that jurisdiction and that genre of legal writing? Are spelling, PUNCTUATION, and GRAMMAR all correct? Where appropriate, are legal conventions observed?

3. Start at the top of the list in step 2 and make comments appropriate to that kind of document. Much of editing concentrates on 2(c) and (d), so when suggesting changes try to step inside the writer's shoes to make comments consistent with that writer's voice and STYLE rather than with your personal writing style. Then, rather than explain any questions or problems you have in terms of right or wrong, explain them in terms of the reader's needs.

If possible, create a sense of partnership early and obtain the writer's permission to make certain changes in accord with the writer's style and understanding of the problem. This partnership can quicken the editing process and increase its quality.

EDITING QUOTES

Although some editing of quotes is desirable for effective focus and for READABILITY, too much can make the reader suspicious, as in the following example.

The court stated its reasoning explicitly when it said, "[w]e cannot ignore the plaintiff's complaint . . . . [because] [i]n this case, the issue of mutuality . . . requires . . . examin[ing] . . . the parol evidence . . . ."

When faced with this situation, PARAPHRASE or summarize the quote rather than overediting. For specific ways to edit quotes, see PUNCTUATING QUOTES.

EFFECT OR AFFECT?
See AFFECT OR EFFECT?

E.G.
See SIGNALS.

ELEGANT VARIATION
Elegant variation means using different words for the same idea, solely for variety. Do not use this technique in legal writing.

This contract supersedes all previous contracts.

rather than

This document supersedes all previous contracts.

For discussions of related general points, see REPETITION, READABILITY, PRECISION, and WORD CHOICE.

ELLIPSES
An ellipsis is a series of three spaced dots (. . .) used to show omissions in quotes. See PUNCTUATING QUOTES for the details of the use of ellipses.

EMOTIONAL FACTS
Used in persuasive writing, these facts are carefully chosen and included in a STATEMENT OF THE CASE to subtly persuade the reader. They have no bearing on the legal reasoning, nor are they chronological or informational facts necessary to complete a legal analysis. Rather, they play on the reader's emotions. For example, if Malcolm assaulted Alice one Saturday night with an unloaded gun, the writer may tell the reader that they had a sexual relationship in the past. This is an emotionally significant fact that has no bearing on the legal definition of assault. For related information, see TONE, EMPHASIS, PERSUASIVE WRITING, and POINT OF VIEW.

EMOTIONAL LANGUAGE
Emotional language is appropriate only in PERSUASIVE WRITING, and then only if used sparingly. Use emotional language to describe significant EMOTIONAL FACTS, emotional arguments, or possibly POLICY arguments. Use emotional language only if it is necessary to convey the point and if it does not impair your TONE.

Emotional language can impair credibility if used inappropriately, personally, or excessively.

Admitting this evidence would rob the defendant of his due process rights.

rather than

The plaintiff's counsel foolishly suggests the court admit the evidence; such a move would be unjust and wrong.

For related problems, see CONNOTATION.

EMPHASIS

When emphasizing a point, you want to emphasize the content, not the writing itself. For this reason, avoid heavy-handed use of any emphasizing techniques. With that caveat in mind, try using one or more of the following techniques to emphasize your point.

1. Put the point to be emphasized at a position of emphasis: the beginning or end of a sentence or a paragraph. Conversely, bury phrases you want to de-emphasize in the middle, because the middle of sentences, paragraphs, and even whole sections gets less attention than the beginnings or ends.

In addition, in legal writing the beginning gets more attention than the end because the legal reader does not always finish reading. Therefore, get your main points in early. This technique is particularly useful for introducing KEY TERMS and TERMS OF ART that will reappear throughout the text, because the terms can both gain emphasis and serve as TRANSITIONS. See ORGANIZATION, POSITIONS OF EMPHASIS, and PARAGRAPHS.

2. State the point to be emphasized in concrete, specific terms. Conversely, use more abstract terms to de-emphasize a point. When a point is stated in concrete or specific terms, the reader creates a mental picture of the point; this picture makes the point easier to remember. In contrast, something stated abstractly or generally does not leave a picture in the reader's mind and is less easy to remember.

When asked where he had been at 10:00 p.m. on the night of the assault, the alleged assailant looked away and mumbled, "Nowhere."

rather than

When asked where he had been, he seemed uneasy.

The concrete version also is more factual. For related information, see ABSTRACT NOUNS.

3. Put the point to be emphasized in a short sentence. Because SHORT SENTENCES are relatively rare in legal writing, they are particularly effective for emphasis. A short sentence will make a stronger statement and will also be easier to read. Both these facts work together to make the point easier to remember.

The defendant then fired three shots.

Watch out, however, for using several short sentences in a row, because this can create an impatient, slightly angry tone. For occasions when you want to create this tone, see TOUGH, SOUNDING THAT WAY. For related information, see SENTENCE STRUCTURE, subsection 1.

4. Put the point to be emphasized in a one-sentence paragraph. Use this technique only when you have a sentence that can stand on its own logically. When you can use a one-sentence paragraph, however, it can make the point stand out from other paragraphs, just as a short

sentence stands out from other longer sentences. For more information, see ONE–SENTENCE PARAGRAPHS.

5. Use strong SUBJECT–VERB COMBINATIONS that use terms central to your point, which may include TERMS OF ART or other words you want to emphasize.

The Family Car Doctrine holds parents liable for their children's accidents.

or

The defendant was slowing down his car at the time of the accident.

Conversely, de-emphasize points by putting them in DEPENDENT CLAUSES. For example, the following sentence de-emphasizes **the defendant had not come to a full stop** by placing it after **although**.

Although the defendant had not come to a full stop at the official stop sign, he had slowed to less than five miles per hour and was not accelerating at the time of the accident.

For related information, see SUBJECT–VERB COMBINATIONS, KEY TERMS, and TERMS OF ART.

6. Put the point to be emphasized in an inverted sentence structure. In general, something unusual gets more attention just because it is unusual.

Imprudent it was, but not illegal.

But beware of overusing this technique. Inverted sentence structure draws attention to the writing itself as much as to the content; if you use it frequently, the reader will start to think about your writing style and may be distracted from your content. For more of this, see SENTENCE STRUCTURE, subsection 4.

7. Use CITATIONS at the ends of sentences, not as introductions to a sentence.

Only under exigent circumstances may police enter a person's home without a warrant or consent. Dayton v. New York, 945 U.S. 573, 590 (1990).

rather than

Dayton v. New York, 945 U.S. 573, 590 (1990) states that only under exigent circumstances may police enter a person's home without a warrant or consent.

END RESULT

Result is adequate unless you are discussing complicated math formulas with both interim results and end results.

EQUITY

Equity refers to justice and fairness. If, for example, legal procedures and existing laws give inadequate or no redress for a grievance, then **equity** would require creating some redress.

Equity has several shades of meaning, which are beyond the scope of this book, but be sure to consider equity in making a complete analysis in your DISCUSSION SECTION, ARGUMENT SECTION, or explanation in an opinion letter. See also POLICY.

ETC.

Use etc. only in informal writing, because it looks rather informal and can be vague in some circumstances. Instead, use and so forth, and others, or another appropriate phrase. Better yet, complete the phrase with specific terms.

EVERYBODY

Everybody takes a singular verb.

Everybody has the right to his or her own fair trial.

Everybody is rather informal; consider substituting everyone.

EVERYONE

Everyone takes a singular verb.

Everyone is writing an outline for the course.

Do not confuse everyone with every one; every one refers to each person or thing of a specific group, and is usually followed by of.

Every one of the defendants is at fault.

EVIDENCE

Evidence always takes a singular verb.

All the evidence points to this conclusion.

This is true even if there are many bits of evidence, because evidence is a collective noun. If you want to use a plural verb, you will need to make some other word the subject.

All the pieces of evidence point to this conclusion.

For related information, see COLLECTIVE NOUNS.

EX–

As a prefix, use ex with a hyphen.

ex-wife, ex-Governor Smith

As a part of a Latin phrase, write it as a separate word.

ex post facto

EXACTNESS

See ACCURACY.

EXCLAMATION

Exclamations are used in legal writing only as part of a quote. For related information, see also INTERJECTIONS.

EXCLAMATION POINT

An exclamation point is rather like shouting and thus is not used in legal writing, except as part of a quote. Let someone else do the shouting. For better ways to emphasize a point, see EMPHASIS and POSITIONS OF EMPHASIS.

EXPLANATORY PHRASES

For ways to include these gracefully, see APPOSITIVES and UNOBSTRUSIVE DEFINITIONS.

EXTENDED QUOTES

Resist the urge, please, to use quotes that extend for whole pages. No matter how good the quote is, many readers will skip over it, so use quotes of more than one long paragraph only when PARAPHRASE or EDITING QUOTES are not viable alternatives. If you must quote an extended passage, such as the full text of a statute, do so, but make sure the explanation surrounding it is adequate to make the reader see the essential use. If possible, append the full text and then refer to that APPENDIX, unless flipping too often to the appendix will distract the reader. See also PUNCTUATING QUOTES and ACCURACY.

FACT OF THE MATTER, THE

This phrase can almost always be omitted with no loss of meaning.

The plaintiff did not raise this claim until she learned of the defendant's affluence.

rather than

The fact of the matter is that the plaintiff did not raise this claim until she learned of the defendant's affluence.

For a discussion of related problems, see CONCISENESS and SUBJECT–VERB COMBINATIONS.

FACT THAT, THE

Avoid this phrase. Usually it adds extra words without adding extra meaning.

This failure was caused by the machine's inadequate design.

rather than

This failure was caused by the fact that the machine was inadequately designed.

For related information, see CONCISENESS.

FACTS

See EMOTIONAL FACTS, BACKGROUND FACTS, and LEGALLY SIGNIFICANT FACTS.

FARTHER OR FURTHER?

Farther refers to literal distance.

She moved farther away from me than I had wanted.

Further refers to all other senses, such as additional degree, time, or quantity.

The attorney stretched the argument further than anyone could have imagined.

Further also denotes figurative distance.

That line of reasoning is further from the truth than would be acceptable.

FEWER OR LESS?

Fewer refers to things that can be counted. As such, it takes a plural verb.

Fewer students are enrolling than the university would have liked.

Less refers to things that cannot be counted.

Plaintiffs believed there was less likelihood of success if they waited too long to file.

We need less talk, more action.

Less also refers to things that could be counted, but are being referred to as a group rather than as individual units. Examples of this include periods of time, sums of money, measures of distance, and weights.

Plaintiff must file in less than sixty days.

The prayer asked for less than one million dollars.

The engine lasted for less than 45,000 miles.

While the plaintiff weighed almost 200 pounds, the defendant weighed less than 130 pounds.

FIGURATIVE MEANING

In legal writing do not use a word figuratively, rather than literally, if there is any chance that the legal reader could take you literally.

When he tried to drive his car out of the marsh, he actually drove it farther into the mud.

rather than

When he tried to drive his car out of the marsh, he foundered in a swamp he himself created.

You may use a word figuratively when (1) you are writing for legal readers and (2) the figurative term is commonly used by those readers.

The plaintiff's own word bars his suit.

In this example, nothing is **barred** in the sense of **barred from entering the room**, but any legal reader will know what you mean.

For related concerns, see AMBIGUITY, LITERAL MEANING, and JARGON.

FIND

Courts **find**; counsel does not.

FLOWERY LANGUAGE

Avoid flowery language, or the use of unnecessarily ornate words in legal writing. Usually the ideas in legal writing are so complicated that flowery language will only serve to make them more complicated. The only time that flowery language might be appropriate would be if requested by an AUDIENCE, such as a client requesting it in a will.

In law review articles you may bend this rule a little; a few **arcane** words are allowable if they do not hide crucial meaning. Do not, however, **surfeit your reader with a multifarious array of sententious phrases.** Too quickly that becomes obnoxious and loses the reader.

See also JARGON, LEGALESE, ELEGANT VARIATION, and READABILITY.

FOOTNOTES

1. Using Footnotes.

Use footnotes in articles, treatises, and opinions but avoid them in LETTERS, MEMOS, pretrial documents, or BRIEFS. For example, when an explanation would distract from the presentation's flow in the main part of the text, put the explanation in a footnote. Or use footnotes to expand a point beyond the information essential to the purpose of the presentation. For example, a footnote in an opinion might give the text of a statute or case that is better read on that page than appended to the main text. Thus footnotes in law review articles and treatises are helpful to document authority, but footnotes in a memo or brief generally distract the reader.

2. Citing Footnotes.

Refer to footnotes when they contain pertinent text, just as a PINPOINT CITE would refer to a specific page.

(a) Cite a footnote from a case as follows.

Brown v. Smith, 469 U.S. 27, 34 n. 3 (1988).

(b) Cite a footnote from an article as follows.

1988 Wis. L. Rev. 349, 358 n. 89. For further reference, see Blue Book rule 3.3.

FOR

Sometimes **for** is used as a subordinating conjunction.

She had no patience with imprecise language, for she had a background in legal drafting.

Although this use of **for** is not grammatically wrong, it suggests a rather fuzzy logical relationship. **For** is not as precise as **because**. If you mean to show a causal connection, use **because**.

The operator cannot be considered negligent because he was not told that it was his job to check the hoses before starting the motor.

If you mean something less precise, try to revise to state exactly what you mean. For related information, see TRANSITIONS and CONJUNCTIONS.

FOR THE PERIOD OF

For CONCISENESS, leave out the last three words.

FORCEFUL WRITING

See EMPHASIS and POSITIONS OF EMPHASIS.

FORM BOOKS, USE OF

Referring to forms can save time and avoid the problem of missing a needed element in a routine task. Using forms, however, can also cause problems, such as including contradictory clauses in a contract or nonsensical phrases in a letter. Therefore, do not use forms as a substitute for your own thinking about the writing task you face. With this caveat in mind, when you do refer to forms, you can make good use of them if you remember to do the following three things.

1. Compare forms.

Compare different forms before you settle on one form to follow. Comparing different forms, whether from form books or from samples you have collected, helps you see which content and formats are common and which are unique to certain forms. This comparison in turn helps you get a clearer sense of the options you have and of the standard content and FORMAT used for this kind of legal document.

2. Prepare your form.

Prepare by identifying all the elements needed to complete your document, omitting any unneeded elements found in the forms but inappropriate to your document, and checking for logical inconsistencies between these elements. Check carefully for those logical inconsistencies, so that your document is not the next in the line of cases that outlines the problems of ambiguous and inconsistent clauses. Resist the temptation to include even one word you do not understand.

3. Repair your form.

Finally, repair the elements you have chosen. Most of the forms have unneeded FLOWERY LANGUAGE, obtuse SENTENCE STRUCTURE, and unnecessary words. You have used the forms to get a sense of content, structure, and format; you can retain those elements and still revise to gain increased READABILITY. For help in omitting unnecessary words, see CONCISENESS. For related information, see CONTRACTS, DRAFTING.

FORM CONTRACTS, USE OF

Form contracts can be useful as long as they are used as a resource rather than a substitute for your own thinking about the agreement. To use forms effectively, follow the three steps listed under FORM BOOKS, USE OF. For a checklist for drafting contracts, see CONTRACTS, DRAFTING.

FORMAT

Legal readers are particular about format because they want the structure to be transparent enough to make the substance clearly visible. For example, know and follow the requirements of the format peculiar to your jurisdiction when writing BRIEFS. Similarly, know and follow also the demands of your employer for format in memos and opinion letters. For specific formats, see MEMOS, BRIEFS, and OPINION LETTERS.

FORMER

If the reference of **former** is more than a few words back, repeat the word to which you are referring rather than using **former**. To understant what **former** means, the reader must remember the items listed, remember which was first, and then insert that information into the sentence. As a result, **former** is inconvenient for the reader. The reader should never be inconvenienced for the convenience of the writer.

Also remember that **former** and **latter** can be ambiguous when they refer to a list of more than two items.

FURTHER OR FARTHER?

See FARTHER OR FURTHER?

FUTURE PERFECT TENSE

See VERB TENSES.

FUTURE PROGRESSIVE TENSE

See VERB TENSES.

FUTURE TENSES
See VERB TENSES.

GENDER–FREE PROSE
See SEXIST LANGUAGE, WAYS TO AVOID.

GENERAL CORRESPONDENCE LETTERS
One common problem legal writers have with letters is time; letters take too long to write. Often this happens because writers spend a long time deciding how to begin and how to organize each letter.

Only four kinds of general correspondence letters are commonly written: (1) letters delivering information the reader requested, (2) letters delivering information the writer needs the reader to have (for-your-information, or FYI letters), (3) letters delivering bad news, and (4) letters trying to persuade the reader to do something. You can use a standard organization for each of these kinds of letters, which means you no longer have to decide how to begin or how to organize. All you have to decide is what kind of letter you are writing. Then you need only choose the appropriate TONE for your letter and the appropriate SALUTATION and CLOSING.

To decide what kind of letter you are writing, first jot down in one sentence the point of your letter. Be blunt; this is for your private use, not necessarily for inclusion in the letter. For example, your point might be (1) **Here, for your review, is your revised will;** (2) **You may need to change your method of keeping tax records;** (3) **After meeting you, I know that there is no way I would hire you to work for our company;** or (4) **I want to get you to pay even though I can't sue you because suit would cost more than it is worth.** Then decide which of the four kinds of letters this point requires.

1. Letters delivering requested information.

If the letter is delivering requested information (as in the first example: **Here for your review, is your revised will.**), refer to the request and then respond to that request.

At our conference on January 23, you asked me to help you make several changes in your will. I have subsequently drafted a new will incorporating these changes and am including a copy of this draft with this letter.

Elaborate or explain as needed in the second paragraph.

Please review this draft carefully. Specifically, consider the following questions:

(1) .   .   .

Then close politely in the last paragraph.

If you have any questions or wish to make any further changes in the will, do not hesitate to call. I will have the final will prepared and you may come to the office to execute it on February 12, as we have scheduled.

2. Letters delivering information the writer needs the reader to have (for-your-information, or FYI Letters).

If it is an FYI letter (as in the second example: **You may need to change your methods of keeping tax records.**), start with a statement of the point of the letter.

As your attorney, I want to notify you of some recent changes in the tax law that may require a change in your record-keeping practices.

If needed, include this opening in a brief description of who you are or an explanation of why you are writing. In subsequent paragraphs, elaborate as needed.

Specifically, the new law requires you to keep a log of your use of the computer, so that you can document the percentage of time . . . . Additionally, the law requires . . . .

In the final paragraph, close politely.

Please feel free to call to set up an appointment if you have any questions about this or other tax matters.

3. Bad News Letters.

If the letter is delivering bad news (as in the third example: **After meeting you, I know that there is no way I would hire you to work in our company.**), try organizing the letter in three parts that do the following: (1) set the TONE of the letter; (2) deliver the bad news; and (3) re-establish the tone. Think of this as the sandwich organization, because in effect you place your meat between two slices of bread to make it more palatable.

(a) The first slice of bread: set the tone.

In the first paragraph, establish the tone you want to take with the reader. For example, you might want to be kind.

It was a pleasure to have the opportunity to interview you last week . . . .

Or you may be tough.

Mr. William Marshfield has asked me as his attorney to answer your demands that he pay for computer software he neither ordered nor received . . . .

You may choose to be warm and personal.

Thank you for inviting me to speak at the Society's annual awards banquet. Regrettably, ...

You may prefer to be distant.

Your request for a reduction in your child support payments has been received by . . . .

If answering a request, you may want to restate that request, so that the reader knows you paid attention to the request before saying no.

In your letter dated March 3, 1986, you requested a restructuring of your payment schedule for the land contract on . . . . Your reasons were that . . . .

(b) The meat: deliver the bad news.

At the beginning of the second paragraph, state the bad news plainly so that the reader cannot misinterpret what you are saying. Follow this statement with your reasons, if appropriate. This paragraph will be unemotional and matter of fact, no matter what the tone of the other paragraphs. This section may also extend for several paragraphs if needed.

(c) The second piece of bread: re-establish the tone.

In the final paragraph, re-establish your tone while you state closing technicalities. For example, you may suggest that the reader call if he or she has questions.

If you have any further questions concerning this matter, you may call me at (505) 555–1234.

If you are being kind, you may wish the reader some sort of relevant good fortune.

I enjoyed our conversation at the convention, and look forward to reading your article on . . . .

If you are being tough, you may close with a declarative statement.

I trust that this settles the matter.

For related information, see BAD NEWS, SOFTENING IT; LETTERS REQUESTING PAYMENT; and TOUGH, SOUNDING THAT WAY.

4. Persuasive Letters.

If the letter is being written to persuade the reader (as in the third example: **I want to get you to pay even though I can't sue you because suit would cost more than it's worth.**), you may use the same organization used for bad news letters.

Start with a paragraph that sets the TONE of the letter, such as a kind tone.

Throughout the years, Everly Auto Parts has valued Morgan Auto as a customer. Because Everly hopes to maintain this solid working relationship, Bob Everly has asked me to write to you concerning the rather large outstanding balance in your account.

You may set a tough tone.

Despite receiving three statements from my client, Everly Auto Parts, your company has not yet paid the balance of $2,015 owed for parts purchased four months ago.

Or you may choose something in between.

My client, Everly Auto Parts, has asked me to write to you concerning the outstanding balance on your company's account.

Do not go on too long, however, because a lengthy introduction can make the writer look rather timid or can make the reader impatient.

At the end of the first paragraph or the beginning of the second, state your point. Write this sentence with care; it must be unambiguous and yet inoffensive, if possible.

Everly will not be able to extend further credit to your company until this balance has been paid.

Then launch into your reasons, which may go on for several PARAGRAPHS. Make one point at a time, rather than rambling back and forth between several points.

Everly Auto Parts, as a general policy, limits credit to any company to . . . . Additionally, ...

In the last paragraph close politely, or at least civilly.

Everly Auto Parts will appreciate your prompt payment of this outstanding balance and looks forward to your continued patronage.

In general, persuasive letters will take more time and care than the other three kinds because you must tailor your argument and tone to suit the individual circumstances. Choose not what persuades you, but what will persuade your reader. If you are trying to persuade a party to settle out of court, for example, do not use threats if you think the party would view that threat as a challenge and submission as a weakness. In that situation, you might instead explain that the suit is not worth the expense of trial. For related suggestions, see SETTLEMENT LETTERS; LETTERS REQUESTING PAYMENT; and TOUGH, SOUNDING THAT WAY.

Similarly, if you think the reader is someone motivated by certain values, try to explain how the action you recommend is consistent with those values. For example, you might argue that paying a bill is essentially the same as keeping a promise. In short, try to explain how the action you recommend is consistent with some goal the reader has. Try to help the reader feel good, or at least not defeated, about taking the action you recommend.

In general, use an unemotional, polite tone. In most legal writing situations, the emotions you would arouse would work against you rather than for you. There are some exceptions to this, such as fundraising letters to sympathetic constituents or letters advising clients to do what they want to do already. Even here, however, you will usually want to present yourself as a logical, reasonable person who, although impassioned about a cause, is still capable of making a coherent and logical argument. For a discussion of related points, see TONE, EMPHASIS, PERSUASIVE WRITING, and COHERENCE.

5. TONE IN LETTERS.

TONE is especially important in letters. As your general demeanor in an interview creates an impression in the mind of the interviewer, the tone of your letter creates an impression in the reader's mind. Thus, although your tone in various letters may range from friendly to tough, it should always be within the limits of temperate, businesslike communication. A chatty tone will seem slightly unprofessional in all but personal letters. An intemperate tirade will also seem unprofessional, even in the toughest collection letter.

Within these limits, however, you must make your own choices, based on what is appropriate to the situation and what suits your personal communicating style.

Using tone effectively in letters involves three tasks: (a) choosing the appropriate tone, (b) creating that tone through word choice and sentence structure, and (c) keeping the tone consistent.

(a) Choosing the appropriate tone.

Before you begin writing the letter, consider what your relationship is to the reader. For example, if your reader is a judge or your supervisor at work, you will probably want to use a tone that is both businesslike and respectful. This means that you will state your points as concisely as possible but will not omit appropriate opening and closing amenities, such as the following closing to a letter requesting a favor.

Thank you for your help in this matter.

If your reader is a client, you may choose to be polite and businesslike, or you may choose an appropriately friendly tone.

Please call if you have any further questions.

or

I am looking forward to our next tennis match.

If your reader is your client's opponent or a client who has not paid you for one year, you may choose a tough, businesslike tone.

I trust this settles the matter.

or

Please pay this bill promptly.

(b) Creating the appropriate tone through WORD CHOICE and SENTENCE STRUCTURE.

Choosing your words carefully is one effective way to establish your tone. For example, if you want to create an informal, friendly tone, use less formal words, such as **talk** and **meeting**. If you want to create a more formal tone, use more formal words, such as **confer** and **discussion**.

Avoid, however, using formal words to the point that your letter becomes stuffy or hard to read.

77

Regarding this question, I have conferred with Ms. Jamison's attorney, who explained that . . . .

rather than

In pursuit of this query, I have held consultations with counsel for Ms. Jamison, who elucidated the point by stating that . . . .

Another way to avoid a stuffy tone is to avoid inappropriately using the third person, such as **this attorney**, when the first person, **I**, is accurate. In general, letters are addressed from one person to another, and so the use of I is appropriate, or **we** if you are speaking officially for a group of people, such as a whole law firm.

You may also establish your tone by using appropriate sentence structures. For example, if you want to create a friendly, informal tone, use longer sentences rather than terse ones.

Thank you for your kind invitation to speak at your annual banquet honoring outstanding alumni from the law school.

rather than

Thank you for the invitation to speak at the alumni banquet.

Conversely, if you want to create a tough, no nonsense tone, use short, rather choppy sentences.

My client, Ms. Ambrose, does not intend to pay this bill. She has no reason to pay this bill. She did not receive any software from your company. She did not order any software from your company. Until receiving your bill, she did not know your company existed.

rather than

My client, Ms. Ambrose, does not intend to pay this bill because she has no reason to do so. She did not receive or order any software from your company, and in fact did not know your company existed until receiving your bill.

(c) Keeping the tone consistent.

Inconsistent tone occurs when a letter includes words that are noticeably more formal or informal than the rest of a letter. For example, a writer may use a formal phrase, such as **please be advised that**, in an otherwise informal letter. Or a writer may use a colloquialism, such as **ripped off**, in an otherwise businesslike letter.

Avoid using any unnecessary legal terms, or LEGALESE. Dexterity with legal terms does not impress all readers. What does impress readers is correspondence that gives them the information they need without making them work hard to get it, so try to be concise and organized. For related information, see CONCISENESS, FANCY LANGUAGE, and ORGANIZATION.

6. Opening and Closing Letters.

(a) Including or omitting SALUTATIONS.

In general, include a salutation. Some writers omit the salutation in business letters, substituting instead a subject line, and this is not technically wrong. Omitting the line, however, makes the letter seem rather abrupt and impersonal, which is not usually the tone you want in a letter.

(b) Writing non-sexist openings.

If you do not know the sex of the person to whom you are writing, substitute the name without a title.

Dear D.A. Young:

Dear Terry Holmes:

If you do not know a name, use the person's title, or some appropriate generic term.

Dear Administrator:

Dear Client:

If you cannot come up with even a generic term, you may use the following.

Dear Sir or Madam:

Use **Dear Sir** only when you are sure the reader is male.

(c) Choosing commas or colons for salutations.

Use colons in business writing. If you are writing something that is a social courtesy, such as a thank you note or an expression of congratulations, you may use a comma. A colon would also be appropriate, except in a note that is much more personal than businesslike in tone.

(d) Choosing an appropriate closing.

Choose the standard closing that suits your writing STYLE and the tone of your letter. If the tone of your letter is businesslike and yet friendly, use **Sincerely** or **Sincerely yours**. If your tone is more formal, use **Yours truly** or **Very truly yours**. Do not worry about seeming insincere; these closings are not taken literally.

Using innovative alternatives, rather than underscoring your sincerity, would only create undesirable responses. If you used something more accurate, like **Don't bother me anymore**, you would seem unprofessional or petulant. If you omitted the closing, you would create a distant, impersonal tone, which is not usually what you want.

For related information, see TONE.

GENERALLY

Generally is an adverb that means **for the most part** or **usually**. Be careful to use it in its exact meaning, rather than as a meaningless introduction.

Generally, states do not consider a non-viable fetus a "minor child."

rather than

Generally, the defendant would like a pardon.

GERUNDS

Gerunds are NOUNS formed from the -ing form of a verb.

Seeing is believing.

Using gerunds can often make a sentence more concise.

Imagining alone does not constitute intent.

rather than

The act of imagination alone does not constitute intent.

GETTING ORGANIZED

For help here, choose the entry most closely related to your concern: GETTING STARTED, OUTLINES, ORGANIZATION, WRITING BLOCKS, WRITING PROCESS, or ORGANIZATION FOR THOSE WHO CAN'T OUTLINE.

GETTING STARTED

You may have trouble getting started for any of several reasons. You may dread the job because it is boring, difficult, or crucial to your career. You may not know where to start. Or you may be stuck in the first step. Do not despair; all of these problems are fixable. But to solve these problems you may have to change your approach to the problem. For related information, see WRITING BLOCKS and HABITS, WRITING.

1. When you dread it.

Try listing what needs to be done and then dividing the tasks on the list into subtasks. Keep dividing them until you get down to small tasks that each seem manageable. Even if the list seems very long, just start completing the tasks one by one. If time is short, do first those tasks essential to the job, such as clear organization, and then those tasks desirable but not necessary, such as emphatic sentence structure. For more ideas, see DEADLINES, MEETING THEM.

2. When you do not know where to start.

Start anywhere. Many people think that they have to start with an outline, but in reality you can start in any of several places. For example, you might start drafting one subpoint of the Discussion of a memo because you understand that particular point best. Or you might start by trying to get your QUESTIONS PRESENTED exactly right. In a law review article, you might start with one sentence that sums up the point of your whole article, not worrying about whether that sentence will appear in the final draft. Then you could list the points needed to back up that statement and develop that list into an OUTLINE. For more ideas, see PREWRITING.

3. When you are stuck.

Try starting somewhere else. For example, if you cannot get the Question Presented right, try writing the Discussion or the Argument.

If the Discussion or Argument is rambling, try writing your Conclusion; that may help you see how to organize the Discussion. You may discover that starting with any one of these always helps you get the job done more efficiently. The best starting place for one person is not the best for another, so experiment to discover what works for you. Remember, good writing does not depend on whether you start in the right place; it depends on whether you do all you need to before you stop.

GOOD OR WELL?

Use **good** to modify a noun.

She had good reason to doubt his word.

Use **well** to modify a verb or an adjective.

She could hear well enough to understand the general topic of the defendants' conversation.

Use **good** after **feel**, because **good** here modifies the subject, not the verb.

I feel good about this decision.

Well would be correct only if you were talking about your ability to feel physically, which almost never comes up in writing. For related information, see BAD OR BADLY?

GRAMMAR

Grammar counts in legal writing. Grammatical mistakes are potholes in the superhighway of a presentation. Therefore, use grammar carefully to convey your legal ideas clearly, and revise specifically for its proper use.

For specific grammar questions, see PARTS OF SPEECH, SENTENCE STRUCTURE, VERB TENSES, MODIFIERS, PARALLEL STRUCTURE, and PUNCTUATION. Also see BENDING THE RULES. For a more extensive discussion of grammar rules, see a grammar handbook such as J. Hodges & M. Whitten, *Harbrace College Handbook* (Harcourt Brace Jovanovich 9th ed. 1982).

HABITS, WRITING

Habits form in writing just as they do everywhere else. Because legal writing often requires high efficiency in short periods of time, keeping bad writing habits can cost both you and your client. But old habits die hard; you must consciously kill them. Therefore, in moving from the PREWRITING stage through WRITING, REWRITING, REVISING, and POLISHING, consider which habits work for you and which habits do not. Then start with the most troublesome habit and eradicate it by replacing it with a better habit. For example, if you habitually try to revise each sentence as you write, you will probably find that the writing process has become very time-consuming and agonizing. Instead, try giving yourself a time limit and forcing yourself to write without any revision until you finish your first draft. Then go back and rewrite. Similarly, if you spend too much time doing research and as a result do not have enough time for the actual writing, set a deadline by which the first draft has to be written and force yourself to meet that deadline by finding someone to give it to, whether a secretary or a coworker who is willing to read it at that point.

For suggestions for breaking habits in each stage of the WRITING PROCESS, see PREWRITING, WRITING, REWRITING, REVISING, and POLISHING. For help in facing the writing process itself, see GETTING STARTED and WRITING BLOCKS.

HANGED OR HUNG?
If you are talking about a person being hanged by the neck until dead, use hanged. If you are talking about hung in any other sense, such as a thing hung on the wall, use hung. Informally, you may refer to a hung jury.

HARDLY
Hardly is more informal than its synonyms scarcely or nearly, so use it sparingly in formal writing, such as MEMOS and BRIEFS. See also CAN HARDLY OR CAN'T HARDLY?

HE OR SHE?
When the sex of the person referred to is unknown, he or she is preferable to s/he or he. For a general discussion of this question, see SEXIST LANGUAGE, WAYS TO AVOID.

HEADINGS
In most legal writing, headings identify the subsections of memo, brief, letter, or article. Headings should ease the eye and the mind of the reader, so that the legal analysis is easier to follow. In BRIEFS, headings take the specific form of POINT HEADINGS, subheadings, and sub-subheadings, which outline the specific legal points of the argument and the reasoning behind those points. In MEMOS, headings distinguish each part of the memo, such as Questions Presented, BRIEF ANSWERS, Discussion, and Conclusion. Subheadings may be used to divide the DISCUSSION SECTION, so that the reader can see at a glance which legal issues are being discussed where. Usually these subheadings take the form of a label, such as False Imprisonment or Jurisdiction, although a sentence can be even more helpful.

This District Court Has Jurisdiction.

In long OPINION LETTERS, subheadings similarly subdivide the explanation. The same is true with articles.

In your headings and subheadings, try to convey a definite message to the reader; avoid headings that clutter the writing unnecessarily. Also avoid using headings as a substitute for clear, specific TOPIC SENTENCES.

For related information, see ARTICLES, PUBLISHED.

HEADNOTES

Headnotes are numbered paragraphs that summarize the legal points of a court's opinion. These summaries are written by the editors of the reporter in which the case appears, and they appear before the actual text of the case begins.

Headnotes are designed as research tools to aid the reader in using the case. For example, if you are researching intentional torts and a case contains, among others, a procedural headnote on jurisdiction and a substantive headnote on intentional torts, then you can use the headnote number to find the section of the case discussing intentional torts where that number reappears. Similarly, that headnote is Shepardized so that you can update just that section of the case on intentional torts. See SHEPARD'S.

Because headnotes are research tools and are not written by judges, never cite to a headnote.

HELP

If you have turned to this, you are probably in the midst of your writing process and under pressure. Consult the most relevant of the following entries: GETTING STARTED; OUTLINES; ORGANIZA-TION FOR THOSE WHO CAN'T OUTLINE; WRITING BLOCKS; WRITING PROCESS; or DEADLINES, MEETING THEM. Also look for an entry under the particular kind of writing that concerns you, such as ARTICLES, PUBLISHED; BRIEFS; CASE BRIEFS; CON-TRACTS, DRAFTING; GENERAL CORRESPONDENCE LETTERS; MEMOS; and so forth. If none of these entries seems right, consult the master list of entries in the front of the book. Do not panic. Divide the tasks and conquer.

HELPING VERBS

See VERB TENSES.

HOLD

Courts hold; counsel does not.

HOLDINGS

The holding is the decision a court reaches in a case. A holding thus disposes an issue raised in the case, whether procedural or sub-stantive and as such binds that court and those under it in making subsequent holdings based on similar facts. Therefore, holdings provide the focal point for research constructing arguments, and measuring the strength of a client's case. Consider the following in using case holdings.

1. In CASE BRIEFS, use the holding to state the answer to the issue and give a reason for that answer.

Yes; Curtis falsely imprisoned Butterworth because he used words or acts that intended to confine Butterworth, he actually confined her in the car, and Butterworth was aware that she was confined.

For related information, see ISSUES, DICTA, and CASE BRIEFS.

2. In MEMOS, use holdings to explain RULES.

Hospitalization for alcohol abuse does not preclude being awarded custody of a child. Nagle v. Nagle, 999 Utah 2d 84, 101, 941 P.2d 1, 3 (1989).

Or use **holdings** to describe ANALOGOUS CASES.

There, the mother was awarded custody of the daughter despite her previous hospitalization for alcohol abuse. Nagle v. Nagle, 999 Utah 2d 84, 101, 941 P.2d 1, 3 (1989).

3. In BRIEFS, use holdings to argue.

Even a mother who has been hospitalized for alcohol abuse can win custody of her daughter. Nagle v. Nagle, 999 Utah 2d 84, 101, 941 P.2d 1, 3 (1989).

4. In PARENTHETICALS, state the holdings as they relate to the use of the cases.

Artists must look outside the moral rights doctrine for protection. See Peabody v. Percival, 999 F.2d 17, (9th Cir.1999) (No moral right exists in the U.S., so breach of contract must be used to compensate artists whose work is mutilated).

HOPEFULLY

Use **it is hoped** or **I hope**. Use **hopefully** only when you mean that something was done in a hopeful way.

The pilgrims sailed hopefully for America.

It is rare that you will mean this. While **hopefully** is used widely in speaking, it is not yet accepted as meaning **it is hoped** in formal writing.

HOWEVER

However has two different uses, each of which can cause problems for the legal writer.

1. Use **however** as a transition. As such, it is a concise way of saying something roughly equivalent to **on the other hand**; it signals a shift to the other side or a contrasting subpoint. One way this may be done is to place **however** right after a semicolon joining two sentences.

The defendant has testified that he was not present at the scene of the crime; however, two witnesses have contradicted this.

When using **however** this way, do not use it with only a comma. You must put a semicolon before **however** and a comma after. The semicolon is necessary because however is not a conjunction, like **and** or **but**.

The court remanded the case; however, the plaintiff did not receive an appreciably higher reward.

rather than

The court remanded the case, however, the plaintiff did not receive an appreciably higher reward.

Another way **however** may be used as a transition is to place it a few words into a sentence.

The defendant has testified that he was not present at the scene of the crime. Two witnesses, however, have contradicted this.

2. Use **however** as an adverb. As such, it modifies a part of the sentence rather than serving as a transition between sentences.

However it happened, the fact remains that the defendant lost use of his arm as a result of this accident.

Often this use of **however** sounds awkward in formal writing. In this situation, you may substitute another phrase.

No matter how it happened, ...

or

Regardless of the cause of the accident, ...

Avoid overusing the word. If, for example, you see **however** appearing in every paragraph you write, you are probably overusing it. To correct the problem, first check your organization: Are you trying to cover two points that would be better presented in two separate paragraphs? Are you wavering between two views, avoiding taking a stand when it is your job to take a stand? If so, see ORGANIZATION and PARAGRAPHS for possible solutions. Second, check the accuracy of your word choice: Are you using **however** when you really mean **nevertheless, additionally,** or something else? See TRANSITIONS for a list of transition words that may communicate your point more accurately. Usually the answers to these questions will show you how you must revise. If not, consider using synonyms for **however** to avoid overusing it. For related information, see REPETITION.

HUNG OR HANGED?
    See HANGED OR HUNG?

HYPERBOLE
    Hyperbole is an excessive exaggeration used as a figure of speech; avoid it generally, because its excesses often reduce the writer's credibility, as in the following examples.

Defendant was dying to get out of the courtroom.

The judge hung the defendant out to dry.

HYPHENS

Hyphens have three uses: (1) dividing words at the end of a line, (2) joining MODIFIERS that work together, and (3) connecting some prefixes to words.

1. You may use a hyphen to divide a long word coming at the end of a line. Check the dictionary if you are not sure where the hyphen should go. Do not hyphenate proper names and avoid hyphenating at the end of a page, as a favor to your reader.

2. Use a hyphen to signal that the words hyphenated work together to modify a subsequent word in the sentence: **bone-jarring blow, high-pitched voice, work-related expenses, owner-occupied housing, thirty-seven-year-old male,** or **three- to five-year sentence.** There is one exception to this. Proper names are not hyphenated: **Southeast Asian conflict, Supreme Court opinion, West Coast phenomenon.**

3. Also use a hyphen to connect some prefixes to words.

(a) You may use a hyphen when adding a prefix to a proper name: **un-American, ex-President Carter.**

(b) Use a hyphen when the prefix ends with the same vowel that begins the main word: **re-examine, semi-independent.**

(c) Use a hyphen with **self-**: **self-employed, self-sufficient.**

(d) Use a hyphen with **ex-** when it means **former**: **ex-wife.**

(e) Use a hyphen whenever omitting it will confuse readers.

He wanted to re-lease the apartment.

Or reword the sentence to avoid the problem.

He wanted to lease the apartment again.

I

Use **I**, or the first person, in business letters when you are writing as an individual. Do not use **I** in MEMOS, BRIEFS, articles, or any other writings where the content, not the writer, is important to the reader. For a general discussion of the reasons behind this use of **I**, see TONE. For related information, see AMBIGUITY, WAYS TO AVOID, subsection 2; and PERSON: FIRST, SECOND, OR THIRD?

IDIOM

An **idiom** is an expression or phrase that is acceptable English even though it cannot be understood by interpreting the literal meaning of its elements.

We gave them up.

or

I dropped off the package.

Idioms are often metaphors that have become so common that the original metaphorical image is lost: **to catch a cold, How do you do?** or **to strike a bargain.** Avoid idioms that are ambiguous in context or that sound too informal.

I.E.

The abbreviation **i.e.** stands for **id est,** or **that is.** As an abbreviation, you may use **i.e.** in place of those two words, particularly in the context of further explanation, as in an explanatory footnote.

The 12(b)(6) motion failed, i.e., the case was dismissed.

Avoid using **i.e.** in text, such as a business letter or formal documents, such as wills. Use **that is** or another appropriate phrase instead, surrounded by commas.

On June 4, 1982, she initiated the action, that is, filed the motion.

rather than

On June 4, 1982, she initiated the action, i.e., filed the motion.

He agreed to the condition when he signed the waiver.

rather than

He agreed to the condition, i.e., he signed the waiver.

IF

If is useful in legal writing because **if** has only one meaning, and therefore provides a precise transition between CLAUSES. Because **if** is precise and because you will often be writing about points that logically are **if . . . then** situations, do not worry too much about overusing **if.** Worry only when several sentences in a paragraph contain **if** and when those **if**'s are not logically parallel. For related information, see SENTENCE STRUCTURE, PARALLEL STRUCTURE, REPETITION, and TRANSITIONS.

If the **if** phrase is quite long, use a **then** after the comma at the end of the **if** phrase.

If the court extends this reasoning to include all victims of industrial accidents, then Harris can establish a cause of action.

IF AND WHEN

Delete the **and when;** **if** says it all.

IMPACT

Use **impact** as a noun.

The impact caused extensive damages to defendant's vehicle.

The impact of such a decision would be far reaching.

Although **impact** is sometimes used as a verb, as in **to impact a decision**, this use is not yet acceptable English. As a verb, **impact** should refer only to such things as teeth.

His wisdom tooth was impacted.

IMPERATIVE MOOD
See VERB TENSES.

IMPLY OR INFER?
These words are not interchangeable. **Imply** means **to suggest** or **to express indirectly**. **Infer** means **to surmise** or **to derive a conclusion from the information**. As a result, use **imply** when the subject is a piece of writing, a thing, a speaker, or a writer.

This reasoning implies that . . . .

Use **infer** when the subject is a reader or a listener.

The court inferred from this phrase that . . . .

IN ADVANCE OF
Use **before** for a cleaner, more concise sentence. For a discussion of the general principles behind this, see CONCISENESS.

IN, INTO, OR IN TO?
In means **inside of, during** or **as part of the act or process of, among other things.**

He is in the room.

Into means to the inside of, or **to the action or occupation of.**

She will go into law.

In to is used only informally.

My friend is in to body building.

For related information, see PREPOSITIONS.

IN QUESTION
This phrase is often used to describe issues under consideration in the present memo, brief, or opinion. If used frequently, this phrase robs the text of CONCISENESS. Therefore, when possible, avoid this phrase by using **these** or **this**: **these facts,** rather than **the facts in question; these parties** rather than **the parties in question,** or **this issue** rather than the **issue in question.**

INDENTED QUOTES OR QUOTATION MARKS?
Use quotation marks around direct quotes of forty-nine words or less and around titles of articles. When a direct quote is longer than forty-nine words, indent it, single-space it, and omit quotation marks.

The only time you will use quotation marks in an indented, single-spaced quote is when there is a quote within the indented quote.

For related information, see QUOTATIONS, WHEN TO USE; EXTENDED QUOTES; and PUNCTUATING QUOTES.

INDENTING
See QUOTATIONS, WHEN TO USE.

INDEPENDENT CLAUSE
See CLAUSES or SENTENCE, PARTS OF.

INDICATIVE MOOD
See VERB TENSES.

INDIRECT OBJECTS
See SENTENCE, PARTS OF and CLAUSES.

INFER OR IMPLY?
See IMPLY OR INFER?

INFINITIVE VERBS
See VERB TENSES.

INFORMAL LANGUAGE
See COLLOQUIALISMS.

–ING WORDS
See MODIFIERS, DANGLING; GERUNDS; and VERB TENSES.

INSERTED PHRASES
See INTRUSIVE PHRASES and SENTENCE STRUCTURE, sub-section 7.

INSTRUCTIONS TO THE JURY
See JURY INSTRUCTIONS.

INTERJECTIONS
Interjections are just that, interjections of exclamation.

Hurray!

Because they are emotional and informal, do not use them in legal writing, except as part of a quote.

INTRUSIVE PHRASES
Intrusive phrases are phrases inserted into a sentence.

Anorexics, *by failing to eat*, **passively expose themselves to harm.**

You may use short intrusive phrases to emphasize a legal or argumentative point because they will force the reader to stop and think about the content of the intrusive phrase.

These facts, which are outside the knowledge of most people, illustrate the kind of information expert witnesses can provide.

These issues, controversial and crucial, must nevertheless be resolved.

Dr. Janssen, who attended the defendant in the emergency room, testified that her injuries were caused by the faulty design of the steering wheel.

Do not use phrases longer than approximately seven words, however, because phrases that long will cause the reader to lose track of the point the rest of the sentence was making.

Without realizing she would be punished by this court for her action, the defendant committed perjury.

rather than

The defendant, without realizing she would be punished by this court for her actions, committed perjury.

Avoid using intrusive phrases if you do not want the reader to stop; also avoid overusing intrusive phrases if they make your style too cumbersome.

For more information, see SENTENCE STRUCTURE, subsection 7.

INVERTED ORDER
See SENTENCE STRUCTURE and EMPHASIS.

IRREGARDLESS OR REGARDLESS?
Use **regardless**, always.

ISSUE STATEMENTS
An issue is that question to be decided in a legal argument; it is the question that, when answered, determines the outcome of the case. The issue is the lens of the legal analyst's camera, so focusing it in legal writing is of utmost importance.

The Issue or Issues are part of CASE BRIEFS, memoranda of points and authorities, PRETRIAL BRIEFS, TRIAL BRIEFS, or APPELLATE BRIEFS. The Issue is often the first part the reader consults to focus on the law, the facts, and the question their combination raises.

In OBJECTIVE WRITING, the issue focuses the reader without persuading. For related information, see QUESTION PRESENTED AND MEMORANDUM OF POINTS AND AUTHORITIES.

In PERSUASIVE WRITING, the Issue must not only focus, but also persuade the reader. To do this, it should contain (1) a reference to the general law under which the question is being asked; (2) the legal question, which combines the law and the facts of this case; and (3) the LEGALLY SIGNIFICANT FACTS. Sometimes the reference to the general statement of the law is omitted. Many jurisdictions require the Issue to be fair and neutral, although most legal writers make the Issue fair but persuasive. The following are examples of issue statements from appellate briefs.

Petitioner's Issue:

Is a large law firm exempt from Title VII of the Civil Rights Act of 1964, and therefore free (1) to discriminate on the basis of sex, race, or religion and (2) to discharge those associates whom they did not admit to partnership based on reasons of sex, race, or religion merely because the firm is organized as a partnership and has an established "up-or-out" policy?

Respondent's Issue:

1. Are law partners organized for advocacy entitled to constitutionally protected freedom of association?

2. Through Title VII of the Civil Rights Act of 1964, did Congress intend to give the Equal Employment Opportunity Commission, a politically appointed advocacy agency engaged in litigation, jurisdiction over invitations to join law firm partnerships?

From a pretrial motion:

Under Iowa Code Section 99.99.99, *Custody of children, is it in the best interests of two young children to award custody to their mother when she has a history of alcohol abuse, has shown no signs of abstention from alcohol, and is given to emotional outbursts?*

IT

Minimize the use of this pronoun because too often its ANTECEDENT is unclear. See PRONOUNS; IT IS SAID THAT; AND AMBIGUITY, WAYS TO AVOID, section 2.

IT IS SAID THAT, IT WOULD SEEM THAT, IT MIGHT BE SAID THAT

If you have reservations about the point you are making, state them. Do not rely on these phrases, because they make you seem uncertain without indicating the sound reasons for your lack of certainty.

IT IS . . . THAT

Often this phrase can be omitted for a stronger, more concise sentence.

The attorney must prepare a thorough and accurate statement of fact.

rather than

It is important that the attorney prepare a thorough and accurate statement of fact.

For related information, see CONCISENESS.

ITALICS

Italics are the typesetting equivalent of UNDERLINING. Like underlining, they should not be used to add emphasis in the general text of formal legal writing. Italics should, however, be used to indicate emphasis added to quotes. Italics are also used conventionally for some words in some legal documents, such as *resolved* in a bill and *ordered* in a court order. They may be used to indicate defined terms, as in a contract or for signals and cases in footnotes. Italics are also used to mark words from a foreign language, like *savoir faire*. Finally, italics are used for book titles. For more detail, see Blue Book rules 1 and 7.

ITS OR IT'S?

It's = it is. **Its** = belonging to it. Legal readers are highly annoyed if one is confused with the other. See also APOSTROPHES and POSSESSIVES.

JARGON

Jargon is a pejorative term for technical language that the reader does not understand, such as **price/cost elasticity**, although the writer and others in the writer's field of expertise would understand it. LEGALESE is jargon used by lawyers. Legalese includes both specialized words unfamiliar to nonlegal readers, such as **estopped**, and flowery words that (1) are unfamiliar to the reader, such as **abovementioned** and **heretofore**, and (2) could be avoided by using a more familiar word, such as **this** or **previously**.

Because you as a writer are trying to communicate to the reader, you want to avoid using jargon. Remember that nonlawyers are not the only ones who will resent jargon; judges are just as likely to resent an unfamiliar or unnecessary technical term.

Therefore, if you must use the technical word to make your point, add a definition in text so the reader does not have to look it up elsewhere. See UNOBTRUSIVE DEFINITIONS for ways to do this.

JUDGES, HOW TO ADDRESS

Use **your honor** in person and **the honorable Judge [name]** for lower court judges, or **the honorable Justice [name]** for higher court justices in third person writing. Always precede the judge's name with **Judge** or **Justice**. This is what the **J.** following a court's name in an opinion represents. For more details on terms of court, see Blue Book rule 9.

JUDGMENT

A judgment is a court's final determination of the parties' rights in a legal controversy. In America, judgment has only one e.

JUMP CITES

See PINPOINT CITES.

JURY INSTRUCTIONS

Jury instructions are submitted to the court by the attorneys for each side. The following techniques can help you in drafting your instructions and in making them a part of your advocacy. Whatever your method, make sure you check your jurisdiction for any specific requirements.

1. Drafting jury instructions.

When drafting jury instructions, you must reconcile conflicting matters in two different areas. First, you must strike a workable balance between two audiences. Jury instructions explain the law to jurors, yet they have to be accepted by the judge. As a result, you need to use some legal terms but also explain them in everyday language.

Second, you must conform patterned jury instructions to the specifics of your case. Most states provide patterned jury instructions that are established general statements of the law. Although these are good places to start, they need editing to be relevant to the particular facts involved in your case. For example, you may have to delete statements addressing issues settled before trial or you may have to combine several instructions to address the multiple issues in your case.

The following checklist can help you balance these factors when writing jury instructions.

(a) Use elements of the standard jury instructions. For example, you might retain the legal terminology in the instructions, but increase understandability by adding definitions if you think they are needed. Similarly, you might keep the wording of the standard instruction but break it into several shorter sentences to make it more readable. For help here, see UNOBTRUSIVE DEFINITIONS and READABILITY, subsection 1.

(b) When appropriate, include supporting CITATIONS or explanations with your submitted instructions, so that the judge knows there are legitimate reasons for your changes.

(c) When choosing instructions, list all the legal questions the jury must resolve to decide in your client's favor. Then lay out the specific law they need to know to resolve those questions. This can help you avoid gaps and present a logical overall package.

(d) Additionally, the jury often hears but does not read the instructions. As a result, you must reorder your priorities to meet the needs of the listener: you must worry more about CLARITY and less about CONCISENESS. The following checklist can help you achieve clarity.

(i) Use understandable words.

Use words that will be familiar to the jury. For example, use **automobile** rather than **motorized vehicle.**

Use verbs instead of nouns whenever possible.

You should *consider* all the evidence as a whole.

rather than

You should give *consideration* to all the evidence as a whole.

Avoid using several negative words in one sentence.

Mr. Allen should have come to a complete stop at the crosswalk.

rather than

Mr. Allen must *not* have *failed* to come to a complete stop at the crosswalk.

Use TRANSITIONS or phrases that precisely communicate the logical relationship between two points.

Even if Mr. Allen did stop at the crosswalk, he should have also stopped again at a point where his view was not obstructed.

rather than

Mr. Allen should have also stopped at a point where his view was not obstructed.

(ii) Use understandable SENTENCE STRUCTURE.

Keep sentences simple by making only one legal point per sentence.

You may decide that the testimony of one witness is entitled to greater weight than that of another witness, or even of several witnesses. In weighing the evidence, you may consider your own knowledge, observations, and life experiences.

rather than

In weighing the evidence, you may consider the testimony of one witness as entitled to greater weight than that of another or several others, your own knowledge, what you have observed, and the experiences you have had in life.

Use only one word for one idea. For example, use **capable** rather than **capable and able.**

Place lists at the end of a sentence.

In weighing the evidence, you may consider your own knowledge, observations, and life experiences.

rather than

You may consider your own knowledge, observations, and life experiences in weighing the evidence.

(iii) Personalize the instructions if permissible in your jurisdiction. You can still remain objective by using only objective, factual terms.

If Mr. Ellis had a gun concealed . . . .

rather than

If the defendant had a weapon concealed . . . .

2. Making jury instructions part of your advocacy.

To help make your instructions an extension of your advocacy, consider framing the instructions early in the litigation process, when you are drafting your brief, or at least before the start of the trial. Then you can word your arguments so that they lead to the conclusions you want to reach, based on the law laid out in the instructions.

JURY, PLURAL OR SINGULAR?

Use a singular verb with **jury** when it is a collective noun, which it usually is.

The jury receives instructions at the end of the trial.

Use a plural verb only when you refer to the jury as a collection of individuals.

The jury appear nervous.

Better yet, avoid this awkward-sounding phrase by using **members of the jury** or another similar phrase.

The members of the jury appear nervous.

or

Each jury member appears nervous.

KEY TERMS

Key terms are words describing facts crucial to an issue. As such, key terms work in tandem with TERMS OF ART to define and discuss legal issues. As terms of art are derived from the law, key terms are derived from BACKGROUND FACTS, EMOTIONAL FACTS and LEGALLY SIGNIFICANT FACTS. Thus, key terms may be definitions, facts, or descriptions of desired results, among other things.

For example, in a custody dispute where **best interests of the children** are the TERMS OF ART from the statute, the key terms in the discussion or argument might be **custody dispute, father-son relationship,** or **son's wishes.** For related information, see ISSUE STATEMENTS and QUESTION PRESENTED.

LARGE-SCALE ORGANIZATION

See ORGANIZATION, LARGE-SCALE.

LATTER

See FORMER.

LAW REVIEW ARTICLES

See ARTICLES, PUBLISHED.

LAWYER OR ATTORNEY?

See ATTORNEY OR LAWYER?

LAY OR LIE?

Lay is a transitive verb that always takes a direct object. It means **to place or set down** or **to produce or deposit,** among other things. The conjugation of this verb is **today I lay, yesterday I laid, I have laid.**

The attorney laid the exhibit carefully on the bench before the bailiff.

She laid her briefs down before she left the office.

Lie is an intransitive verb that never takes a direct object. It means **to recline** or **to remain in a specific condition,** among other things. It is conjugated **today I lie, yesterday I lay,** and **I have lain.**

The site of the crime lies between Fargo and Grand Forks.

When I lay down yesterday, the phone rang.

LEGALESE

Legalese is a pejorative term for technical legal words or phrases, and it implies that the legal words are unneeded. To avoid the problem, avoid legal terms whenever common language terms can convey the meaning.

The testator, William James (James) then signed the will, which was witnessed by Ellen Brady, Katrina Birchler, and Mella White.

rather than

The *said* testator, *one* William James, (*hereinafter referred to as* James) then *duly* signed the *aforementioned said* will, *in witness whereof* were Ellen Brady, Katrina Birchler, and Mella White.

Similarly, although you will find that you do need to use many technical legal terms, you do not need to overuse them. You will be able to keep your writing style more direct and concise if you avoid the terms whenever possible.

If you must use a technical term and you are not sure the reader will know the meaning, add a definition.

The tortfeasor, who is the person committing the tort, ...

For ways to do this, see UNOBTRUSIVE DEFINITIONS.

For a discussion of a related problem, see JARGON.

LEGALLY SIGNIFICANT FACTS

Legally significant facts are facts that, if they were changed or deleted, would affect the outcome of the case. To determine what facts are legally significant, you therefore need to read the law. Then, by comparison, certain facts will emerge as significant, just as white emerges under a black light.

For example, a case may state that the waving of a loaded gun in someone's face is an assault. In the fact situation being analyzed, Michael waved a gun that was not loaded. The fact that it was unloaded is legally significant because it may mean Michael is not guilty of assault.

In a MEMO, legally significant facts should appear in the Statement of Facts, in the QUESTION PRESENTED, in the Brief Answer, in the application during the Discussion, and in the Conclusion. Any legally significant facts used in the application should appear in the Statement of Facts first, in detail. No surprises.

Similarly, in a BRIEF, legally significant facts should appear in the Statement of the Case, the ISSUE STATEMENTS, the POINT HEADINGS, the application during the Argument and in abbreviated form in the CONCLUSIONS.

In an OPINION LETTER, include legally significant facts in the separate section on facts, in the application during the explanation, and in the recommendation.

For an explanation of other kinds of facts, see BACKGROUND FACTS and EMOTIONAL FACTS. For related information, see ISSUE STATEMENTS and BRIEF ANSWERS.

LEGISLATION

Drafting legislation requires particular skill, for legislation must bear up under generations of scrutiny. Consider those generations of audiences, as well as the current AUDIENCE of legislators. The following guidelines can help you do this when drafting legislation.

1. Draft the original idea you have in mind as clearly as you can, in your own words.

2. Consider all the legal problems raised by the legislation, both the original problem and any previously unanticipated corollaries. Run the draft past several readers from different audiences if possible.

3. Check the draft against other sections within that part of the statute to catch any possible ambiguities or other problems that may arise in this larger context.

4. Similarly, see if any terms used in your legislation are defined elsewhere in the statutes and make sure your use is consistent with those definitions.

5. Adjust the language to accommodate any ancillary problems created in the process of revising the legislation.

(a) Avoid extra phrases that raise, rather than answer, problems. For related information, see PRECISION.

(b) Use PLAIN ENGLISH.

(c) Eliminate any JARGON or LEGALESE.

(d) Define all terms that might lead to ambiguity. For help here, see AMBIGUITY, WAYS TO AVOID.

6. Unify STYLE when the legislation has been drafted by more than one person. For ways to do this, see EDITING OTHER PEOPLE'S WRITING.

7. When using quotation marks in legislation, put other punctuation marks, such as periods or semicolons, outside the quotation marks unless that punctuation mark is part of the quote.

"Dwelling", when used in this section, means . . . .

This differs from the use of quotation marks in general writing, where commas and periods always are placed inside the quotation marks. For more on this, see QUOTATION MARKS WITH OTHER PUNCTUATION.

Because there are so many audiences to please and so many things to consider in drafting legislation, do your best under the circumstances to create the clearest results.

LENGTHY QUOTES
See EXTENDED QUOTES.

LESS OR FEWER?
See FEWER OR LESS?

LETTERS
In letters, your information is not the only thing you communicate to the reader. Just as the clothes you wear to an interview communicate something about your general personality, the way you put together a letter communicates your attitude. Fortunately, you can use three basic writing tools to establish the appropriate impression by establishing the appropriate tone: WORD CHOICE, SENTENCE STRUCTURE, and overall structure.

For details about how to structure your letters, see specific kinds of letters: GENERAL CORRESPONDENCE LETTERS; OPINION LETTERS; BAD NEWS, GIVING IT; BAD NEWS, SOFTENING IT; and REQUESTS FOR PAYMENT. Further, for help in choosing and creating the appropriate tone, see TONE IN LETTERS. And if you are taking too long to get the letters written, see GENERAL CORRESPONDENCE LETTERS, PERSUASIVE LETTERS, OPINION LETTERS, and WRITING BLOCKS.

LIE OR LAY?

See LAY OR LIE?

LIKE OR AS?

See AS OR LIKE?

LINKING VERBS

See VERBS, LINKING.

LISTS, STRUCTURE OF

The following rules can help you use lists effectively and correctly.

1. Make sure the items in the list are both logically and grammatically parallel.

You may decide that the testimony of one witness is entitled to greater weight than that of another witness, or even of several witnesses. In weighing the evidence, you may consider your own *knowledge, observations,* and *life experiences.*

rather than

In weighing the evidence, you may consider the testimony of one witness as entitled to greater weight than that of another witness or several others, *your own knowledge, what you have observed,* and *the experiences you have had in life.*

In the first example, two ideas (**weighing evidence** and **using personal experience to weigh the evidence**) are divided into two sentences. Additionally, the list of kinds of personal experience in the second sentence is revised to be grammatically parallel. For related information, see PARALLEL STRUCTURE.

2. Use commas to separate items in the list.

The defendant moved his car into the left lane to pass, lost control on the snow-packed pavement, slid back into the right lane, and collided with the plaintiff's truck.

When writing a list in legal writing, put a comma before the **and** or **or** that introduces the final item in the list. For example, in the following sentence, the comma before the **and** makes it clear that there are four shares, not three.

My estate is to be divided equally among my nephew, my son, my daughter, and my son-in-law.

3. Use commas even if the list is set off from the text. Do not use semicolons just because the list is set off from the text. See subsection 4.

"Remanufacturing equipment" includes the following processes:

(1) disassembly to a predetermined standard established by the manufacturer for each model,

99

(2) cleaning,

(3) refinishing,

(4) inspecting and testing to new machine test standards,

(5) installation of all retrofits, and

(6) operational testing.

4. Use semicolons only if there is a comma within one of the items on the list; otherwise use commas, no matter how long each item in the list is. See subsection 3 for an example of the correct use of commas. The following examples show the correct use of semicolons with commas.

The Company warrants for one year that its compressors (1) are free from defects in material and workmanship; (2) have the capacities and rating set forth in the Company's catalogs, provided that no warranty is made against corrosion, erosion, or deterioration; and (3) meet all relevant federal safety standards.

The Company is not liable for any delay in performance due to any of the following:

(1) any act of God, including but not limited to floods, epidemics, fires, storms, or earthquakes;

(2) any acts of others beyond the reasonable control of the Company, including but not limited to strikes or other labor disturbances, riots, wars, acts of civil or military authority, or acts of the Customer; and

(3) any cause beyond its reasonable control, including but not limited to delays in transportation, inability to obtain necessary materials or components, or labor shortages.

5. Whenever possible, put the list at the end of the sentence. It is much easier to read there.

In justifying the exclusion of expert psychiatric evidence, the court listed three concerns: maintaining the integrity of the bifurcated trial procedure, avoiding allowing the guilty to go free, and preserving the defendant's right against self-incrimination.

rather than

The court listed the concerns of maintaining the integrity of the bifurcated trial procedure, avoiding allowing the guilty to go free, and preserving the defendant's right against self-incrimination in justifying the exclusion of expert psychiatric evidence.

For related information, see READABILITY.

6. Choose the format for your list by considering the complexity of the list. In general, the more complex the items on the list or the longer the list, the more graphically you should set off the list. You may use your COMMON SENSE here, and also consider the following guidelines.

(a) Run the list in text if (1) each item is one to three words long and (2) there are three to five items in the list.

100

The plaintiff paid the defendant $2,550 in installments of $510, $700, $850, and $490.

(b) As this sentence illustrates, run the list in text and insert parenthetical numbers before each item if (1) each item in the list is several words long and (2) the list includes three or fewer items. This can be useful in those awkward situations when you need to include a list within a list.

The defendant agreed to provide the roofing materials needed and (1) construct the new roof or (2) subcontract the job to a bonded roofer.

(c) Introduce the list with a colon and insert parenthetical numbers if the list does not occur in a highly formal rhetoric situation and if (1) most items are more than three words long or (2) there are more than five items in the list.

Before drafting this warning letter, I will need the following information: (1) copies of all previous written correspondence you have had with Mr. Jones regarding this matter, (2) any information you may have forgotten during our interview regarding your conversations with Mr. Jones, and (3) copies of the relevant pages of your bookkeeper's records on accounts receivable.

(d) Introduce each item on the list with the same word (1) if you want to remain more formal, (2) if the items on the list are more than three words long, or (3) if the repeated word contains an idea you want to emphasize.

A doctor may forego disclosure to his adult patient if any of the following situations occur: if the patient is unconscious, incompetent, or otherwise incapable of understanding the information; if in the doctor's opinion the information would have a disproportionately adverse reaction on the patient's ability to make a rational decision; or if an emergency exists which allows no time to safely consult with the patient.

(e) Use a colon and parenthetical numbers and also set the list off from the text if (1) most of the items on the list are more than ten words long, (2) the items are phrases but not complete sentences, and (3) there are more than three items in the list.

The Company's liability does not include any of the following:

(1) any damage occurring in connection with the use of the equipment in any nuclear facility;

(2) any consequential or incidental damages, including but not limited to loss of profit, damage to associated equipment, cost of capital, and cost of substitute products;

(3) any costs beyond the price of the product and service that gives rise to the claim; or

(4) any claims arising from advice or assistance given by the Company without separate compensation for that advice.

(f) Set off complete sentences in a list, each introduced with a number, if (1) each item is a complete sentence of more than ten words, (2) there are more than two items, and (3) that format is appropriate in this writing situation.

During the period of this maintenance agreement, if the Company determines that it cannot maintain the equipment in good working order, then the Company must replace the equipment with another unit in good working order. This requirement is subject to the following provisions.

1. If the Company replaces the equipment within two years of the warranty expiration date, then the replacement unit must be one that is newly manufactured, remanufactured, or reconditioned.

2. If the Company replaces the equipment more than two years after the warranty expiration date, then the replacement unit will be one that is refurbished in accordance with the process used to refurbish rental units.

3. If the Company cannot replace the equipment with another unit of the same model, then the replacement unit will be substantially similar or will have greater capabilities.

4. . . . .

7. Set off complete sentences with **first, second,** and so on, if the items in the list introduce points that will be discussed at length or if you are writing in a situation where a set-off list seems inappropriate.

The appellate process has two major objectives, and it must meet both of them to be considered successful. First, the appellate process must give litigants a fair opportunity to have legitimate claims resolved by a court of law. Second, the appellate process must provide a framework within which the common law can develop in an orderly manner.

For related information, see PARALLEL STRUCTURE and LISTS, WHEN TO USE.

LISTS, WHEN TO USE

Use a list whenever you have three or more items that are logically parallel. Also use a list when you have a lot of information that the reader needs to remember, because grouping items into a list makes both reading and remembering easier. For help doing this, see LISTS, STRUCTURE OF. Two particular problems with lists are handling multiple lists and long lists.

1. Handling multiple lists.

Avoid using too many lists at once. For example, avoid using more than one list in a sentence.

If you need to include several lists, try to put each lengthy list in a separate sentence. Also try to separate clearly any small lists of two or three items.

102

Seller is to comply with all requirements of laws and regulations, whether federal, state, or local. For example, these requirements include but are not limited to compliance with laws and regulations relating to labor, worker's compensation, wages and hours, unemployment compensation or insurance, old age benefits, other social security and welfare laws, and payment of payroll taxes.

rather than

Seller is to comply with all requirements of federal, state, and local laws and regulations, including, for example, but not limited to, compliance with laws and regulations relating to labor, worker's compensation, wages and hours, unemployment compensation or insurance, old age benefits, any other social security and welfare laws and all requirements concerning the payment of payroll taxes.

2. Handling long lists.

If you can reduce the number of items listed, do so, because lists are hard to read if they run long, such as more than five items. The reader has difficulty remembering that many items at once. But, because often you cannot shorten the list in legal writing, you may have to try some other techniques. Try grouping the listed items into logical subgroups. For example, four lists of four items each is much easier to read than one list of sixteen items. If subdividing is not possible, use graphic devices to make the list easier to follow. For samples of these see LISTS, STRUCTURE OF, subsection 6.

LITERAL LANGUAGE

Literal language is used almost exclusively in legal writing because it is precise and accurately defines things exactly as they are. For a definition, see LITERAL MEANING. For some uses of figurative language, rather than literal, see FIGURATIVE LANGUAGE.

LITERAL MEANING

A word's literal meaning is its actual or exact meaning. Literal meaning avoids exaggeration, metaphor, or embellishment; it therefore conveys the explicit meaning of the word or words.

Four witnesses gave statements after the accident.

rather than

A handful of witnesses painted a vivid picture of the tragedy.

Legal writers expect literal language, particularly in drafting and OBJECTIVE WRITING. Save precise figurative language for persuasive or scholarly style.

LITERALLY

Literally in a strict sense means **really** or **actually**. **Literally** is often misused to mean **figuratively**. The following sentence uses **literally** correctly.

There were literally three hundred people in the courtroom.

This means that there were actually three hundred people there. The following example uses literally incorrectly.

I am literally dying of boredom.

I am dying of boredom is sufficient to communicate the HYPERBOLE; boredom does not literally cause death. For related information, see LITERAL MEANING.

LOGICAL LINKS

Logical links are those clues that show the reader how your sentences and paragraphs fit together logically. For ways to show the logical links in your argument, see CONNECTIONS, MAKING THEM; TRANSITIONS; ORGANIZATION, SMALL–SCALE; and PARAGRAPHS.

LONG QUOTES

See EXTENDED QUOTES.

LOOSELEAFS

See UPDATING THE LAW.

LUCIDITY

See ACCURACY, PRECISION, and READABILITY.

–LY OR NOT?

The suffix -ly is used to make ADVERBS out of ADJECTIVES, such as carefully from careful or generously from generous. When using -ly, make sure that the word is being used as an adverb, that is, it modifies a verb, an adjective or another adverb. If the word is modifying a noun or pronoun, there should be no -ly.

MAIN SENTENCES

See TOPIC SENTENCES.

MATTER OF FACT, AS A

See AS A MATTER OF FACT.

MAY OR CAN?

See CAN OR MAY?

MEANING OF WORDS

For topics in this area, see LITERAL MEANING, FIGURATIVE MEANING, CONNOTATION, PRECISION, and WORD CHOICE.

MEMORANDUM OF POINTS AND AUTHORITIES

A memorandum of points and authorities is a PRETRIAL BRIE[F] that outlines the legal arguments to be made on a pretrial issue. In some jurisdictions, this terminology is used because the format requires the writer to make each legal point separately and give authority for it. Check your jurisdiction for the appropriate terminology and FORMAT. For an example of one kind of format, see BRIEFS.

MEMOS

Memos are intraoffice communications that convey information from researchers to decision-makers before, during, and after litigation. Memos use OBJECTIVE STYLE to inform the reader of how the law measures the strengths and weaknesses of the client's position, to predict the court's decision, and to advise the reader on what decision to make. For related information, see OBJECTIVITY. The usual format for a memo follows.

MEMO

To: [This caption contains information

From: that gets the memo filed accurately and

Re: makes it useful for future reference.

Date: For more information see CAPTIONS.]

STATEMENT OF FACTS

The STATEMENT OF FACTS summarizes the LEGALLY SIGNIFICANT FACTS and fills in any needed BACKGROUND FACTS. Check with your reader to see if this section should follow the Brief Answer, rather than precede the Question Presented.

Applicable Statute(s)

QUESTION PRESENTED

This section includes the final version of the preliminary QUESTION PRESENTED as it was formulated in Step 3 of the RESEARCH STRATEGY. It should contain the following three elements.

Under [general rule of law],

did (or was) [legal question]

when [legally significant facts of this case]?

Under Wyoming law on false imprisonment, did Cornbloom falsely imprison Abernathy when he drove Abernathy around in the car for seven hours without letting him out?

Check with your reader to see if the particular facts of your case should be included in the Question Presented or if the facts should be stated more generally, as in the following example.

Under Wyoming law on false imprisonment, does the driver of a car falsely imprison a passenger when he drives the passenger around for seven hours without stopping and letting him out of the car?

BRIEF ANSWER

The BRIEF ANSWER gives the writer's predicted answer to the question and gives the reason for this answer, usually in one sentence.

Yes; Cornbloom falsely imprisoned Abernathy because he intended to confine Abernathy in the car, because Abernathy was actually confined in the car, and because Abernathy was aware of his confinement.

DISCUSSION

This section discusses the application of the law to the facts; generally, it will be organized around the structure of the law being used. For example, a discussion of a statute with several elements will progress element by element; a discussion of a balancing test will weigh the two sides. For each element, the DISCUSSION SECTION begins with the general RULES of law, describes useful ANALOGOUS CASES, and then applies that information to the facts of this situation. For related information, see APPLICATION.

Thus you will not necessarily have all the law in one place and all the application in another, but rather for each point of the analysis, you might state the law and then apply it. For more help, see ORGANIZATION, LARGE–SCALE and ORGANIZATION, SMALL–SCALE.

CONCLUSION

This section summarizes the main points made in the Discussion, giving a capsule of the reasoning that led to the Brief Answer. It may also contain recommendations to the reader. It does not, however, include any information or reasoning not covered in the Discussion.

MIGHT

See VERB TENSES.

MISSPELLINGS, HOW TO AVOID

Fortunately, spelling problems can often be best cured by relatively painless measures. Here are two ideas.

1. Take a 3 × 5 index card and write on it three words you need to use frequently but have trouble spelling, such as **defendant** or **conceive**, and underline the part that gives you trouble. Then put the index card somewhere where you will see it frequently, such as on your bathroom mirror or inside your brief case. Do nothing more for two or three weeks. By that time, you will probably find that you can close your eyes and see the card in your mind, thus seeing how to spell the problem words. As you gain confidence with these three words, substitute new ones on the list.

2. Make an alphabetized list of words that commonly give you trouble, but keep the list to one page. Then carry this list with you and look up the problem word any time you need to write it. With this technique,

you are not trying to learn to spell the words; you are finding a way around the problem, which is a practical alternative.

MODELS, USE OF
See FORMS, USE OF.

MODIFIERS
A modifier adds information about a noun or verb and can be either a single word or a group of words. Avoid using too many modifiers because they weaken the sentence. Particularly avoid using two modifiers that mean the same thing, such as **first and foremost** or **separate and apart**. Also avoid modifiers that have little substantive meaning, such as **in this manner**, **very**, or **obviously**.

These are the specific words of Minnesota lawmakers; consequently, the works must be given special significance.

rather than

Clearly these are the specific and precise words of Minnesota lawmakers regarding the issue; consequently, the words must be given special significance and appropriate attention.

The court in *Higgins* does not establish a standard for viability any more specific than the fetus' ability to exist separately from its mother.

rather than

Obviously, the court in *Higgins* appears to fail to definitively establish an unambiguous and undebatable determining standard for when a fetus reaches the medical state of viability that seems to be any more clearly specific than ascertaining medically the fetus' ability to exist separately and apart from its biological mother.

For more general information on modifiers, see ADJECTIVES, ADVERBS, and PREPOSITIONS. For more on problems associated with the use of modifiers, see MODIFIERS, DANGLING; MODIFIERS, MISPLACED; and MODIFIERS, SQUINTING.

MODIFIERS, DANGLING
A dangling modifier is a modifying phrase that does not modify any word in the sentence. This situation invites ambiguity. Usually these dangling modifiers occur at the beginning of a sentence.

To argue contributory negligence, all elements of negligence must be shown.

It is not clear here who will be doing the arguing. In contrast, see the following revision.

To argue contributory negligence, the defense must show all elements of negligence.

You can avoid this problem by doing the following: when you start a sentence with an introductory phrase beginning with a verb, such as **to argue**, make sure that the subject of that verb is also the subject of the sentence following the introductory phrase. For related information, see AMBIGUITY, WAYS TO AVOID.

MODIFIERS, MISPLACED

Sometimes a modifying phrase, because of its position, modifies the wrong phrase in a sentence.

The defendant refused to service the car belonging to the man who insulted him with good reason.

Here **with good reason** should modify **refused** rather than **insulted**. To avoid ambiguity, place the modifying phrase right next to the word modified, such as **refused** in this example.

The defendant, with good reason, refused to service the car belonging to the man who had insulted him.

For other problems associated with modifiers, see MODIFIERS, DANGLING and MODIFIERS, SQUINTING.

MODIFIERS, SQUINTING

Squinting modifiers create ambiguity because they can modify terms either before or after the modifier. To correct this problem, move the modifier to an unambiguous location in the sentence.

Only Ms. Sparks suggested filing a suit for adverse possession.

or

Ms. Sparks suggested but did not recommend filing a suit for adverse possession.

rather than

Ms. Sparks only suggested filing a suit for adverse possession.

For a discussion of related problems, see ONLY and AMBIGUITY, WAYS TO AVOID.

MOODS

Mood refers to changes made in the form of the verb to indicate whether or not the action described by the verb happened in fact. These changes in the form of the verb are called inflections, and create three moods. These moods are important conveyors of meaning in legal writing.

1. Indicative

The indicative mood refers to actions that have in fact happened or will in fact happen. This mood is used most often in legal writing.

The defendant filed a motion for failure to state a claim upon which relief can be granted.

or

The plaintiff invited the defendant to dinner on the night of the robbery.

2. Subjunctive

The subjunctive mood refers to actions that will not necessarily happen, but are being discussed hypothetically.

If I were you, I would not use that argument with Judge Carwell.

or

If the defendant were younger, such an assault might have been possible.

3. Imperative

The imperative mood states commands. The subject of the sentence is **you,** which is understood.

Return the bottom portion.

Meet me at the hearing at 10:30.

Use it when explaining how to do something. Do not use the imperative mood when talking to courts.

MOTIONS

A motion is an application to a court for a rule or order in the moving party's favor. In most jurisdictions, the motion must be filed with the court as a separate document. In some jurisdictions, it is combined with a NOTICE OF MOTION, which tells the opposition when the court will hear the motion. Check your jurisdiction for specific FORMAT and filing requirements.

Often you will file a brief in support of the motion. This brief is designed to persuade the court to rule in your client's favor. When the opposition responds to the motion, it will usually file a brief in opposition to the motion. For a basic format, see BRIEFS. For related information, see PERSUASIVE WRITING.

MS., MRS., OR MISS?

If possible, find out from the person addressed what she prefers. If this is not possible, use **Ms.**

NAMES

There are two schools of thought on whether or not to use clients' names in any piece of legal writing. The first school holds that names are appropriate because they focus the reader on the specific outcome of the case being analyzed. The second school prefers using more general terms because the reader can get a concept of the legal question being analyzed, which in a memo will also be of use in future cases. Consider your AUDIENCE, and write accordingly.

Under Washington Law on false imprisonment, did Cornbloom falsely imprison Abernathy when he drove Abernathy around in the car for seven hours without letting him out?

or

Under Washington Law on false imprisonment, does the driver of a car falsely imprison a passenger when he drives the passenger around for seven hours without stopping and letting him out of the car?

Whichever format you use, remain consistent throughout any piece of legal writing. If you choose to use names in OBJECTIVE WRITING, use them in each subsection of the memo or opinion letter. Choose the form of name most appropriate to the setting, such as **Mr. Jones, Theodore Jones,** or **Ted,** depending upon your familiarity with the party and the formality of the document you are writing. Similarly, if you choose to use names in PERSUASIVE WRITING, use them in each part of the brief or opinion letter. Choose the form of name most favorable to your client. For example, use **Mr., Ms., Miss,** or **Mrs. Smith** if you wish to dignify the party by using a formal tone. In briefs, use first names only if needed for clarity or if referring to a juvenile. For example, if two brothers were contesting a will, you might use first and last names, such as **Allen Anderson** and **Andrew Anderson,** to distinguish the two. If one party was an eight-year-old girl, you might use the first name only, such as **Betty,** to underscore the sympathy the court might feel for the child.

Avoid using names of anyone other than the parties, such as the names of opposing counsel. Such references detract from the purpose of your argument.

NEGATIVES

Negative statements are harder to understand than positive ones, so state things positively whenever possible.

Come to the meeting at 3:00 p.m. or later.

rather than

Do not come to the meeting before 3:00 p.m.

The negative statements that are hardest to read are those including **unless, neglect to, not unlike, hardly, scarcely,** and other such words. These negative words can be easily misread and so should be avoided when possible.

Multiple negatives are also hard to read, so try to avoid them.

Come to the meeting only if you are required to do so.

rather than

Do not come to the meeting unless you are told not to neglect to come.

NEITHER

Use **neither** only when listing two items. Like **either, neither** is a helpful signal for the reader when it is followed by two listed items; it is much less helpful when it is followed by a list of more than two items, because **neither** leads the reader to expect only two. Therefore, if you are introducing a list of more than two items, try using **none of the following,** which will prepare the reader for a longer list.

Further, make sure that the terms after **neither** and **nor** are logically and grammatically parallel.

Neither the defendant's own testimony nor her written records support this assertion.

rather than

Neither the testimony offered by the defendant nor the defendant's own written records support this assertion.

For related information, see PARALLEL STRUCTURE.

NOBODY

Nobody takes a singular verb.

Nobody has shown up on time for the hearing yet.

Nobody knows the trouble I've seen.

Nobody sounds slightly informal, so you may prefer **no one** in most legal writing.

NOMINALIZATION

Nominalization refers to the process of turning ADJECTIVES, ADVERBS, and VERBS into NOUNS. Nominalizations are grammatically correct, but their overuse can make the writing stodgy or hard to read. Whenever possible and appropriate, replace a nominalization with the verb, adjective or adverb form.

Use the following phrases	rather than these.
stated	made the statement that
Machines operated by inserting a coin	Machines operated by means of insertion of a coin
Counsel objected to the expert's testimony.	Counsel made an objection to the expert's testimony.
He was devoted to his father.	He showed great devotion to his father.

But use nominalizations where they make more sense, such as when the noun forms are TERMS OF ART.

He is accused of alienation of affection.

rather than

He alienated her affections toward her husband.

NO ONE

No one takes a singular verb; related personal pronouns and adjectives must also be singular.

No one has testified to plaintiff's innocence.

No one has all of his or her [not their] pretrial discovery ready.

111

NONRESTRICTIVE PHRASES

Nonrestrictive phrases are those phrases that describe but do not limit the words preceding them. They are surrounded by commas, which act as a kind of parentheses, because if the nonrestrictive phrases were taken out of the sentence the sentence would still be accurate. Nonrestrictive phrases often begin with **which** or **who**.

The defendant, who thinks he is innocent, looks terrified.

The fourth amendment, which protects citizens against unlawful searches and seizures, provides the foundation for this suit.

For related information, see THAT OR WHICH?

NOR

Nor is a conjunction that continues the negative force of **neither, never,** or **not**, and therefore can be used effectively in PERSUASIVE WRITING.

The defendant was never read his rights, nor was he allowed to make a phone call, nor was he allowed to talk with an attorney within the first twenty-four hours of his internment.

Respondent objected neither to cross-examination nor to introduction of the evidence at trial.

The statute has never been construed to have such a result, nor is such a result possible under the Constitution.

NOT

Not is a small word that changes the meaning of a whole sentence. Therefore, proofread your text to make sure **not** is placed accurately. Additionally, whenever possible, try to write so the point will not be lost if the reader overlooks **not**.

NOT ONLY . . . BUT ALSO

These two phrases belong in partnership as conjunctions. In PERSUASIVE WRITING, use the pair to foreshadow and emphasize the logical parallels of two arguments.

Not only has the plaintiff failed to show that the father gave the son implied consent, but the plaintiff has also failed to show that the father provided the car for the son's use.

In OBJECTIVE WRITING, use the pair to connect legal concepts clearly.

The plaintiff must show not only that the father gave implied consent, but also that the father provided the car to the son.

In using this pair of conjunctions, remember to use **but also** after **not only**. Do no use **not only . . . but**. The mismatched **not only . . . but** is particularly confusing to readers because **not . . . but** means almost the opposite of **not only . . . but also**.

112

Also make sure that the term following **not only** is structurally and logically parallel to the term following **but also**. See PARALLEL STRUCTURE.

The defendant abused not only the privileges offered him, but also the procedure designed to protect him.

NOT SO MUCH . . . AS

Like NOT ONLY . . . BUT ALSO, these words work together as conjunctions and should be used together.

The key is not so much the existence of central authority as the frequency with which that authority is exercised.

rather than

The key is not so much the existence of central authority but the frequency with which that authority is exercised.

NOTES

Develop an effective system of note taking so that PREWRITING is comfortable for you. Your system is personal, of course, but taking effective notes throughout RESEARCH and PREWRITING will make WRITING and REWRITING much faster. In developing your own system, consider the following.

1. Whatever form you use, such as note cards, legal size paper, or cut-and-pasted scraps of paper, write on only one side of the paper so that information can be moved easily.

2. If an authority looks at all usable, write down the entire correct citation right at the beginning. This will save you time when you use that authority later; you will not have to spend time in the library looking up citations. The time you save will outweigh any extra time you take to record citations at the beginning.

3. When using quotes, RULES, propositions, REASONING, or HOLD-INGS from any case, note the exact page number so that you can incorporate PINPOINT CITES in the final draft without returning to the original source.

4. Try to develop a system, such as one using headings, using colors, or using tabs, one that organizes notes by topic, so that the notes can be easily organized according to issue.

5. Write legibly so you will not waste time later deciphering your notes.

6. Focus on the legal issue you are researching by translating your notes into relevant TERMS OF ART. Once you have formulated the QUESTION PRESENTED in step 3 of the research process described in RESEARCH STRATEGY, begin reading your cases with that issue in mind; then record holdings, propositions, rules with the terms of art important to that issue. For example, if you are researching whether

or not your client committed an intentional tort, use **intend** as your main verb when stating the holding.

A five year old could not intend to injure an elderly woman because five-year-olds are not capable of forming intent.

7. Leave space for adding notes, which may include either cross-references or your own thoughts as the research and writing process progresses.

8. Take notes with your own thoughts in mind; work those thoughts into your theory of the case, whether writing a memo, a letter, or a brief. This will help you begin to organize and understand the significance of your research and will help you build your case.

NOTICE OF MOTION

A Notice of Motion accompanies a motion to a court. It notifies the other party of the time and place the motion will be heard. The Notice of Motion is accompanied by the motion itself and often a brief in support of or in opposition to the motion. In some jurisdictions, you may incorporate the notice into the motion's preamble, as shown in the following example. Combining the two, however, may create an awkwardly long sentence. For related information, see MOTIONS and BRIEFS.

STATE OF WISCONSIN   CIRCUIT COURT   DANE COUNTY

OLAF PETERSON, HENRY PETERSON and DOROTHY PETERSON,
 	
                    Plaintiffs,
vs.
BUDGET INSURANCE COMPANY, et al.,
                   Defendants.
	NOTICE OF MOTION AND MOTIONS AFTER VERDICT
	Case No: 000–999

TO: Attorney David A. Salverson
      Salverson & Johnson, S.C.
      Suite 6032
      9101 West Wisconsin Avenue
      Milwaukee, Wisconsin 53203

PLEASE TAKE NOTICE that on September 29, 1989, at 10:30 A.M., at the Courthouse in the City of Madison, Circuit Court, Branch IX, the Honorable Albert Purdy, presiding, the Defendants, by their attorneys, will move the Court on Motions After Verdict as follows:

    1.   For judgment notwithstanding the verdict, dismissing the Complaint of the Plaintiffs, for reasons evident in the record and stated in these Motions;

2. In the alternative, to change the answers to Questions No. 1 and 2 from "Yes" to "No", dismissing the Complaint of the Plaintiffs on the ground of insufficiency of the evidence to sustain the answers;

. . .

8. In the alternative, to set the judgment aside and order judgment in favor of the Defendants, dismissing the Plaintiffs' Complaint on the ground that the Plaintiff's negligence was a superseding cause of his injuries.

Dated August 15, 1981.

POTTERS, PEARSON, PEEPLES, & PRINCE

BY: _____

JOSEPH E. POTTERS,
Attorney for Defendants,
Budget Insurance Company
and Far Horizons Foundation,
Inc.

P.O. Box 6666
Madison, Wisconsin   53701

NOUNS

To lawyers, nouns are probably second only to verbs as the most important part of speech because nouns name clients, theories, causes, damages, results, and rights. Thus legal writers must choose nouns with care and use them with precision. In order to do so, first understand the uses of the various noun classifications. Second, avoid the common problems associated with the use of nouns in legal writing.

1. Classifications of nouns and their uses.

(a) Proper nouns name specific persons, places, or things, and are capitalized.

San Francisco, Sandstrom, Bill of Rights

(b) Common nouns do not refer to specific persons, places, or things, and thus are not capitalized.

lawyer, courtroom, fairness, alienation

(c) ABSTRACT NOUNS name concepts or ideas, rather than tangible things.

fairness, right, protection, weapon

Abstract nouns are necessary and useful in legal writing, but if misused or overused they make the content less memorable for the reader.

Equity dictates that the plaintiff be reimbursed for this loss.

rather than

Fairness dictates that plaintiff's rights should be protected.

(d) In contrast, concrete nouns name tangible things.

lawyer, courtroom, Doberman, knife

These concrete nouns are easier to remember and are thus more helpful to the legal reader. Therefore, use concrete nouns often, especially to emphasize a point.

The testimony of four witnesses proves Mr. Noble was mentally incompetent, and should therefore be spared the death penalty.

rather than

Fairness dictates that my client's mental state should absolve him of guilt.

For more examples of the uses of concrete nouns, see EMPHASIS, subsection 2.

(e) Collective nouns name groups that are to be treated logically and grammatically as a single unit.

The Supreme Court holds . . . .

With collective nouns, use the singular form of the verb, such as **holds**, even though the noun refers to a group, such as a court made up of several justices.

(f) GERUNDS are nouns formed from the **-ing** form of a verb. Often using gerunds makes a sentence more concise.

Imagining alone does not constitute intent.

rather than

The act of imagination alone does not constitute intent.

2. Common problems with nouns in legal writing.

Two common problems occur with nouns in legal writing: they are used imprecisely and inconsistently. Therefore, consider your choices carefully. First, choose the noun that most precisely states your meaning. To paraphrase Mark Twain, "the difference between the right word and the almost right word is the difference between **internment** and **interment**." Second, do not change a noun solely for VARIETY. The legal reader will assume a different noun represents a different idea. For more explanation and examples, see WORD CHOICE and REPETITION.

NUMBERS

See NUMERALS.

NUMERALS

The common question here is whether a number should be spelled out in words or written as a numeral.

1. Spell out a number that begins a sentence.

One hundred twenty-five pieces of evidence were admitted at trial.

The one exception to this rule is years.

1984 was not what we expected.

2. Spell out zero to ninety-nine in text and zero to nine in footnotes in law review articles. Different sources list different upper limits on spelling out numbers, but Blue Book rule 6.3(a) lists ninety-nine as the limit.

3. Spell out round numbers larger than ninety-nine, if you choose, as long as you are consistent throughout the text.

4. Spell out numbers and then insert numerals in parentheses only in drafting legal documents, and then only when the duplication is needed to avoid the possibility of a critical inaccuracy.

In consideration for these agreements, Howard Industries agrees to pay Liveson Construction the sum of four thousand dollars ($4,000).

5. Use numerals for numbers larger than ninety-nine.

The prosecution introduced 173 separate documents to support this claim.

6. Use numerals if, in one series, you have numbers both over ninety-nine and under.

The numbers of computers taken in these four robberies were 7, 25, 102, and 130.

7. Use numerals when you are referring to a section of a document and that section itself is identified by a numeral.

This exception is covered in subsection 5.

OBJECT
See SENTENCE, PARTS OF, subsections 3, 4, and 5.

OBJECT OF A PREPOSITION
See PREPOSITIONS and SENTENCE, PARTS OF, subsection 6.

OBJECTIVE WRITING
Objective writing informs and predicts, using a neutral POINT OF VIEW. For example, use objective writing in MEMOS to inform the reader of the current status of the law, or in OPINION LETTERS to inform the reader of the current status of a case. In either situation, the reader is looking for an unbiased assessment of the circumstances.

The reader may also expect a prediction of the outcome of the case. This prediction should be based on objective analysis of the law that measures the strengths and weaknesses of the client's position and balances them. In doing so, objective writing does not minimize the weaknesses of the argument, as PERSUASIVE WRITING does.

The majority of states draws the viability line at around six months; only two states have drawn the line earlier.

rather than

117

Even though a majority of states has drawn the viability line at six months, two states have carefully considered the valid arguments for drawing the line earlier and have done so.

Consider the following in preparing objective writing, such as a memo or an opinion letter.

1. Keep an objective point of view, as a reporter would.

2. Report what the law or the status of the case is by giving an objective summary of the law.

3. Make sure both the strengths and weaknesses of the client's arguments are clear.

4. Make sure the reader sees the balance of those arguments, that is, what weight law, POLICY, and EQUITY give to each.

5. Avoid overuse of MODIFIERS, because objective writing informs but does not persuade. Concentrate instead on precise use of nouns and verbs.

The majority of states draws the viability line at around six months; only two states have drawn the line earlier.

rather than

The vast majority of states have clearly decided to draw the viability line at approximately six months, although two dissenting states have deviated somewhat from that popular course.

When using modifiers, also avoid those that argue, such as **unjust** or **unmistakably**; use only those modifiers that clarify the presentation, such as **unsettled** or **previously**.

6. Make sure the information in the memo is complete, despite your personal bias; do not omit unfavorable points the other side may raise.

For related information, see OBJECTIVITY and POINT OF VIEW, OBJECTIVE OR PERSUASIVE?

OBJECTIVITY

Objectivity is essential to all forms of legal writing at some stage. An attorney must remain particularly objective when planning the client's case so that the attorney can correctly anticipate all possible arguments on both sides of the issue. Equally important, an attorney must remain objective in any oral presentations designed to inform the court or another attorney of the law, such as in pretrial or intraoffice conferences.

Objectivity is paramount in pretrial work because the attorney must accurately assess the strength of the arguments. This objectivity paves the way for accurate use of law and POLICY to persuade the court in BRIEFS and oral arguments. Therefore, in intraoffice documents, such as MEMOS, present information objectively. For related information, see OBJECTIVE WRITING and ORAL PRESENTA-TIONS.

OBLIVIOUS OF OR OBLIVIOUS TO?

If you mean **unaware**, use **oblivious of**. If you mean **forgetful**, use **oblivious to**. Of the two, **oblivious of** is the narrower meaning. To avoid confusion, consider using another word, such as **unaware** or **unmindful**.

The defendant was unaware of the significance of this waiver.

rather than

The defendant was oblivious of the significance of this waiver.

The defendant was unmindful of her duty to see that all the children's seat belts were properly fastened.

rather than

The defendant was oblivious to her duty to see that all the children's seat belts were properly fastened.

OBVIOUSLY

Use **obviously** only when the point is indeed obvious. Use **obviously** sparingly in legal writing, because you seldom state an obvious point, and even when you do state it you seldom want to underscore its obviousness. If the point is not obvious, labelling it as such insults your reader and impairs your credibility. For related concerns, see MODIFI-ERS and LITERAL MEANING.

OF COURSE

This phrase is best avoided in legal writing; **of course** implies that the point is obvious, but the legal reader may not see your point as being this clear cut. Do not use **of course** to gloss over assumptions that need to be supported. For related problems, see IT IS SAID THAT, OBVIOUSLY, and MODIFIERS.

OK, O.K., OR OKAY?

Probably use none of the above in formal writing. If you need to use one of the three, **OK** is the most widely used form.

OMITTING WORDS FROM QUOTES

For when and how to do this, see PUNCTUATING QUOTES, subsections 7, 8, and 9. Also see EDITING QUOTES.

ONE

One as a pronoun indicates a single person, a single unit, a single thing. It takes a singular verb.

One of the defendants is moving to have the case dismissed.

One of the problems with teaching legal analysis is that not all professors agree on the best way to teach it.

ONE–SENTENCE PARAGRAPHS

Occasionally you may use one-sentence paragraphs for EMPHASIS, but only occasionally. If you have several in one brief or memo, you are probably overusing them. The following one-sentence paragraph, following a detailed explanation of a Congressional policy statement, effectively emphasized a point.

While this statement of Congressional policy has no direct effect on the commerce regulations, it may be such a strong policy statement that future Presidents will think twice about restricting scientific or scholarly transnational communications.

For problems one-sentence paragraphs may signal, see PARAGRAPHS and ORGANIZATION. For related information, see ORGANIZATION, SMALL–SCALE.

ONLY, WHERE TO PLACE

Each time you use **only**, check its placement; in general, place it immediately before the word it modifies. A misplaced **only** can create ambiguity, and often in legal writing that ambiguity is serious. For example, what does the following sentence mean?

Shares are sold to the public only by the parent corporation.

Are shares sold only to the public, or only by the parent corporation? Although the reader might be able to reason out the meaning in context, the sentence should be written so the meaning is unmistakable. See MODIFIERS, SQUINTING.

Often ambiguity occurs because **only** comes too early in the sentence.

You should only introduce this evidence if the defendant chooses to testify.

The writer did not mean to say that the reader should **only introduce** this evidence and do nothing else with it. To avoid this ambiguity, try placing **only** as late in the sentence as possible without creating an inaccuracy.

You should introduce this evidence only if the defendant chooses to testify.

For related information, see also ACCURACY, subsection 6.

OPENINGS FOR LETTERS

In general, open with a sentence or two explaining the point of your letter or why you are writing.

In response to your inquiry, I am enclosing . . . .

or

Last Monday, we met to discuss . . . . This letter formalizes our agreement that I would act as your attorney concerning . . . .

This is preferable to starting with a sentence explaining who you are; that opening tempts the reader to say, "Who cares?" You can, however, explain who you are in the second or third sentence, after the reader has some reason to care, or you can add an explanatory reference as part of another sentence.

As your attorney, I want to notify you of some recent changes in the tax law that may require a change in your record-keeping practices.

In some cases, you may want to be slightly less direct, including a brief explanatory paragraph before your point. See BAD NEWS, GIVING IT; BAD NEWS, SOFTENING IT; and PERSUASIVE LETTERS for ways to handle these situations. For more detail on ways to structure other letters, see GENERAL CORRESPONDENCE LETTERS.

Have stock phrases for opening routine letters, so that you avoid reinventing the wheel. But take care in selecting these stock phrases, because these opening phrases give the reader an impression of your personality, just as your demeanor creates an impression when you meet someone for the first time. In general, avoid stuffy openings, like **Pursuant to your request**, and long-winded ones, like **In regard to the matter of your request** . . . . When you receive a letter that appeals to you, notice the opening. If you like it, modify it as needed and add it to your own collection of stock openings. For related information, see SALUTATIONS and GENERAL CORRESPONDENCE LETTERS.

OPINION LETTERS

Opinion letters serve the client in two ways: (1) they inform the client of the writer's legal analysis of the situation and any updating information and (2) they predict a possible outcome or recommend a certain path. In order to do both well, consider carefully your POINT OF VIEW, TONE, and AUDIENCE.

For example, choose OBJECTIVE WRITING if you are merely informing the client of the situation. Choose PERSUASIVE WRITING if you are trying to convince the client to do something, such as settle out of court or pay a bill. For more information on handling bad news, see BAD NEWS, GIVING IT and BAD NEWS, SOFTENING IT.

Likewise, choose the TONE appropriate to your AUDIENCE. If you know the client well and it seems appropriate, use a friendly tone; if you do not know the client well, be formal but not stuffy. Choose a style that considers the client's experience in law and the client's needs.

Additionally, because an opinion letter advises the client about a legal question, do make sure you answer the question. Do not write an abstract essay or a law review article on the general topic, but instead answer the specific question as best you can.

Finally, write in clear and understandable language unless you know the client prefers you do otherwise. Clients who want legalese may exist, but they are rare. See LEGALESE, READABILITY, and CLARITY.

Opinion letters should contain any or all of the following, depending upon the status of the case.

1. A heading, including the date.

2. A salutation.

Dear Dr. Brand:

For more information, see SALUTATIONS.

3. An opening or introduction that states the question the letter will answer and refers to the request you received.

If the news is good, you may want to include the conclusion and recommendation to the client here. If the news is bad, you may state the conclusion later. (See subsection 5.) Either way, include a caveat stating that the validity of the answer depends on the accuracy of the facts you were given. This caveat can serve as a transition into the next section. For related information, see OPENINGS FOR LETTERS.

4. A summary of the LEGALLY SIGNIFICANT FACTS, the BACKGROUND FACTS, and any other facts you think the client should know that you know.

If the letter is long, set this section off with a subheading, such as the following.

FACTS OF THE CASE

or

RELEVANT FACTS

or just

FACTS

Clients may omit facts unfavorable to their position, so before writing you may want to probe to get those unfavorable facts that might influence your opinion. If appropriate, you may even draft the facts section and get the client to review it for accuracy before drafting the opinion itself. Ask the client to advise you of any additions or corrections needed in the letter, because your analysis depends on the accuracy of these facts.

5. Your conclusion, if this was not included earlier.

Make sure you answer the client's question. If the conclusion is long, you may set if off by using another subheading. See CONCLUSIONS.

6. An explanation of your conclusion, including a summary of the law and the application of the law to the facts.

If you are using subheadings, include one for this section. In the explanation section, lay out your reasoning step by step (see ORGANIZATION). Also take care to avoid using unneeded legal terms (see LEGALESE) and to define those legal terms that are needed (see UNOBTRUSIVE DEFINITIONS). Whether and when you include CITATIONS is a matter of judgment, depending on the sophistication of your reader, the extent to which your opinion rests on the case cited, and the possibility of the client misunderstanding the significance of the cites. Including citations, however, does not greatly affect READABILITY; readers can skip over citations easily if they so choose.

7. A prediction of the outcome of the case, based on the balance of the strengths against the weaknesses in the application of the law to the facts.

8. A recommendation of a course of action.

You will be balancing here your professional responsibility to inform the client fully and your need to protect yourself against potential malpractice problems. Do cover yourself, but do it by explaining the caveats and reasons behind your opinion, not by using spineless phrases that only create ambiguities. Avoid phrases like **in effect, it is said that**, and **of course**. For example, the following paragraph hedges by explaining the writer's position rather than by inserting spineless phrases.

It is my opinion that you should try to settle this claim because litigation would not be economically worthwhile. My research indicates that New York law may favor Mr. Polewski's position, and that your legal position is therefore unclear. As a result, although the outcome of a trial is not certain, you would be running a substantial risk of losing this claim even after investing the substantial amount required to litigate the case.

Sometimes you will have to say that the client cannot do what he or she wants. When possible, make this bad news more palatable by offering alternatives that lead to the same objective or to similar ones. For example, you may have to state that a lawsuit would probably be financially unfeasible, but may be able to add that negotiation might bring about some of the desired result. When your answer is no, also include in your conclusion a brief outline of your strong reasons for the no, in case an unhappy or angry client skips reading the reasons section. For related information, see BAD NEWS, GIVING IT and BAD NEWS, SOFTENING IT.

9. A specific directive to the client to call or come in to discuss the matter further.

Unless the letter is meant to do so, add a sentence explaining to your reader that your letter does not create any legal rights. For related information, see OPINION OR ADVICE?

10. A closing.

Sincerely yours,

or

Yours truly,

For related information, see CLOSINGS FOR LETTERS.

For a discussion of letters in general, see GENERAL CORRESPONDENCE LETTERS. For related information, see TONE IN LETTERS.

OPINION OR ADVICE?

When writing an opinion letter or conferring with a client, an attorney may give a client a legal opinion on a matter as long as that opinion is based on the law and the reasonable boundaries of the law. An attorney may also advise a client to pursue a certain legal course. Be careful, however, of personal, as opposed to legal, advice that could cross the line from professional opinion to coercion. Such advice could violate the Model Code of Professional Responsibility, a question beyond the scope of this book. For related information, see OPINION LETTERS.

OPINIONS

When reading an opinion, consider the steps listed below to increase both your effectiveness and your efficiency.

1. Keep in mind the purpose for which you are using that opinion. For example, if you are reading an opinion to learn about a particular subject for class, such as personal jurisdiction, read the opinion for what it offers to enhance the analysis of personal jurisdiction. If you are reading the opinion for research, read with the thesis or issue of your memo, brief, or paper in mind.

2. Read through the opinion once to get the gist of it, without marking the text or taking extensive notes. This aids your understanding by helping you see the overall framework of the case before you begin dealing with the details.

3. While reading, focus on the holding, or the result of the case, and relate that holding to your topic or issue. For example, if a new trial was granted because evidence was not properly suppressed, then study the case to find some definition of when evidence should be suppressed.

4. If you are working on an appellate brief, also note the STANDARD OF REVIEW, because this may affect your use of the case.

5. Then reread the case, briefing it according to your preference. For suggestions on how to do this, see CASE BRIEFS.

OR

Or is a conjunction that signals to the reader that you mean **any one of the listed items**, rather than **all of them**. Thus or is disjunctive. In legal writing, misuse of or can create AMBIGUITY in two situations.

1. Or alone is not always enough to communicate your meaning. If you mean to signal something else besides **any one of the listed items**, you must add other explanatory phrases, such as

by any of the following means

or

any of the following subsections.

2. Or alone is not always enough to signal that a long list is disjunctive. When you rely solely on or to show the structure of the list, the

reader has to read through most of the list before finding out whether this is an **and** or an **or** situation. Therefore, if your list is very long, let the reader know before the list that this is an **or** situation.

Either party may notify the other of a delay *by any of the following means*: telephoning the other party, sending an agent with a written message, sending an agent with an oral message, sending a telegram addressed to the other party personally, sending a certified letter, or meeting with the other party in person.

rather than

Either party may notify the other of a delay by telephoning the other party, sending an agent with the message, sending a telegram, sending a certified letter, *or any combination of these*.

For related information, see CONJUNCTIONS and LISTS, STRUCTURE OF.

ORAL OR VERBAL?

Verbal refers to any communication using words, in contrast to **nonverbal**.

A successful lawyer is usually a master of verbal communication.

Oral refers to any communication that is spoken, rather than written. Do not use **verbal** when you mean **oral**.

The contract was based on an oral agreement made July 6, 1991.

rather than

The contract was based on a verbal agreement made July 6, 1991.

ORAL PRESENTATIONS

Oral presentations must convey the essence of written presentations, but in less time and more simply. Whether it is an objective presentation to a senior partner or a persuasive argument before a court, the presentation should focus first on the issue to be resolved. It should focus second on the answer and, third, on a clear explanation.

1. In an objective oral presentation, consider the following.

(a) State the issue to which the listener wants an answer. Incorporate the same three parts used in ISSUE STATEMENTS or Questions Presented: the general law under which the question is being asked, the legal question, and the legally significant facts pertinent to that question.

(b) Give the answer. Do not make the listener wait for this.

(c) Make sure your listener is familiar with the facts of the case; if not, give a succinct presentation of the LEGALLY SIGNIFICANT FACTS, the BACKGROUND FACTS, and any significant EMOTIONAL FACTS, as they relate to the issue and answer.

(d) Explain the answer as succinctly as possible, stating the applicable rule or RULES, any pertinent ANALOGOUS CASES, an

APPLICATION of the rule or rules that connects this case to those analogous cases, and a conclusion.

(e) Be extremely flexible in answering questions. It is likely you will get interrupted by any legal listener, so use the questions to explain to the listener what the answer is and to move gracefully through the pre-planned parts of your presentation. For example, if you are asked a question about the third issue you wanted to discuss while you are discussing the first, answer the question about the third issue and move gracefully back into the first by saying something like **which is why we are arguing under the first issue that** . . . .

2. In persuasive oral presentations, consider the following.

(a) State the issue to be resolved and the answer to that issue. State it first, so you can get this information out before you are interrupted.

(b) Explain the plan of your argument to defer questions about later issues.

(c) Make sure the listener knows the facts. If you are the moving party, you must give the listener the facts of the case. But if they so choose, let the listeners waive that presentation of facts.

(d) State the conclusions the court should reach, including a brief statement explaining that a decision in your client's favor is consistent with principles of law and fair under these facts.

(e) Know the record and the law thoroughly. There is no substitute for this. If you are comfortable with the record and the law, there will be no hesitation or weakness in your argument. Your confidence should then come automatically.

(f) Address the case's impact on the law in general, especially if addressing an appellate court. The listener wants to know how the decision in this case will affect subsequent cases.

(g) Be candid and flexible; deal with weak points directly and welcome questions as an opportunity to explain the answers to the listener.

(h) Be respectful, showing good manners and good humor and keeping personalities out of the argument.

ORGANIZATION

Effective organization guides the reader through the text, just as a map guides a traveler through the country. This organization is not easy to achieve, but it is worth the effort. More than any other single aspect of legal writing, clear and logical organization distinguishes excellent writing from mediocre.

1. When to organize.

You must organize any piece of writing, but you need not do it at one particular point in the WRITING PROCESS. Instead, you may develop your organization at any of several stages. For example, you may organize by outlining during PREWRITING. Alternatively, you may first collect your thoughts or even write a loose rough draft before you develop your organization. For further help, see OUTLINES and ORGANIZATION FOR THOSE WHO CAN'T OUTLINE.

2. How to organize.

Develop your own system. You may begin by trial and error, but keep trying until you find some way to organize that works for you. You probably know already what does not work, so begin by eliminating bad habits. Then build in techniques that foster your thinking and writing process. You might try by organizing big concepts in stacks of paper, then adding notes to the stacks as you go. Or you might use yellow stickers you have labelled in the margins of your notes or case books, and then draw the legal points all together on one page later on.

For further help, see HABITS, WRITING and WRITING PROCESS. For various ways to organize, see OUTLINING, ORGANIZATION FOR THOSE WHO CAN'T OUTLINE, GETTING STARTED, and PREWRITING.

3. How to present your organization to the reader.

In legal writing, worry more about making your organization clear to the reader, less about being too obvious. For example, use enumeration, such as **first, second, third,** or **(1), (2), (3)**. Use TRANSITIONS, such as **additionally** or **in contrast**. Use HEADINGS and subheadings.

Use focused PARAGRAPHS that include TOPIC SENTENCES, usually at the first of the paragraph, and that include support for that point only.

For more information, see CONNECTIONS, MAKING THEM; ORGANIZATION, LARGE–SCALE; ORGANIZATION, SMALL–SCALE; TOPICAL ORGANIZATION; and CHRONOLOGICAL ORGANIZATION.

ORGANIZATION FOR THOSE WHO CAN'T OUTLINE

The following steps can help you organize successfully, even if you have never been able to master the more traditional method of organization, OUTLINES.

1. Brainstorm.

Try listing all the points you want to make or might want to make, or just list everything you can think of. Do not worry about order, quality, or anything else at this stage except coming up with ideas. Allow enough time for this stage, so you do not cut it short.

2. Group your ideas.

Read through all your listed points and see if they fall into any logical groups. Try grouping the points several different ways before you settle on one way that makes the most sense to you. Often the organization that occurs to you first will be adequate, but not optimal.

Alternatively, if your list of points includes six or fewer items, you may already have your logical groups. If so, fill in more supporting points on those items and then check to see if you are still satisfied with those groups.

3. Organize the groups.

Look at each group and decide which point is the major one and which are subordinate, or supporting, points. At this stage you may still find some errors in your grouping, but you can revise those groups as needed. You may also find that you have stated the same thing in two different ways, so that you can strike out redundant points.

4. Subdivide further, if needed.

Divide your arguments, and divide the subpoints made in those arguments. Check each item to make sure that it should not be subdivided further. Remember that you need to make only one point at a time. Even though all your points are inextricably interrelated, you must divide them into manageable portions, or PARAGRAPHS, for the reader.

5. Order the groups, points, and subpoints.

After the points are divided, decide how to order them. To determine this order, think about what will be logical to your reader, rather than what seems important to you. To help determine what is logical to the reader, ask yourself the following three questions.

(a) Is there some point that logically comes first? For example, if your case involved a jurisdiction question, that question would logically come first because the court will not look to any other issues until they have determined that it is the court's job to decide those issues.

(b) Is one point more significant than the others? For example, if your case involves clear-cut violations of freedom of speech and also involves some technical violations of proper notice, you may want to start with the violation of the freedom of speech. This point may convince your reader that justice favors your side, and will probably make more compelling reading. The technical point may then provide a convenient peg upon which to hang the hat of justice.

(c) Is one point stronger than the others? For example, if your case involves a clear-cut violation of proper notice but also involves a potential-but-debatable violation of freedom of speech, you may start with the violation of proper notice. This way you can establish some justification for your client's position before you present more questionable justifications.

6. Write.

At this point you will have all the information provided by a traditional outline, and you can rewrite it in outline format, if you wish, or go directly to writing your rough draft. If you had started trying to outline by writing a Roman numeral at the top of the page, you would have been expecting yourself to do all of these previous steps in your head, which is why trying to write a traditional outline is futile for many people.

7. Check the organization.

Once you have written your rough draft, recheck your organization. In fact, many successful writers write a rough draft first and then outline or go through the organization steps listed above. One way to check your organization is to read the first sentence of each paragraph throughout the document. This should give you a summary of the points of the paper, although it will not document the proof of those points.

For related information, see GETTING STARTED and OUTLINES. See also PARAGRAPHS; ORGANIZATION, LARGE–SCALE; ORGANIZATION, SMALL–SCALE; and WRITING PROCESS.

ORGANIZATION, LARGE–SCALE

Large-scale organization conveys the overall logic of any piece of writing. Large-scale organization is communicated in HEADINGS, TOPIC SENTENCES, introductions, and CONCLUSIONS. The logic of this organization should grow from the logic of the content. For example, if one of the issues in a memo is whether or not the district court has jurisdiction over the issue, that procedural question should be discussed before any substantive question, because if the answer is no, the substantive questions will not matter. See MEMOS and PROCEDURAL OR SUBSTANTIVE?

Look at the overall picture in deciding what your large scale organization should be, so that your choice of organization communicates to the reader how each subpart fits in the whole. For example, if there is a question of governmental immunity and two subissues must be raised to answer the larger issue of immunity, organize both the QUESTION PRESENTED and the DISCUSSION SECTION so that the reader sees how the subissues fit into the larger question of immunity.

Work on the large-scale organization early in the WRITING PROCESS, and keep working on it until it is clear to you. Most issues can be organized in several ways, and your paper must be organized in a way that makes sense to you. Consider your possible large-scale organization as you gather research in PREWRITING, as you outline, and as you rewrite. If the large-scale organization is not working at any of these three points, try rearranging. If you wait until REVISING or POLISHING, it may be too late and too frustrating to change. For related information, see OUTLINING and REWRITING.

ORGANIZATION, SMALL–SCALE

Small-scale organization refers to the organization between and within PARAGRAPHS and sentences; it communicates the LOGICAL

LINKS between those paragraphs and sentences. In contrast, large-scale organization refers to the overall format of the analysis or explanation.

Small-scale organization involves five skills, each of which is explained in detail in a separate entry. These skills include (1) using effective TOPIC SENTENCES, (2) clarifying logical connections (see CONNECTIONS, MAKING THEM), (3) choosing the most effective SENTENCE STRUCTURE, (4) choosing accurate TRANSITIONS, and (5) making lists readable (see LISTS, STRUCTURE OF).

The revision for small-scale organization should take place after WRITING and REWRITING, so that you are not struggling with fundamental ideas at the same time you are straightening out the expression of those ideas. For related information, see WRITING PROCESS and REVISING.

ORNATE LANGUAGE
　　See FLOWERY LANGUAGE.

OTHERWISE
　　　Otherwise means in another way or apart from that.

We cannot locate our expert witness, but otherwise the case is in good shape.

Avoid overusing **otherwise** or using it loosely.

If they accept this offer, we will settle. If they refuse, we will sue.

rather than

If they accept this offer, we will settle. Otherwise, we will sue.

OUTLINES
　　Outlines can help writers before or after writing a draft. Outlines can take any form, whether lists, barely legible scratching, flow charts, or Venn diagrams. Whatever the form, outlines help the writer make sure any reader can follow the document's logic.

Make an outline, either before or after writing, by sketching a general portrait of the large-scale ideas, such as the following.

　　Custody disputes
　　Was "tender years"
　　　　not any more
　　　　ERA contributed
　　　　changed in 1973
　　Now statutory—five factors + 1 = "best interests"
　　Apply here—probably mother
　　Conclusion

Then fill in the details as you reread authority and rethink your ideas.

Custody disputes

    Was "tender years"

        "best interests of child" paramount then <u>Jones</u> at 48, 50.

        Mother used to be thought best <u>Id.</u>

        ERA, general social changes say father or mother can "mother" <u>Smith</u> at 97

        Led to partial codification, some changes in 1973

    Statute R.C.W. 29.09.999 (quote)

        Court must show they looked at factors <u>Smith</u> at 85, all five + anything else relevant

        Broad discretion, but must be more structured now. <u>Id.</u>

Apply here

    Factor 1—wishes of parents

        both want, but both will give visitation rights

    Factor 2—wishes of child

        nothing expressed

    Factor 3—Interrelationship of children w/ parents

        mother drinks (<u>Johnson</u> mom drank too—distinguish)

        father strict (<u>Pines</u>—father got son—same?)

        mother stable? (see <u>Schwartz</u>—not as crazy as this woman: distinguish)

    Factor 4—Child's adjustment to home & community

        with mom now, no adjustment

        father will live in same city, but move required

    Factor 5—Mental and physical health

        mother stable? (see <u>Schwartz</u>; distinguish this mother, not that crazy)

        father unemotional

    Other factors—adultery, moral character

        father having an affair, missed meeting with kids

        cf. <u>Hildebrand</u>—doesn't mean he can't "mother"

    Conclusion

        Mom probably gets them because she is more responsive to their needs, has them now, hasn't missed any time with them.

If you outline before writing the first draft, then at the writing stage you can just fill in the blanks left in the outline. Therefore, if writing is uncomfortable for you, try doing a detailed outline first.

Make lots of notes in the margin if necessary; this will make WRITING easier.

If you outline after writing, you can use the outline to check logic and details. Any reader should be able to write your outline after reading your writing, so you might make sure your writing is clear by outlining it yourself.

If ORGANIZATION is a problem for you, outlining may offer a solution. For other aids to organization and related problems, see WRITING PROCESS; WRITING BLOCKS; ORGANIZATION, LARGE–SCALE; and ORGANIZATION FOR THOSE WHO CAN'T OUTLINE.

OVERDONE
See FLOWERY LANGUAGE, MODIFIERS, and EMOTIONAL LANGUAGE.

OVERREFINEMENT
This term refers to the kind of errors writers commit when they are trying hard to be correct but do not quite understand the rules. For example, a writer might use **I feel badly** even though **I feel bad** is correct. For other common overrefinement problems, see GOOD OR WELL?, BETWEEN YOU AND ME OR BETWEEN YOU AND I?, CAN OR MAY?, PRIOR TO, IN ADVANCE OF, and WHO OR WHOM?

In a broader sense, **overrefinement** refers to the tendency some writers have to revise their writing too much. For example, a writer might remove important TRANSITIONS in the name of CONCISENESS, or create FIGURATIVE LANGUAGE when LITERAL LANGUAGE conveys the point better. Fight the temptation to overrefine, which can rob your STYLE of its spontaneity and READABILITY. Overrefinement can also add unnecessary time to your schedule. For ways to refine effectively, see REVISING and POLISHING.

PADDING
In legal writing, avoid padding, or adding content not because it is needed but solely to increase length. Legal readers prize CONCISENESS; padding will not impress them.

PARAGRAPH BLOCKS
A paragraph block is a group of PARAGRAPHS that fit together as a visual and substantive unit, just as sentences fit into the unit of a single paragraph.

1. When to use.

Paragraph blocks are most likely to be useful when your analysis requires a sub-subsection of explanation in the text; in this situation, you often will not want to add another level of heading because you already have headings and subheadings, and a third level might fragment the ORGANIZATION too much. The visual separation of a paragraph block is not as strong as that created by a subheading, and thus it is useful without distracting from the headings already in place. The paragraph block is most likely to be useful in documents that run thirty or more pages. In shorter documents, HEADINGS, SUBHEADINGS, and PARAGRAPHS should provide sufficient organizational tools.

2. How to use.

To create a paragraph block visually, put an extra blank line between the previous text and the first paragraph of the block. At the end of the paragraph block, again add an extra blank line. Paragraph blocks work best if they are limited to three to six paragraphs; if the blocks are longer, the reader forgets about the paragraph block and its organizing value is lost. If the block consists of only two paragraphs, the reader may think that the blank lines are typographical errors.

Remember that substance dictates the form of your writing. Therefore, avoid creating a paragraph block solely for looks. Create one only when your analysis requires the sub-subsection.

PARAGRAPH LENGTH

In a brief, memo, or longer opinion letter, you should average about three paragraph breaks per page. In business letters, you will have more paragraphs per page. Whatever the setting, however, you should divide paragraphs logically rather than periodically. Therefore, first divide paragraphs logically and then change this paragraph division, if needed, using the following guidelines.

1. Long Paragraphs.

If you find one paragraph that runs two-thirds of a page, leave it undivided if it is logically one unit. If you have one paragraph that runs for more than two-thirds of a page, try to divide it, because the reader needs a visual break. If you have many paragraphs that run two-thirds of a page, check for general organization problems. See ORGANIZATION, LARGE–SCALE.

2. Short Paragraphs.

If you have written a one-sentence paragraph or many short paragraphs, check to see if you have supported your points adequately.

Occasionally a one-sentence paragraph can be used for EMPHASIS, but not more than once in ten pages. Occasionally a one-sentence paragraph also serves as a transition or an introduction, but again it should not occur too often.

For related writing problems, see SENTENCE LENGTH.

PARAGRAPHS

In legal writing, each paragraph should focus on only one point, and each should have a topic sentence that states that point, often at the beginning of the paragraph. In other disciplines, such as literary criticism, this more obvious form of logical ORGANIZATION is often disfavored, but obvious organization is rarely criticized in legal writing. Instead, your reader will be grateful to you for making it easy to see the point. For example, in the following paragraphs, the points are much clearer when two paragraphs are used, one for each point made, and when each point is stated in a topic sentence at the first of the paragraph.

To complain about the illegality of a search, the defendant must, as the State correctly asserts, have an expectation of privacy in the place searched. United States v. Park, 999 U.S. 314, 316 (1996); United States v. Toyle, 999 U.S. 115, 118 (1993). The State implies that solely because the defendant's office, desk, and files were within a public building, he knowingly exposed them to the public. This is incorrect. The uncontroverted testimony in this case established that defendant did expect his office, desk, and files to be private because he exercised exclusive use and control over these areas and in things present in those areas. (R. 207–209).

This expectation of privacy must be justified under the law. In this case, the defendant was justified in expecting privacy in his private office. There was no free public access to these areas. The sole fact that a private office is located in a public building does not satisfy the "plain view" doctrine as restated in United States v. Peabody, 999 U.S. 22, 26 (1996). The trial court in this case thus found that defendant had rights guaranteed by the fourth amendment of the United States Constitution and by article I, section 2 of the Constitution of the State of Iowa, and that these rights were violated.

rather than

The trial court in this case found that defendant had rights guaranteed by the fourth amendment of the United States Constitution and by article I, section 2 of the Constitution of the State of Iowa, which were violated. To complain about the illegality of a search, the defendant must, as the State correctly asserts, have an expectation of privacy in the place searched. United States v. Park, 999 U.S. 314, 316 (1996); United States v. Toyle, 999 U.S. 115, 118 (1993). The State implies that because the defendant's office, desk, and files were within a public building, he knowingly exposed them to the public. This is simply not the fact in this case. The uncontroverted testimony indicates defendant did expect his office, desk, and files to be private and that he exercised exclusive use and control in these areas (R. 207–209). There was no free public access to these areas. The location of a private office in a public building does not satisfy the plain view doctrine as restated in United States v. Peabody, 999 U.S. 22, 26 (1996). Further, the defendant's expectation of privacy in his private office is justified under the law.

134

For related information, see ONE–SENTENCE PARAGRAPHS; TOPIC SENTENCES; PARAGRAPH LENGTH; OUTLINES; ORGANIZATION; TRANSITIONS; and ORGANIZATION; SMALL–SCALE.

PARALLEL CITATIONS
See CITATIONS, PARALLEL.

PARALLEL STRUCTURE
Parallel structure means using the same grammatical structure for things that are logically parallel. For example, parallel adjectives can describe parallel qualities.

Defendant was hostile, abusive, and violent.

Parallel prepositional phrases can describe parallel situations.

Plaintiff admits he was driving without his license, without his lights on, and with an open six-pack of beer in the front seat.

Parallel structure creates a grammatically transparent framework that allows substantive points to shine through in clear relation to each other. This structure is extremely useful in legal writing because it simplifies syntax and focuses on substance. Therefore, three common places to use parallel structure are in lists, in comparisons or contrasts of cases, and in persuasive writing to add emphasis.

1. Use parallel structure in lists.

The plaintiff parked his car, turned the wheels toward the curb, and set the handbrake.

This point was established in the testimony of the defendant, of the police officer investigating the accident, and of a passerby who observed the accident.

Parallel structure is also useful for emphasizing the logical parallels between the items in a list, such as in the following list of facts. See EMPHASIS.

The trial court found that Cox Realty displayed the Realax logo at its office, signs, and forms; that Cox's employees each wear a blue blazer with the Realax logo on it; and that Cox Realty benefits from nationwide advertising identifying Realax franchises as "local professionals."

2. Use parallel structure to compare or contrast cases. One place where parallel structure is particularly desirable is in the analogy of two similar cases, as shown by the following example taken from the middle of a paragraph.

In Rickaby, the court found that the plaintiff's reputation in the community was not impaired even though the employer disclosed his reasons for discharging the employee in a judicial proceeding. Similarly, in this case Elmore's reputation in the community has not been impaired merely because the employer disclosed her reasons for discharging Elmore in conferences with union officials.

As this example shows, using accurate TRANSITIONS, such as similarly, can also enhance the point of the parallel.

Parallel structure can also underscore a contrast. By making similarities obvious, parallel structure allows the differences to stand out.

In Rickaby, the court found that the plaintiff's reputation in the community was not impaired even though the employer disclosed his reasons for discharging the employee in a judicial proceeding. In contrast, Elmore's reputation was impaired, because his employer not only disclosed her reasons for discharging Elmore in conferences with union officials but also disclosed those reasons at an officer party and in a reference letter written to Elmore's prospective employers.

For more information on this technique, see COMPARISON.

3. Use parallel structure to add emphasis. In the following example, two points support the implied point that the defendant deserves no sympathy. The parallel structure thus reflects the logical parallels of the content and also allows the writer to use REPETITION to emphasize a point.

The defendant company failed to schedule routine maintenance for the press, failed to have a technician check the press when operators complained of its malfunction, and failed to warn the plaintiff about those malfunctions.

For more information on this technique, see EMPHASIS.

PARALLELISM
See PARALLEL STRUCTURE; LISTS, STRUCTURE OF; and EMPHASIS.

PARAPHRASE
Paraphrasing means restating someone else's ideas in your own words. There is nothing illegitimate about paraphrasing as long as you give credit when you have used a specific source, such as on opinion or article, and as long as you avoid misstating the original point. Paraphrasing is more useful than quoting when the original language is hard to understand, is lengthy, or incorporates other information that could confuse your reader.

The court stated that it must intervene in this case to resolve the issue of mutuality despite the emotional pleas for freedom of contract.

changed from the original

Despite the defendant's emotional plea regarding the centrality of upholding contracts to the free working of a democracy, we cannot ignore the plaintiff's complaint. In this case, the court must intervene; the issue of mutuality, not to mention that of duress, requires that the court examine both the contract's wording and the parol evidence surrounding the signing of that contract.

Quote only when the exact language is needed, as when discussing the interpretation of a phrase in a statute, or when you could not say it better yourself, as with an apt and relevant phrase in an opinion.

In writing MEMOS or BRIEFS, it is permissible to quote a commonly used rule, without quotation marks, as long as you use a Pinpoint Cite.

Use of a criminal defendant's silence for impeachment purposes violates the defendant's due process rights. <u>Boyle v. Kentucky,</u> 999 U.S. 810, 817 (1996).

For more information, see QUOTATIONS, WHEN TO USE. For related information, see UNDERLINING, subsection 5 and PINPOINT CITES.

PARENTHESES

Use parentheses in legal writing only in the situations listed below. If the matter is important enough to be in the text, it should be stated outside the shadow of parentheses. Additionally, avoid overuse of parentheses because it can create the impression that the writer is disorganized. For related information, see PARENTHETICALS.

1. When to use parentheses.

(a) Use parentheses to enclose information useful to the reader if that information is not an integral part of the text itself. For example, use parentheses to refer to the transcript, such as (**Tr. 37**), or an appendix, such as (**See Appendix A**).

The defendant testified he had never seen the plaintiff (Tr. 349).

or

The defendant testified that he had never seen the plaintiff. (Tr. 349).

(b) Use parentheses to introduce abbreviations. For example, if one of the parties in your brief is **Leitner Systems, Inc.,** and you want to use **LSI** in the text, write out the complete name the first time you use it and then put the abbreviation in parentheses afterwards.

Leitner Systems, Inc. (LSI).

Do not state **hereinafter referred to as** before the abbreviation. See LEGALESE.

(c) Use parentheses in drafting contracts to enclose a numeral repeating a number spelled out.

For the sum of five hundred dollars ($500) . . . .

(d) Use parentheses to enclose examples when the examples are necessary but do not require a separate definition. See UNOBTRUSIVE DEFINITIONS.

Crimes against persons (murder, rape, and the like) are usually considered more serious than crimes against property.

2. How to punctuate within parentheses.

If they are written inside another sentence, parenthetical sentences (this is an example of a parenthetical sentence inside another sentence) are not begun with capital letters or ended with periods; but when other punctuation marks are appropriate (do you understand this rule?), they are used.   If they are written outside other sentences, parenthetical sentences are begun with capital letters and ended with periods inside the parentheses.   (This is an example of a parenthetical outside a sentence.) Parentheticals coming at the end of a sentence may be punctuated either as a parenthetical outside the sentence,

Defendant's car was parked facing north.   (R.P. 31.)

or as a parenthetical within the sentence.

Defendant's car was parked facing north (R.P. 31).

PARENTHETICALS

Parentheticals appear in specific places in legal writing to give the reader information about authority.   Proper use of parentheticals saves time and text.   While the Blue Book outlines all technical uses of parentheticals, the most helpful uses include the following.

1.   Use parentheticals after basic citations to add information about the source.

Arnold v. Butters, 999 F. Supp. 111 (W.D. Wis.1998) (moral right is not cause of action for artist whose painting was separated into four pieces).

For further reference, see Blue Book rule 2.5.

2.   Use parentheticals after cases to indicate that the holding is not the single clear holding of a majority of the court, or to indicate the weight of authority.

State v. Blunt, 999 U.S. 99 (1999) (per curiam) (an "indicia of reliability" is necessary for an informer's information to support a search warrant).

For further reference, see Blue Book rule 10.6.

3.   Use parentheticals in statute citations to convey the following information.

(a) Use them to show the code location of statutes cited to session laws or secondary sources.

Popular Names Act of 1999.   Pub. L. No. 102–113, 999 Stat. 111 (codified at 99 U.S.C. §§ 2222 to 2232 (1999)).

(b) Use them to give the unofficial section when an unofficial code is numbered differently from an official code and when the section does not yet appear in the official code.

Mich. Comp. Laws § 999.09 (1990) (Mich. Stat. Ann. § 111.01 (Callaghan 1999)).

(c) Use them to identify useful dates, such as the effective date of a statute.

Alaska Stat. § 99.09.090 (1999) (effective July 1, 1999).

(d) Use them to indicate the repeal, amendment, or prior history of a statute.

99 U.S.C. § 999(b) (1999) (repealed 2001).

(e) Use them to give any other relevant information about a statute.

99 U.S.C. § 999(b) (1999) (requiring IRS agents to give proper notice of auditing procedures to those being audited).

For further reference, see Blue Book rules 12.6 and 12.7.

PARTICIPLES
See VERB TENSES.

PARTS OF A SENTENCE
See SENTENCE, PARTS OF.

PARTS OF SPEECH
Parts of speech is the grammatical term used to summarize the eight categories into which all words are divided. These eight categories include NOUNS, PRONOUNS, ADJECTIVES, VERBS, ADVERBS, PREPOSITIONS, CONJUNCTIONS, and INTERJECTIONS.

PASSIVE VERBS
See PASSIVE VOICE and ACTIVE VOICE.

PASSIVE VOICE
In general, use ACTIVE VOICE rather than passive, both in OBJECTIVE WRITING and PERSUASIVE WRITING, because the active voice keeps the reader's eye moving forward and clarifies both the subject and the action. Active voice thus promotes CLARITY and PRECISION.

Passive voice, on the other hand, makes the reader's eye move backwards because the subject of the sentence receives the action, rather than causes the action. As a result, passive voice forces the reader to stop at the end of the sentence and think back through the sentence to sort out who did what.

The plaintiff was hit by the defendant. [passive voice]

but

The defendant hit the plaintiff. [active voice]

A decision was made by the court. [passive voice]

but

The court made a decision. [active voice]

or

The court decided.   [active voice]

Passive verbs also sometimes leave the actor out of the picture.

The plaintiff was hit.

A decision was made.

This use of passive voice often creates ambiguity. For example, the following regulation would be inadequate if it did not specify who has the responsibility for the clean-up.

Any manufacturer who generates toxic waste must dispose of that waste by one of the following means.

rather than

Toxic waste must be disposed of by one of the following means.

Passive voice is useful, however, in four specific situations. In legal writing, use it consciously and for these reasons only; otherwise eliminate it.

1. Use passive voice to de-emphasize unfavorable facts or law. For example, the attorney for the defense might want to write the following.

The plaintiff was assaulted by the defendant.

The attorney for the prosecution, however, might write the following.

The defendant assaulted the plaintiff.

2. Use passive voice to hide the identity of the actor.

A decision was made to cut your salary.

Here passive voice avoids telling who made the decision.

3. Use passive voice when the subject is very long. In this situation, using passive voice creates a more readable sentence because the active voice would put the subject and verb so far apart that the sentence would be too hard to read.

This action is required by statutory law, by the common law principle of due care, and by a general sense of justice.

rather than

Statutory law, the common law principle of due care, and a general sense of justice require this action.

4. Finally, use passive voice when the subject is much less important than the object.

Freedom of speech cannot be encumbered by concerns of propriety.

rather than

Concerns of propriety cannot encumber freedom of speech.

For related information, see ACTIVE VOICE.

PAST PARTICIPLES

Past participles are the **-ed** form of regular verbs, such as **decided, moved, assaulted**. Irregular verbs form past participles differently, such as held, gone, and been. See VERBS, PARTICIPLES; VERB TENSES; and VERBS, IRREGULAR.

PAST PERFECT TENSE
See VERB TENSES.

PAST PROGRESSIVE TENSE
See VERB TENSES.

PAST TENSE
See VERB TENSES.

PEOPLE OR PERSONS?
Use **people** to refer a group of individuals collectively. Use **persons** when referring to a small and specific number.

All people of this country have constitutional rights.

but

Defendant has assaulted nine persons in the last month.

PER
Per means **for each** and is useful when talking about ratios.

The defendant company promised different rates of pay to different sales personnel, ranging from the $5 per call paid to secretaries who worked in the company headquarters, to $1 per call paid to employees who made the calls from their homes.

Per should not be used, however, in other contexts.

Regarding our previous request for payment, ...

rather than

As per our previous request, ...

PERCENT OR PER CENT?
Use **percent**, which is preferred by most authorities.

PERFECT TENSES
See VERB TENSES.

PERFECTIONISM
Perfectionism can be the enemy of creative thought. Relegate your perfectionism to REVISING, REWRITING, and POLISHING in the WRITING PROCESS. In PREWRITING, contain your perfectionist tendencies by balancing time constraints against scholarship and by

concentrating on substantive ideas rather than the methodology of note taking, outlining, and other prewriting tasks.

When WRITING, do not allow your perfectionist editing voice to restrict your creative writing voice. Try not to perfect each sentence as you go, but rather to write the entire paper without revising. This will allow your ideas to flow more smoothly as you focus on content, not form. Then go back to perfect your paper in the REWRITING, REVISING, and POLISHING stages. In those stages, let your perfectionism work within your time restraints.

For further help, see WHEN TO STOP. For a discussion of related problems, see PROCRASTINATION; WRITING BLOCKS; GETTING STARTED; and DEADLINES, MEETING THEM.

PERIOD OR QUESTION MARK?
See QUESTION MARKS.

PERIODS
Periods have three common uses in legal writing.

1. Periods as ends to sentences.

If your sentences routinely run for more than four lines of text, use more periods. See SENTENCE LENGTH and READABILITY.

2. Periods with abbreviations.

When an abbreviation comes at the end of a sentence, use just one period.

The meeting is scheduled for 9:00 p.m.

3. Periods in parentheticals.

If they are written inside another sentence, parenthetical sentences **(this is an example of a parenthetical sentence inside another sentence)** are not ended with periods; but if other punctuation marks are appropriate **(do you understand this rule?)**, they are used. If they are written outside other sentences, parenthetical sentences are ended with periods inside the parentheses. **(This is an example of a parenthetical outside a sentence.)** Parentheticals coming at the end of a sentence may be punctuated as a parenthetical either outside or inside the sentence.

Defendant's car was parked facing north. (R.P. 31.)

or

Defendant's car was parked facing north (R.P. 31).

4. Periods with quotation marks.

A period goes inside quotation marks, even if the period is not part of the quote.

The term on which we must focus is "intent."

This rule is the same for both double quotation marks ("—") and single ones ('—'). The rule is not meant to reflect logical concerns, but

142

rather graphic ones. It looks funny to see the period sitting out there alone.

One exception to this rule is LEGISLATION, where periods are treated like all other punctuation marks.

PERSON: FIRST, SECOND, OR THIRD?

First person is **I** or **we**, second person is **you**, and third person is **he, she, it,** or **they.** Because person identifies the reader and writer, knowing the AUDIENCE determines which to use. In any given piece of legal writing, choose one person and use it consistently throughout.

1. Use first person singular, **I**, when giving a personal opinion. Use first person plural, **we**, when including the reader in the scope of the discussion or when representing the collective opinion of several specific people, as in a letter that speaks for a law firm.

I suggest we try to settle this out of court.

We can argue that a five-month-old fetus is viable, but this issue will probably go to the Supreme Court.

Avoid the editorial or royal **we** because it can be ambiguous. Instead, use **I** or avoid referring to any persons.

I understand your dilemma.

rather than

We recognize your dilemma.

The second element of first degree murder is intent.

rather than

We must next consider the second element of first degree murder.

2. Use second person, **you**, to address the audience directly, when appropriate. For example, GENERAL OPINION LETTERS and other correspondence may include **you** because they require a more personal TONE.

You asked that I write to you about the legal consequences of your unfortunate accident.

Avoid using second person when addressing a court.

Granting this motion is appropriate for three reasons.

rather than

You ought to grant this motion for three reasons.

3. Use third person most often in legal writing, in BRIEFS, MEMOS, MOTIONS, and most formal documents. Identify parties in the third person, your clients as well as their opponents.

Defendant pled not guilty; he denies all charges.

The law favors the plaintiffs in this class action, so they will likely move for a summary judgment.

Respondent further contends that all the facts are not properly before the court.

PERSONAL REFERENCES
Personal references are appropriate in legal writing only if the reader and writer are familiar with each other. Avoid them otherwise; they impair both credibility and meaning.

Although Plaintiff argues that there is a dispute as to the material facts, the affidavits show otherwise.

or

The affidavits show there is no dispute as to the material facts.

rather than

Attorney Cromwell on page sixteen of his brief argues incorrectly again that there is a dispute as to material facts.

For related information, see TONE and TONE IN LETTERS.

PERSONS OR PEOPLE?
See PEOPLE OR PERSONS?

PERSUASIVE LETTERS
Persuading a legal reader to do or decide something in your favor is a bit like finding your way through a mine field; you are trying to reach a certain point without setting off any unfortunate reactions. For this reason, persuasive letters will not be as predictably structured as other GENERAL CORRESPONDENCE LETTERS. In all persuasive letters, however, you will need to make three decisions: (1) what arguments to use, (2) what organization to use for those arguments, and (3) what tone to take. The following guidelines should help you make these decisions.

1. Choosing arguments.

In general, choosing arguments for persuasive letters will take time and care because you must tailor your argument and tone to suit the individual circumstances. Choose not what persuades you, but what will persuade your reader. For example, if you are trying to persuade a party to settle out of court, do not use threats when you think the party would view those threats as a challenge and submission as a weakness. Instead, you might explain that an early settlement might bring better results for the client than a later, more costly, trial.

Similarly, if you think that the reader is someone motivated by certain values or goals, try to explain how the action you recommend is consistent with those values or goals. For example, you might argue that paying a bill is essentially the same as keeping a promise. Try to help the reader feel good, or at least not defeated, about taking the action you recommend.

144

2. Organizing.

The same organization used for other bad news letters will work here. See BAD NEWS, GIVING IT.

Start with a paragraph that sets the tone of the letter, such as the following kind tone.

Throughout the years, Everly Auto Parts has valued Morgan Auto as a customer. Because Everly hopes to maintain this solid working relationship, Bob Everly has asked me to write to you concerning the rather large outstanding balance in your account.

Alternatively, you may choose a tough tone.

Despite receiving three statements from my client, Everly Auto Parts, your company has not yet paid the balance of $2,015 owed for parts purchased four months ago.

Or you may choose something in between.

My client, Everly Auto Parts, has asked me to write to you concerning the outstanding balance on your company's account.

Do not go on too long, however, because a lengthy introduction can make the writer look rather timid or can make the reader impatient.

At the end of the first paragraph or the beginning of the second, state your point. Write this sentence with care; it must be unambiguous and yet unoffensive if possible.

Everly will not be able to extend further credit to your company until this balance has been paid.

Then launch into your reasons, which may go on for several paragraphs. Make one point at a time, rather than rambling back and forth between several points. See PARAGRAPHS.

Everly Auto Parts, as a general policy, limits credit to any company to . . . . . Additionally, ...

In the last paragraph close politely, or at least civilly.

Everly Auto Parts will appreciate your prompt payment of this outstanding balance and looks forward to your continued patronage.

3. Establishing tone.

In general, use an unemotional, polite TONE. In most legal writing situations, the emotions you would arouse would work against you rather than for you. There are some exceptions to this, such as fund-raising letters to sympathetic constituents or letters advising clients to do what they want to do already. Even here, however, you will usually want to present yourself as a logical, reasonable person who, even when impassioned about a cause, is still capable of making a coherent, logical argument. For a discussion of related points, see TONE, EMPHASIS, PERSUASIVENESS, and COHERENCE.

PERSUASIVE WRITING

Writing persuasively entails the use of many specific techniques, none of which alone makes an obvious difference but all of which, when working in harmony, create a masterful piece of persuasion. Each of these techniques takes practice to master. Therefore, choose two or three from the following list and incorporate those into your writing habits. Then, as you master those, add new ones to your repertoire.

1. Use concrete words.

Concrete words create clearer images in the reader's mind than abstract ones, and those clearer images are more memorable. For example, **a 1965 black Stingray** is more memorable than **vehicle**. This tool is especially useful in drafting fact situations for BRIEFS, because you can use concrete words for facts that favor your client and abstract ones for facts that you want to de-emphasize. For example, if you are de-emphasizing the illness of a testator and the medications she was taking, you might write the following.

Because Julia Easley had a history of arthritic and cardiovascular diseases, she was taking a variety of medications.

If, however, you were trying to emphasize the illness and the medications, you might write the following.

Julia Easley's health was poor. She suffered from excruciating tension headaches (R. 925), and during the past year she experienced increasing cardiovascular problems, cataracts, arteriosclerosis, and other problems (R. 928–53). She was also on a large and complex daily regimen of drugs (R. 454). Daily she took three kinds of barbituates: Tuinal (R. 1115–16), Fiornal (R. 1113), and Fiornal with Codeine (R. 1113–14). Additionally, she took greater-than-normal daily dosages of Triavil (R. 114–15), a specialized compound tranquilizer formulated and normally prescribed for mental depression (R. 1148–49).

2. Choose the most appropriate term of address.

This choice is related to the choice of concrete or ABSTRACT NOUNS. In a brief, if you have a situation where your client is a sympathetic figure and the opposition is not, use NAMES, such as **Ms. Jones** or **Julia Easley**, for both parties. This will gently remind the reader of the real people involved here. If the facts are not sympathetic to your client and you are making an argument based more on the impersonal logic of the relevant law, then use generic terms, such as **Plaintiff** and **Defendant**. Use the same kind of term for both sides, however: using **Ms. Jones** for the defendant but then using **Plaintiff** would be too confusing and too obviously biased, even if it seemed appropriate.

3. Repeat key words.

If you want to emphasize a word, repeat it. This is most often useful in the argument section of a brief.

The defendant *abused* the privileges offered him; he *abused* the procedures designed to protect him.

When repeating a term, however, make sure that the idea represented by the term is indeed one you do want to emphasize. For example, repeating **clearly** will create a distraction, not effective EMPHASIS.

Also remember that the effect of a repeated word grows exponentially, rather than linearly. That is, if you use a word twice, it is given perhaps four times the emphasis, not just two. So do not overdo it. This is a place where reading it aloud may work a disservice; you may hear yourself repeating a theme like the master orator Martin Luther King, but your reader, not hearing your impassioned pauses and intonations, may giggle. Let your eye and common sense guide you. See also REPETITION.

4. Repeat sentence or phrase structures.

This tool is particularly useful when analogyzing cases (see COMPARISON) but is also useful and subtly dramatic in CONCLUSIONS and sometimes in fact sections. Repetition of structure creates a sense of rhythm and anticipation. To some extent, it telegraphs to the reader what is coming, so that the reader gets a sense of completion when the expected information arrives.

At best, the City confused its argument by trying to do too much without a full explanation. At worst, the City contradicted itself by misapplying the law.

But this expectation can turn to boredom, so again avoid overdoing it.

5. Adjust sentence length.

SHORT SENTENCES are emphatic. Therefore use them for points you want to emphasize, but do not use them for unimportant points. This tool is particularly useful in fact situations, where tools involving word choice are often limited.

Julia was uniformly described by all the witnesses who had personally known her as a strong-willed, positive, and independent woman. *The plaintiff himself called her "independent and abrupt."*

It is also useful in arguments.

The major purpose of the trial court's established procedures is to give the litigants a fair opportunity to address their claims and have them resolved by a court of law. *The petitioners here had eight years of opportunity.* Therefore, their current procedural arguments . . . .

Several short sentences in a row create a choppy, rather impatient or angry tone. Sometimes this can have a useful effect.

The major purpose of the trial court's established procedure is to give the litigants a fair opportunity to address their claims and have them resolved by a court of law. *That purpose was met here. The litigants had eight years of opportunity. In this context, their arguments on appeal are particularly specious.*

Three sentences is about as far as you should push the series. Any more and the court might sense an intemperate tirade. After a series of short sentences, return to sentences of normal length and make a scrupulously objective statement of your reasoning.

6. Insert information into a sentence with care.

If you want to use a point to set the stage for a punch line, put that point in an introductory phrase at the beginning of a sentence.

Despite the difficulty of this test, the gravity of the situation required that it be done.

If you want to de-emphasize a point, put it in an added phrase at the end of the sentence, like an afterthought.

The minority arrived at the same conclusion, *although for different reasons.*

When you do this, make sure that the word at the end of the sentence is not one you want to de-emphasize. For examples and more details on this technique, see SENTENCE STRUCTURE, subsection 7.

7. Place key phrases at the beginning or end of a paragraph or a sentence.

In general, words at the beginning or end get more attention than those in the middle. In legal writing, things at the beginning have a slight edge because you are never sure the busy and often-interrupted legal reader will finish reading your document with care. While revising, scan your TOPIC SENTENCES to see if the first half-line of each paragraph includes the KEY TERMS of the paragraph. Avoid starting a paragraph with dates or case names unless you have a reason to emphasize that date or name.

Evidence of this concern showed up in the defendant's letter dated January 12, 1980, which stated . . . .

rather than

On January 12, 1980, the defendant wrote a letter that showed *evidence of this concern* when it stated . . . .

For related information, see POSITIONS OF EMPHASIS.

8. Use subtly emotional language, rather than overly emotional.

Emotional language should persuade, not lose, the reader. Therefore choose words precisely to fit the persuasive approach you are taking. Emotional words are not just positive or negative; instead, each word falls somewhere on a continuum between extremely positive and extremely negative. For example, one person who decided to maintain a position on an issue could be described as **ever-faithful, steadfast, unwavering, unchanging, stubborn,** or **pigheaded.** In legal writing, choose words that fall closer to the center of the continuum to color your meanings, but avoid the extremes. For example, if trying to show that someone was overmedicated and thus not capable of making a will, write the following.

Julia Easley was on a large and complex daily regimen of drugs, including . . . .

rather than

Julia Easley was drugged into oblivion daily.

Write the latter only if your facts establish that as her literal state.

Also avoid overly emotional language because it draws the reader's attention to the emotional level of the writing itself, rather than to the content of the persuasive argument. For example, many extremely emotional words, such as **blockhead** or **disaster**, can impair the writer's credibility in court, where another lawyer can point out the silliness of the overstatement.

Finally, avoid overly emotional language because it may be limited by the constraints of legal writing. For example, many words with emotional overtones, such as **derelict** or **nuisance**, are also TERMS OF ART that must be used with PRECISION, whether or not the emotional overtone is appropriate.

9. Play one persuasive technique against another.

As you are applying these tools, you may find some contradictions; applying one principle means you violate another. Practice playing these techniques against each other to get just the effect you want.

10. Avoid overdoing.

Any of these persuasive techniques can be overdone. If you tend to overdo, use Marilyn Monroe's technique to solve the problem. This may be apocryphal, but it has been said that Marilyn tended to overdo it on accessories when she dressed up. To compensate for this, she kept a full length mirror in her entry. Before she left the house, she would walk away from the mirror and then turn quickly to look at her image. She would then take off the first accessory that caught her eye. Similarly, as you read over your last draft of a persuasive piece, take out the most obvious persuasive tools you have used. After all, it worked for Marilyn. Few would have called her overdressed.

PHENOMENA OR PHENOMENONS?

Most dictionaries list either as the acceptable plural of **phenomenon**, but **phenomena** is preferred.

PHRASES

A phrase is a group of words working together, such as prepositional phrases, **in this case**; noun phrases, **the experienced supervising attorney**; and verb phrases, **had been reviewing** . In contrast, a clause is a phrase that includes both a subject and verb.

S   V

The supervising attorney had been reviewing the case.

For an explanation of the use of phrases, see SENTENCE, PARTS OF and SENTENCE STRUCTURE. For related information, see CLAUSES.

PINPOINT CITES

Pinpoint cites are those cites that include the exact page on which the quote, proposition holding, or rule is found. Use pinpoint cites to show your reader the exact source of important points. Pinpoint cites are used more frequently than general cites because most cites refer to quotes, propositions, holdings or rules. When using parallel cites, the pinpoint cite should indicate a specific page for both the official reporter and the unofficial reporter or reporters.

In custody disputes, the appellate court will reverse the trial court only where there is an abuse of discretion. In re Marriage of Smith, 94 Wash. 2d 369, 371, 333 P.2d 43, 44 (1988).

Where there are no exigent circumstances, police must obtain a search warrant before searching the premises. Id. at 486, 483 P.2d at 58.

For other examples of formats for pinpoint cites, see CITATIONS. For related information, see CITATIONS, PARALLEL.

PLAGIARISM

Plagiarism is copying someone else's ideas or words and claiming them as your own. In legal writing, this is as unacceptable as it is in any other kind of writing. But do not confuse plagiarism with paraphrasing; it is perfectly permissible to paraphrase someone else's words, that is, to put their ideas in your own words and then to acknowledge the source of that idea. Thus you may PARAPHRASE and then cite to the authority for any holding, proposition, rule, quotation, or point of law.

But do not use paragraphs and organization from a law review article in place of your own writing. You may quote passages from law review articles verbatim, but they must be marked as quotes and cited. For related information, see PUNCTUATING QUOTES.

PLAIN ENGLISH

In legal writing, plain English is English that is simple, clear, and readable. Many states require plain English in any kind of consumer document. If the document is not drafted in plain English, the consumer has grounds to sue for malpractice against the drafter of the document. Check your jurisdiction for its specific laws on plain English, but in general free your writing of JARGON, LEGALESE, and any undefined terms that will send a reader scurrying to a dictionary. For ways to revise for plain English, see READABILITY, CLARITY, and SIMPLICITY. See also PLAIN MEANING and UNOBTRUSIVE DEFINITIONS.

PLAIN MEANING

Plain meaning is that method of construing statutes that interprets each term by its dictionary meaning. This is a very literal interpretation and is often the point of departure for interpretation of a statute.

For example, when a court is interpreting a statute for the very first time and there is little or no legislative history, the court may resort to the dictionary meaning of each word in the statute in order to apply the statute to the facts before the court.

Therefore, as it relates to legal writing, plain meaning becomes important in drafting legislation. Be sure that each term you use in drafting the statute stands up under the dictionary's scrutiny. See LEGISLATION.

P.M.

It is written **p.m.** and is used only after a number, as in **7:15 p.m.** When it appears at the end of a sentence, only one period is used, as in the previous sentence.

POINT HEADINGS

Point headings, also known as argument headings, are conventions in argumentative writing designed both to tell the reader the legal point made in a section of the argument and to outline the reasons supporting that legal point. Point headings also appear in the tables of contents of APPELLATE BRIEFS. In any brief, the point headings, when read together, should give the reader an outline of the writer's argument.

1. FORMAT for point headings.

Main point headings correspond to the issues. They provide the answer to the legal question asked in each issue, and so there should be a point heading for every issue. Use capital letters, single space, and use a Roman numeral. Include the legal point and the reason if there are no subheadings or multiple reasons; include only the legal point if subheadings will indicate the reasons.

I. THE TRIAL COURT ABUSED ITS DISCRETION WHEN IT AWARDED CUSTODY TO AN ALCOHOLIC MOTHER.

or

I. THE TRIAL COURT ERRED IN DENYING PLAINTIFFS' JURY INSTRUCTION ON DEFECTIVE BRAKES BECAUSE SUBSTANTIAL EVIDENCE INTRODUCED AT TRIAL SUPPORTS THIS THEORY OF PLAINTIFFS' CASE.

Subheadings are used to give more specific reasons for the main legal point. Usually a paragraph or two of summarizing text follows a main heading, and then the first subheading follows that text. In subheadings, indent and capitalize the first letter of each main word, as in a book title; add underlining or bold face if it is customary in your jurisdiction.

A. The Trial Court Did Not Consider the Best Interests of the Children Because It Ignored Mrs. Davis' History of Alcohol Abuse.

Sub-subheadings give particulars of the argument under the sub-heading, and appear most often in appellate briefs. Indent the sub-subheading and capitalize only the first word. Precede it with an arabic numeral.

> 1. Mrs. Davis has been arrested repeatedly for drunken driving.

2. Techniques for writing point headings.

(a) Make one legal point in each heading.

(b) Use a strong, accurate connecting word, such as **because**. See TRANSITIONS.

(c) Include a summary of the reason for the main legal point.

> I. THE TRIAL COURT ERRED IN DENYING PLAINTIFFS' JURY INSTRUCTION ON DEFECTIVE BRAKES BECAUSE SUBSTANTIAL EVIDENCE INTRODUCED AT TRIAL SUPPORTS THIS THEORY OF PLAINTIFFS' CASE.

(d) Use PERSUASIVE WRITING, concentrating on strong SUBJECT–VERB COMBINATIONS and eliminating unneeded MODIFIERS.

(e) Make the point heading no longer than four single-spaced lines, if possible.

(f) Use PARALLEL STRUCTURE in all main headings and in all subheadings.

POINT OF VIEW, OBJECTIVE OR PERSUASIVE?

Point of view in legal writing is either objective or persuasive. The point of view is objective in MEMOS, OPINION LETTERS, opinions, some law review articles, and some GENERAL CORRESPONDENCE LETTERS. Using the objective point of view allows the writer to remain detached from the decision while informing the reader of the law and predicting any outcome or change in trends.

The point of view is persuasive in memoranda of points and authorities, PRETRIAL BRIEFS, TRIAL BRIEFS, APPELLATE BRIEFS, some law review articles, and some general correspondence letters. The purpose of using the persuasive point of view is to persuade the AUDIENCE to accept the writer's argument.

Do not mix the two points of view; remain consistent throughout any given piece of writing. For advice on ways to establish these points of view, see OBJECTIVE WRITING and PERSUASIVE WRITING. For related information, see MEMORANDUM OF POINTS AND AUTHORITIES.

POLICY

Policy refers to matters outside the literal rules and procedures of the law. These matters may include factors such as social change, economic conditions, or unjust results from a literal interpretation of the law. For example, if a state introduced laws for uninsured motorists but in the process created a gap in protection against under-insured motorists, attorneys might argue that, as a policy matter, consumers should be protected from all improperly insured motorists and not just a subgroup.

Often **policy** questions arise in appellate arguments when one party desires the law be reinterpreted in response to changing social or economic values. For related information, see DISCUSSION SECTION, APPLICATION, and EQUITY.

POLISHING

Polishing, the last step in the WRITING PROCESS, includes checking for citation, grammatical, and typographical errors. Always polish your documents, whether MEMOS, LETTERS, BRIEFS, or articles. The legal reader is concerned with detail, so failure to polish the presentation can undermine the legal writer's credibility and can erode the document's meaning.

To insure time for polishing, work backward from the deadline and give yourself a reasonable amount of time to polish smaller details. For example, for a brief, allow an hour; for a memo, thirty minutes; for a short letter, ten.

Develop your own system for polishing, but make sure each aspect gets enough time. You might try the following system.

1. Read from front to back once for each of the following.

   (a) omission of any words, such as **not**;

   (b) punctuation; and

   (c) typographical errors.

2. Read from back to front just for correct citation form.

3. Reread just for spelling, if this is a problem area. For related information, see MISSPELLINGS, HOW TO AVOID.

4. Reread for any problem peculiar to your own writing, such as dangling modifiers, overuse of **however**, or improper use of SEMICOLONS.

POSITIONS OF EMPHASIS

Positions of emphasis are locations in a written text that get more attention than the text in general. They include the beginnings and ends of sentences, paragraphs, sections, and entire works. Use these positions of emphasis to convey major legal points and arguments; all points that you want to emphasize should be at a position of emphasis, with less important or unfavorable information placed in between.

The best interests of children are of paramount concern to courts in *custody disputes.*

rather than

Most courts consider *the best interests of children* in *custody disputes* to be of paramount concern.

Although the trespassers caused much physical damage, their purpose was not to cause *mental anguish*.

rather than

The trespassers caused much physical damage but causing *mental anguish* was not their purpose.

POSSESSIVES

In the law, possessives become important to PRECISION, such as **daughter's half** or **daughters' half** of an estate, so make sure you follow these rules.

1. Add an apostrophe and an **s** to make a singular noun possessive.

John's = belonging to John.

plaintiff's = belonging to a plaintiff.

statute's = belonging to a statute, as in **statute's language**.

2. Add only an **s** to singular pronouns to make them possessive.

its = belonging to it. **It's** = it is. **Its'** is never correct.

yours = belonging to you.

hers = belonging to her.

3. Add **only an apostrophe** to singular or plural nouns ending in **s** already.

Jones' = belonging to one Jones.

Joneses' = belonging to all the Joneses.

plaintiffs' = belonging to all the plaintiffs.

Some authorities allow adding an apostrophe and an **s** to plural nouns, such as **Jones's**. Whatever your choice, be consistent.

4. Add an apostrophe and an **s** to a plural noun that does not end in s.

women's = belonging to women.

For related information, see APOSTROPHES.

PRECISION

Precise writing says exactly what is meant, nothing more and nothing less. It thus focuses the reader on the writer's specific point. In order to be precise, try to answer constantly the question, **What does this mean?**

The following revision techniques can help you increase precision. For the closely related problems caused by inaccurate word choice, see ACCURACY.

1. Make sure the subject-verb combination in your Question Presented or issue says precisely what you mean, including the legal question and the LEGALLY SIGNIFICANT FACTS.

Under Missouri tort law, *did a five-year-old intend to assault an elderly woman* when he pulled a chair out from under her as she was in the process of sitting down?

Intend to assault refers to the specific legal question being asked, and **five-year-old** and **elderly woman** refer to the specific facts of this case.

The issue appellant raises on this appeal is whether *the trial court erred in applying the statute* when it summarized its findings *in only one sentence.*

Trial court erred in applying refers to the error raised on appeal, and the statement **in only one sentence** refers to the legally significant facts of this case. For more help, see QUESTION PRESENTED, SUBJECT-VERB COMBINATIONS, and ISSUE STATEMENTS.

2. In MEMOS, make sure the brief answer indeed gives an answer and explains that answer by giving reasons specific to this case.

No; the five-year-old did not intend to assault the elderly woman because a five-year-old is not capable of forming intent.

or

Yes; the trial court erred because the statute requires the trial court to make specific findings of fact on each subpart of the statute.

For more information, see BRIEF ANSWERS.

3. In argumentative writing, make sure the POINT HEADINGS use appropriate TERMS OF ART and are free of vague or overly general words.

THE TRIAL COURT ABUSED ITS DISCRETION IN FAILING TO SUPPRESS THE EVIDENCE BECAUSE THE GUN WAS PRODUCED AS THE RESULT OF AN ILLEGAL SEARCH OF MS. OLSEN'S APARTMENT.

rather than

THE TRIAL COURT ERRED BECAUSE THE SEARCH WAS IMPROPER.

4. Make sure the STATEMENT OF FACTS or STATEMENT OF THE CASE contains only those facts either (1) used in the analysis, such as the LEGALLY SIGNIFICANT FACTS, or (2) essential to establish context, such as BACKGROUND FACTS and EMOTIONALLY SIGNIFICANT FACTS.

5. Use PINPOINT CITES for any rule, holding, proposition, quotation, or specific reference.

An implied duty exists not to make changes in the work that would render the work a false attribution. Williams v. ABC, 938 F.2d 14, 16 (2d Cir. 1996).

6. Make exact any references to the record, to dates, to numbers, and to authority.

Plaintiff signed the contract on June 22, 1979. (CP 36.)

7.   In general, use concrete and specific words rather than abstract or general ones.

The defendant said that he had a gun as he grabbed Ms. Delaney's arm and poked her in the back.

rather than

The defendant said he was armed as he accosted the victim.

Use the latter version only if you mean to obscure the facts.   For related information, see EMPHASIS and PERSUASIVE WRITING, subsection 2.

PREDICATE
See SENTENCE, PARTS OF.

PREFIXES, WHEN TO HYPHENATE
See HYPHENS.

PREPOSITIONAL PHRASES
A prepositional phrase is a group of words that work together to show the relationship of a noun or pronoun to the rest of the sentence. This noun or pronoun is called the object of the preposition.   A preposition, which is always the first word in a prepositional phrase, shows how the rest of that phrase is logically related to the sentence. Examples of prepositions are **of, to, on, off, between, through, in, at, without, over,** and **under.**   The following examples of prepositional phrases illustrate the variety of information they can convey.

He built the house *with his own hands.*

All nonresidents living *in Illinois for more than three months of a calendar year* must complete the following section.

The contract will have been signed *by that date.*

The settlement seems reasonable *in light of the facts.*

For more information, see PREPOSITIONS.

PREPOSITIONS
Prepositions go before NOUNS, PRONOUNS, or phrases working as nouns (that is the **pre-**), and show the relationship of that noun, pronoun, or phrase to the rest of the sentence (that is the **-position**). Prepositional phrases thus begin with a preposition and end with a noun or pronoun; the noun or pronoun at the end of the phrase is called the **object of the preposition.**

in the car, beyond the cost, of this litigation, without his testimony

Prepositional phrases are useful and necessary, but watch for three problems when using them.

1. Avoid using many in a row. Prepositional phrases have a rhythm something like that of a slow waltz, and many of them in a row can waltz your reader right off to sleep.

The department is required to submit a written explanation if income deviates substantially from predicted income in 1984.

rather than

The department is required to submit a written explanation in the case of deviations of substantial size from the predictions of income for the calendar year of 1984.

2. Avoid using a prepositional phrase when a shorter grammatical phrase could do as well.

If the hearing is delayed, ...

rather than

In the event of the occurence of a delay of the hearing, ...

See CONCISENESS, NOMINALIZATIONS, and PREPOSITIONAL PHRASES.

3. Use the objective case (such as **me, us, him, her,** or **them**) of a pronoun that is the object of a preposition.

This written contract between you and me should help us avoid any confusion in the future.

rather than

This written contract between you and I should help us avoid any confusion in the future.

PRESENT PARTICIPLES
   See VERB TENSES.

PRESENT PERFECT TENSE
   See VERB TENSES.

PRESENT PROGRESSIVE TENSE
   See VERB TENSES.

PRESENT TENSE
   See VERB TENSES.

PRETRIAL BRIEFS
   A pretrial brief is any brief written in support of or opposition to a pretrial motion. A pretrial brief uses PERSUASIVE WRITING to inform the reader of the law and to persuade the reader to accept the client's position, and it is usually filed with the Notice of Motion and Motion or shortly thereafter. For related information, see MEMO-

RANDUM OF POINTS AND AUTHORITIES, NOTICE OF MOTION, and MOTIONS.

Check your jurisdiction for the particular FORMAT requirements. See BRIEFS for a sample format.

PREWRITING

Prewriting includes all work done before writing the first substantial draft of any paper. Clear thought and focused effort at this stage will save hours of time in the later stages of the WRITING PROCESS: WRITING, REWRITING, REVISING, and POLISHING. In a research project, prewriting includes the first five steps of the research strategy, taking NOTES on the research found, in some cases PROCRASTINA-TION, thinking, and outlining or some other means of ORGANIZA-TION. See OUTLINES or ORGANIZATION FOR THOSE WHO CAN'T OUTLINE.

Organization is the key to successful prewriting. As soon as possible, categorize the sections and subsections of your problem so that the work can be done in compartments. For example, if you are writing a three-issue appellate brief, you might organize your prewriting by those three issues and work on only one issue at a time.

Some writers prefer to begin the writing process by writing a very rough preliminary draft as soon as possible, rather than beginning with other prewriting activities. If you are one of these writers, you may apply the techniques below after your preliminary draft.

If you are comfortable with prewriting activities, be careful not to stay in this stage so long that writing, rewriting, and revising are short-changed. The following techniques can help make your prewriting stage successful.

1. Think before you go to the library. In particular, do some version of the first five steps of the RESEARCH STRATEGY CHART first.

2. Make the library work to your advantage by planning your research the way you might plan a trip to the grocery store: before you go, list the books you want to use and order the list.

3. Have your system of note-taking ready to go before you go to the library. See NOTES.

4. Allow yourself to think about the problem even when you are not writing notes; if a good idea comes to your head, jot it down so you can easily file it with its issue.

5. Try to list or outline the important points that you want to make under each issue. Even though this list may be flawed, it will help you focus your research. See OUTLINES.

6. Allow yourself always to make your own comments and commentary as you take notes, to help you pull the pieces together in your own mind.

7. Pull all the pieces together by letting the law itself dicta
organization; resist using a pre-programmed organizational ⌐
but instead respond to the organization of the law. For example, y̌
might discover several elements to a rule and use them as subdivisions.
Or you might have only one test to be applied to the facts in one unit.

PREVIOUS TO
Usually you can substitute **before** for greater READABILITY and
CONCISENESS.

PRINCIPLES OF GOOD LEGAL WRITING
The following checklist is designed to provide a brief overview and
reminder of the principles of good writing. For specific detail on how
to incorporate each of these principles in your writing, see the cross-
referenced entries.

1. Principles regarding the WRITING PROCESS.

   (a) PREWRITING.

   Good writing is good thinking. Make sure you have done
   enough of the second before you start the first. See also OUT-
   LINES and ORGANIZATION FOR THOSE WHO CAN'T OUT-
   LINE.

   (b) WRITING.

   At this stage, focus on getting it written, not getting it right.
   Let your thinking flow onto the page in the first draft, without
   stopping to edit.

   (c) REWRITING.

   Rework main ideas and large-scale organization. Add content
   if necessary. See ORGANIZATION, LARGE–SCALE and ORGA-
   NIZATION, SMALL–SCALE.

   (d) REVISING.

   Reconcile yourself to the fact that it will take several passes
   over the text to get it right. Revise for ACCURACY, CONCISE-
   NESS, READABILITY, TONE, and EMPHASIS. In particular,
   revise POINT HEADINGS, ISSUE STATEMENTS, TOPIC
   SENTENCES, and CONCLUSIONS, because your reader will pay
   special attention to these parts of any legal document.

   (e) POLISHING.

   Use whatever technique works for you: moving back to front,
   reading through separately for each kind of revision needed, reading aloud, or working section by section. Check such things as
   COMMAS, spelling, and FORMAT.

2. Principles regarding the quality of the final product.

   (a) Content.

(i) Select and carefully present all issues relevant to the scope of the paper, with the subjects and verbs presenting the legal question. See ISSUE STATEMENTS.

(ii) In MEMOS, make sure the BRIEF ANSWERS each contain the answer and the reasons for it; in BRIEFS, make sure the POINT HEADINGS contain the legal points and major reasons.

(iii) Include all relevant constitutional provisions, statutes, regulations, and cases.

(iv) Synthesize general RULES from the statute and the cases interpreting it, or the common law rule from the cases. Describe the law completely but concisely.

(v) Apply the law carefully to facts of this case; balance strengths against weaknesses. See APPLICATION.

(vi) Make sure you have adequately examined POLICY and EQUITY.

(vii) Make sure the Conclusion makes a strong prediction based on the information in the DISCUSSION SECTION of a memo, or specific prayer for relief based on the ARGUMENT SECTION of a brief.

(b) Purpose.

(i) Consider the AUDIENCE and tailor the paper to the audience's request.

(ii) Keep TONE and POINT OF VIEW consistently objective in a memo, consistently persuasive in a brief. Avoid editorializing or becoming overly dramatic.

(iii) Make sure the writing is easy for the reader to follow, with clear TRANSITIONS and strong, LOGICAL LINKS. See READABILITY.

(iv) Avoid losing the reader by either skipping steps in reasoning or by overexplaining. Also make sure WORD CHOICE is consistent and accurate. See ACCURACY.

(c) ORGANIZATION and STYLE.

(i) Check organization on all levels: overall, within a section, within a paragraph, and within a sentence. Make sure each subpart is carefully planned and connected to its neighbors. See ORGANIZATION, LARGE–SCALE; ORGANIZATION, SMALL–SCALE; ORGANIZATION; and CONNECTIONS, MAKING THEM.

(ii) Make every word count. See CONCISENESS. Also use ACTIVE VOICE whenever possible.

(iii) Give every paragraph a purpose and say it in the topic sentence. See PARAGRAPHS and TOPIC SENTENCES.

(iv) Use techniques of EMPHASIS, SENTENCE STRUCTURE, and WORD CHOICE to refine your STYLE.

(d) POLISHING.

(i) Do a final check for details; try reading backwards if it helps. Check GRAMMAR, PUNCTUATION, SPELLING, WORD USAGE, and CITATIONS.

(ii) Check to see that all cites conform to the BLUE BOOK or your jurisdiction's citation form.

PRIOR TO

Prior to sounds a bit stuffy and can be ungrammatical. **To avoid prior to, use before.**

Before the accident, he ran three miles each morning.

rather than

Prior to the accident, he ran three miles each morning.

Or use **to.**

To receive this summary of past complaints, the consumer must file . . . .

rather than

Prior to receiving this summary of past complaints, the consumer must file . . . .

PROCEDURAL OR SUBSTANTIVE?

Use these terms precisely, because the distinction between them is critical in legal writing. **Procedural** refers to legal method, or the legal machinery for carrying on a suit. This machinery includes pleading, evidence, process, and similar practical matters. For example, the question of whether a court has jurisdiction over a particular suit is a procedural question; the question of whether post-verdict motions were filed on time is also procedural.

Substantive refers to the law itself, which regulates and defines the rights and duties of parties to the suit. For example, a defendant's right to be represented by counsel is a substantive right; a party's right to bring an action for wrongful death is also a substantive right.

Often substantive rights are referred to as the merits of a case. For example, to say **The judge is ready to make a decision on the merits,** is to say that all the procedural matters have been settled so that the court may judge the remaining issues on the basis of the parties' duties and rights.

PROCRASTINATION

Procrastination works if it is incubation, fails if it is empty postponement. To make procrastination work for you, do the following.

161

1. Do short PREWRITING tasks early and then think. For example, write the Questions Presented as soon as you begin working on a memo and then think about them. Alternatively, gather the research, read it, and then think about it.

2. A little later, brief the cases or take whatever notes work for you. Let the problem sit a while to let it breathe, turn over, move about in your mind. Then jot down ideas as they come to you and put them in your files. See BRIEFING CASES and NOTES.

3. Set a time for completing the research and writing an outline. However cursory this outline may be, this step will usually force the procrastinating to end and the organizing to begin. This is the hardest step to take, but you must take it; skipping it can ruin worthwhile incubating. See OUTLINES and ORGANIZATION FOR THOSE WHO CAN'T OUTLINE.

4. Similarly, set a time to have the draft to a typist, even if you are the typist. By putting interim deadlines on your calendar and tying them to another person or task, you force yourself to avoid further procrastination by sheer embarrassment. If you do your own typing, try to find someone who will be a listener or a reader for your paper at a specific time, again so you have a deadline tied to another person.

5. Finally, schedule many small interim deadlines instead of just the final one and stick to your schedule. This will break down your temptation to postpone.

For related information, see WRITING PROCESS, WRITING BLOCKS, GETTING STARTED, and WHEN TO STOP.

PROGRESSIVE TENSES
See VERB TENSES.

PRONOUN REFERENCE
See AMBIGUITY, Subsection 2.

PRONOUNS
Pronouns take the place of nouns, and they have many uses.

He is the officer *who* gave *me* a ticket.

Without *it, they* have no case.

The plaintiff must take the responsibility upon *himself.*

Each of *you* should write to your senator.

For answers to common problems with pronouns, see the following subsections.

1. When to use commas with relative pronouns.

Relative pronouns, one subcategory of pronouns, deserve special attention because they are used frequently in legal writing and their proper use is often crucial to ACCURACY. Relative pronouns include

who, whose, that, which, whoever, whichever, and **whatever.** These relative pronouns introduce subordinate clauses, or groups of words that include a subject and verb but cannot stand by themselves as sentences.

Your car, *which* was still in the lot at midnight, was towed.

This issue was resolved by the court in <u>Barker v. Holmes</u>, *which* stated . . . .

Any nonresident *who* has lived in the state for more than three months must fill out this portion of the form.

All cars *that* remain in the lot after 10:00 p.m. will be towed.

All operators *whose* licenses expire this month must show the supervisor their renewed license.

Sometimes a subordinate clause adds extra information to the sentence but is not essential to the accuracy of the sentence. To punctuate this clause correctly, place commas before and after the subordinate clause.

Your car, which was still in the lot at midnight, was towed.

Sometimes, however, a subordinating clause is essential to the meaning of the sentence because the clause narrows the subject, or restricts the meaning of the subject. In this situation, removing the subordinate clause would make the sentence inaccurate. To punctuate this kind of subordinate clause correctly, do not put commas before or after the clause.

All cars [ ] that remain in the lot after 10:00 p.m. [ ] will be towed.

Any nonresident [ ] who has lived in the state for more than three months [ ] must fill out this portion of the form.

All operators [ ] whose licenses expire this month [ ] must show the supervisor their renewed license.

2. When to use **who** or **whom.**

Use **who** as a subject, **whom** as an object. First, use **whom** as the object of a PREPOSITION.

To whom did you present the question about the gun?

Second, use **whom** as the object of a verb.

Whom did you see on the night of the incident?

Finally, use **whom** as the subject of a complementary infinitive.

Defendant is the person whom the plaintiff saw on the night of the crime.

Use **who** as a subject of a sentence or of a clause.

Who took my shoes?

You are the person who called me yesterday.

3. When to use **he, she,** or **they.**

Use **they** only when referring to a plural noun. Use **he or she** when you are referring to one person but do not know the sex of the person.

163

For more on this question, see SEXIST LANGUAGE, WAYS TO AVOID.

PROPER NOUNS

Proper nouns are names of specific persons, organizations, publications, and so forth. **Helen Harris, American Bar Association,** *Texas Law Review.* Capitalize them.

PUNCTUATING LISTS

See LISTS, STRUCTURE OF.

PUNCTUATING QUOTES

These rules are picky and extensive but worth observing. It is important to be accurate in legal writing, and particularly important to be accurate when quoting. These rules include (1) when to use quotation marks, (2) when to indent, (3) when to use a comma before a quote, (4) how to use other punctuation marks with quotation marks, (5) when to use single quotation marks, (6) when and how to underline parts of a quote, (7) how to mark changes in a quote, (8) how to mark omissions from a quote, and (9) how to maintain credibility when editing a quote.

1. When to use quotation marks.

Use quotation marks to mark any direct quote. When the quote is forty-nine words or less, put it in quotation marks.

The court reasoned that "any error must in this situation be material."

Also use quotation marks to indicate that a word is being used to refer to the word itself, rather than to the meaning of the word. Thus, put quotation marks around a word when you could insert **the term** or **the word** before that word.

The court focused on "reasonable" when interpreting the meaning of this clause in the contract.

Avoid using quotation marks to indicate slang, sarcasm, irony, or anything other than direct quotes or words used as words. The precision of legal writing requires the precise use of punctuation, including quotation marks. If you feel uncomfortable using a word because it is informal or ambiguous, change the word rather than putting it in quotation marks.

2. When to indent.

When the quote is longer than forty-nine words, indent it and type it single-spaced. Put the citation on the first line of text following the quote, rather than within the indented quote itself.

The court in this case addressed the issue of mutuality.

> Despite the defendant's emotional plea regarding the central-ity of upholding contracts to the free working of a democracy, we cannot ignore the plaintiff's complaint. In this case, the court must

> intervene because the issue of mutuality, not to mention that of
> duress, requires that the court examine both the contract's wording
> and the parol evidence surrounding the signing of that contract.

Hartman v. Legler, 986 F. Supp. 192 (S.D. Ind. 1994).

3. When to use a comma before a quote.

Use a comma if the phrase before the quote introduces it.

She said, "I killed him."

If the quote is an integral part of the larger sentence, do not use a comma.

He said "killed," not "stabbed."

4. How to use other punctuation marks with quotation marks.

Quotation marks go outside commas and periods, even if the comma or period is not part of the quote.

The term on which we must focus is "intent."

This rule is the same for both double quotation marks ("—") and single ones ('—'). The rule is not meant to reflect logical concerns, but rather graphic ones. It looks funny to see the period or comma sitting out there alone.

One exception to this rule is LEGISLATION, where periods and commas are treated like all other punctuation marks.

All other punctuation marks go inside the quotation marks if they are part of the quote, outside if they are not.

Common law recognized a defense to a privacy action where "the incident was a public concern and record"; however, the statutory policy had in effect eliminated this defense.

The semicolon is not part of the quote, so it goes outside the marks.

Smith reports "a majority of the jurors thought 'infer' meant 'assume'!"

The exclamation point is part of the quote, so it goes inside the quotation marks. **Infer** and **assume** refer to the words as words, rather than the concepts the words describe, and so are put in quotation marks. Single marks are used because the words are within another quote. For related information, see EXCLAMATION POINTS.

5. When to use single quotation marks.

In the United States use single quotation marks only for quotes within other quotes.

The defendant said, "He told me to 'get lost.'"

6. When and how to underline parts of a quote.

Underline to add emphasis to the key phrase in QUOTATIONS long enough to be indented and single-spaced in the text. Underlining may encourage the legal reader to read the long quote by making it more visually pleasing. When you underline, add **(emphasis added)** after the citation.

As this court itself has stated, "[T]he court must intervene because the issue of mutuality, not to mention that of duress, requires that the court examine the parol evidence surrounding the signing of the contract." Durant v. Colt, 945 F. Supp. 641 (D.D.C. 1994) (emphasis added).

When the quote is indented, put the cite and (emphasis added) on the first line of text following the indented quote, not within the indented quote itself.

7.   How to mark changes in a quote.

In general, use BRACKETS to mark any changes you make in the wording of a quote.

(a) If you are changing or adding a word to a quote to make it fit grammatically into your sentence, put brackets ([ ]) around that word.

> As the court explained, "Despite the defendant's emotional plea regarding the centrality of upholding contracts to the free working of a democracy, [the court] cannot ignore the plaintiff's complaint."

changed from the original

> Despite the defendant's emotional plea regarding the centrality of upholding contracts to the free working of a democracy, we cannot ignore the plaintiff's complaint.

(b) If you are adding or changing a letter within a word, put brackets around the part of the word changed. Even if all you do is change a letter from lower case (a) to upper case (A), you must put brackets around the change.

> The court made this explicit when it said, "[W]e cannot ignore the plaintiff's complaint."

changed from the original

> Despite the defendant's emotional plea regarding the centrality of upholding contracts to the free working of a democracy, we cannot ignore the plaintiff's complaint.

(c) If you are adding SIC, put it in brackets. Add sic when you want to inform the reader that the error in the text was in the original, rather than being an error you made when copying the quote.

> "In this cause [sic], Ms. Hofner did not realize she was waiving this right."

8.   How to mark omissions from a quote.

In general, use ELLIPSES to mark any omissions you make in a quote. An ellipsis is a series of three periods with spaces between them (.   .   .). To be accurate, you must not only use ellipses to mark any omissions; you must also use accurate spacing and punctuation before and after the ellipses, as the following rules explain. These rules are intricate, but important and useful to the careful reader. If ellipses are used accurately, the reader can tell exactly what changes you made in the original without having to look up the original.

(a) If you are omitting a word or words within one sentence, put a space before and after the ellipsis.

"The issue of mutuality . . . requires that the court examine both the contract's wording and the parol evidence surrounding the signing of the contract."

changed from the original

The issue of mutuality, not to mention that of duress, requires that the court examine both the contract's wording and the parol evidence surrounding the signing of the contract.

(b) If you are omitting the rest of an entire sentence, put a space before the ellipsis and a space and period after the ellipsis. This fourth period represents the period at the end of the original sentence.

"There can be no negligence without duty . . . ."

changed from the original

There can be no negligence without duty, and in this case there is no duty.

(c) If the sentence quoted ended with a question mark or exclamation mark, use that mark rather than a period after the ellipsis.

"The jury thought 'imply' meant 'assume' . . . !"

changed from the original

The jury thought "imply" meant "assume" in this situation!

"Did the defendant take all reasonable precautions . . . ?"

changed from the original

Did the defendant take all reasonable precautions before starting up the mower?

(d) Similarly, if you are omitting the rest of one sentence and then continuing the quote at the first of the next sentence, put a space before the ellipsis, and a space and period after the ellipsis. After the fourth period, add two spaces and then begin the next sentence, just as you would after the period at the end of any other sentence.

"The court cannot base its decision on sympathy . . . . There can be no negligence without duty . . . ."

changed from the original

The court cannot base its decision on sympathy, no matter how great that sympathy may be. There can be no negligence without duty, and in this case there is no duty.

Again, if the sentence you are editing ended with a question mark or exclamation point, repeat that mark instead of the fourth period.

(e) If you are quoting the end of a sentence, omitting one or more sentences, and then continuing the quote with a later sentence, do the following. First, put a period, question mark, or exclamation point immediately after the last word of the quoted sentence right before the ellipsis, just as you would have done if you were not omitting sentences. Second, put in one space and then the ellipsis. Third, space once and then begin the next quoted sentence.

In this case, the court must intervene. . . . The issue of mutuality, not to mention that of duress, requires that the court examine both the contract's wording and the parol evidence surrounding the signing of that contract.

changed from the original

In this case, the court must intervene. Despite the defendant's emotional plea regarding the centrality of upholding contracts to the free working of a democracy, it cannot ignore the plaintiff's complaint. The issue of mutuality, not to mention that of duress, requires that the court examine both the contract's wording and the parol evidence surrounding the signing of that contract.

(f) If you are quoting the end of a sentence, omitting one or more sentences, and then continuing the quote mid-sentence, follow the same procedure explained in subsection (d), but also put brackets around the first word after the ellipsis if you are changing that letter from lower case to upper case.

In this case, the court must intervene. . . . [M]utuality requires that the court examine both the contract's wording and the parol evidence surrounding the signing of that contract.

changed from the original

In this case, the court must intervene. Despite the defendant's emotional plea regarding the centrality of upholding contracts to the free working of a democracy, it cannot ignore the plaintiff's complaint. The issue of mutuality requires that the court examine both the contract's wording and the parol evidence surrounding the signing of that contract.

(g) Never use an ellipsis at the beginning of a quote, even if you have omitted the first word or words of the quoted passage. The ellipsis is unneeded because the fact that the first word of the quote was not originally capitalized is sufficient to indicate that words have been omitted.

[T]here can be no negligence without duty.

rather than

. . . there can be no negligence without duty.

changed from the original

As the defense so aptly argued, there can be no negligence without duty.

9. How to maintain credibility when editing a quote.

Avoid extensive editing of quotes, even though you now know how to do it accurately. If you use ellipses and brackets extensively, the reader will find the quote awkward to read and will probably suspect that you are misrepresenting the original idea. The solution in this situation is not to omit ellipses and thus sacrifice ACCURACY; it is to PARAPHRASE or to find another quote that fits the situation without needing such extensive surgery.

The court stated that it must intervene in this case to resolve the issue of mutuality despite the emotional pleas for freedom of contract.

rather than the edited version

Despite the . . . emotional plea regarding . . . upholding contracts to the free working of a democracy, [the court] cannot ignore the plaintiff's complaint. . . . [T]he court must intervene; the issue of mutuality . . . requires that the court examine both the contract's wording and the parol evidence . . . .

changed from the original

Despite the defendant's emotional plea regarding the centrality of upholding contracts to the free working of a democracy, we cannot ignore the plaintiff's complaint. In this case, the court must intervene; the issue of mutuality, not to mention that of duress, requires that the court examine both the contract's wording and the parol evidence surrounding the signing of that contract.

PUNCTUATION

Punctuation rules are extensive and particular but critical to ACCURACY. For ways to punctuate sentences, see PERIODS, SEMI-COLONS, COLONS, EXCLAMATION POINTS, and QUESTION MARKS. For ways to punctuate phrases within a sentence, see COMMAS, DASHES, SEMICOLONS, and COLONS. For ways to punctuate lists, see LISTS, STRUCTURE OF. For ways to punctuate quotes, see PUNCTUATING QUOTES. See also HYPHENS and APOSTROPHES.

PURPOSE

Have one in mind before you get too far along in the WRITING PROCESS. Although you may brainstorm a first draft or some notes, take time to think about why you are writing as well as what you want to say and to whom you will say it. Taking the time to be honest with yourself about your purpose and to state that purpose clearly can make your writing both more effective and more efficient. For more information on how to develop your purpose, see GETTING STARTED, OUTLINES, ORGANIZATION FOR THOSE WHO CAN'T OUTLINE, and AUDIENCE.

QUESTION MARK OR PERIOD?
See QUESTION MARKS.

QUESTION MARKS

You know to use question marks with questions. The problems occur with sentences like the ones that follow.

1. The question is whether this term applies to the facts of this case.

A period, not a question mark is used.

2. The boy, when confronted by the clerk, said only, "Who, me?"

No period is used after the question mark.

3. Can the issue be raised? is the question.

A question mark is used mid-sentence, after the question, but a period is used at the end of the sentence. This structure is rare and thus looks odd to most readers; try rewording the sentence whenever you can to avoid putting a question mark in the middle, even if it is grammatically correct to do so.

4. The question is, "Does this term apply to the facts of this case?"

A question mark, not a period, is used.

5. May we hear from you within one week.

Here the choice between a period and a question mark is a tactical one. When you are asking a question but implying a demand, you may use a period.

See also PUNCTUATING QUOTES for handling question marks and quotation marks together.

QUESTION PRESENTED

The lens of the legal analyst's camera, the Question Presented focuses on the specific question to be answered in a legal memo. The issue statement in a persuasive piece of writing is also sometimes called a Question Presented. In its objective form, the ideal Question Presented outlines the memo because it has three parts: (1) the general rule of law governing the question, (2) the legal question to be answered in this situation, and (3) the LEGALLY SIGNIFICANT FACTS necessary for the analysis.

Under Fed. R. Civ. P. 4(d)(1), Summons: Personal Service, was a notice effective when it was delivered to defendant's wife and when defendant did not reside at his wife's address, but moved back in with her one week later?

These three parts are combined and written in either question form or **whether** form. The **whether** form enjoys common use among established lawyers, but it is grammatically incorrect because it is an incomplete sentence. The **whether** form also implies a statement rather than a question and can add extra words. In either form, keep subject and verb close together to increase READABILITY.

Whether notice was effective under Fed. R. Civ. P. 4(d)(1), Summons: Personal Service, when it was delivered to defendant's wife and when defendant did not reside at his wife's address but moved back in with her one week later.

170

Put the legally significant facts at the end of the Question Presented so that the reader is focused by moving from general to specific. Placing the legally significant facts at the end also helps keep the question readable because it places the list at the end of the sentence. See LISTS, STRUCTURE OF. For related information, see ISSUE STATEMENTS.

QUOTATION MARKS

Use quotation marks for quotes of forty-nine words or less. Also use quotation marks to indicate that you are referring to a word itself, rather than the thing the words stand for, as in the following example.

"Hearsay" refers to a statement, other than one made by the declarant while testifying at the trial or hearing, offered in evidence to prove the truth of the matter asserted.

For related information, see QUOTATION MARKS OR INDENTED QUOTES?, QUOTATION MARKS WITH OTHER PUNCTUATION, and PUNCTUATING QUOTES.

QUOTATION MARKS IN LEGISLATION

See LEGISLATION.

QUOTATION MARKS OR INDENTED QUOTES?

Use quotation marks around direct quotes of forty-nine words or less and around titles of articles. When a direct quote is longer than forty-nine words, indent it, single-space it, and omit quotation marks. The only time you will use quotation marks in an indented, single-spaced quote is when there is a quote within the indented quote. See also PUNCTUATING QUOTES.

QUOTATION MARKS WITH OTHER PUNCTUATION

Quotation marks go outside commas and periods, even if the comma or period is not part of the quote.

The term on which we must focus is "intent."

The rule is not meant to reflect logical concerns, but rather graphic ones. It looks funny to see the period or comma sitting out there alone.

One exception to this rule is LEGISLATION, where periods and commas are treated like all other punctuation marks.

Whether quotation marks go inside or outside other punctuation marks depends on logic. Put the other mark inside the quotation marks if it is part of the quote; put it outside if it is not. This rule applies to both double quotation marks ("—") and single ones ('—').

Common law recognized a defense to a privacy action where, "the incident was a public concern and record"; however, the statutory policy had in effect eliminated this defense.

The semicolon is not part of the quote, so it goes outside the marks. Smith reports, "a majority of the jurors thought 'infer' meant 'assume'!"

The exclamation point is part of the quote, so it goes inside the quotation marks. **Infer** and **assume** refer to the words as words, rather than the concepts the words describe, and so are put in quotation marks. Single marks are used because the words are within another quote. For related information, see EXCLAMATION POINTS.

QUOTATIONS, LONG
See EXTENDED QUOTES.

QUOTATIONS, WHEN TO USE?
Use quotations if the particular phrasing is central to your issue, such as phrases including TERMS OF ART or key passages from the applicable statute. Otherwise use quotes only if the answer to each of the following questions is **yes**.

1. Does the quotation contain information directly pertinent to the point?

2. Is the quotation no longer than one long paragraph, unless content requires all of it?

3. Does the quotation communicate the information more clearly than you could, even in an accurate PARAPHRASE? Alternatively, does this quotation communicate the information more eloquently than you could in a paraphrase?

See also PUNCTUATING QUOTES and EXTENDED QUOTES.

QUOTE WITHIN A QUOTE
See QUOTATION MARKS WITH OTHER PUNCTUATION.

RAMBLING
To avoid this problem, see ORGANIZATION, PARAGRAPHS, OUTLINES, and ORGANIZATION FOR THOSE WHO CAN'T OUTLINE.

RE
You may use **re** in subject lines for letters or memos, but do not use it in the text of the letter or memo. Instead use **regarding**.

READABILITY
Many factors work together to enhance the readability of a document. Here is a checklist of some of the most useful ones.

1. Use shorter sentences.

Check to make sure that your sentences do not habitually run more than three-and-one-half lines. One easy way to do this is to put a slash after each period in the draft. You can do this without actually reading the text; just skim for the periods. Then, looking at where the slashes fall, check for places where there are several long sentences in a row. Divide at least some of these into shorter sentences.

You may decide that the testimony of one witness is entitled to greater weight than that of another witness, or even of several witnesses. In weighing the evidence, you may consider your own knowledge, observations, and life experiences.

rather than

In weighing the evidence, you may consider the testimony of one witness as entitled to greater weight than that of another witness or several others, your own knowledge, what you have observed, and the experiences you have had in life.

If a sentence contains a list at the end, it may not need to be divided. For ways to handle the list, see the next subsection.

2. Use clear and logical lists.

Careful structuring of lists greatly increases readability. First, always make sure that the elements of your list are both logically and grammatically parallel.

The defendant moved his car into the left lane to pass, lost control on the snow-packed pavement, slid back into the right lane, and collided with the plaintiff's truck.

rather than

The defendant moved his car into the left lane to pass, was losing control, slid back into the right lane, and caused injury to the plaintiff when he hit her truck.

Then structure your sentence so that the list comes at the end. Additionally, when the list is long or complex, use signals, such as parenthetical numbers or tabulation, to help the reader see immediately the structure of the list.

In justifying the exclusion of expert psychiatric evidence, the court discussed (1) maintaining the integrity of the bifurcated trial procedure, (2) avoiding allowing the guilty to go free, and (3) preserving the defendant's right against self-incrimination.

rather than

The court discussed maintaining the integrity of the bifurcated trial procedure, avoiding allowing the guilty to go free, and preserving the defendant's right against self-incrimination in justifying the exclusion of expert psychiatric evidence.

For more detail about ways to do this, see LISTS, STRUCTURE OF.

3. Use familiar words.

Use words that your reader will understand without having to resort to a dictionary.

Counsel, by using apt wording and artful presentation, minimized this weak point in her argument.

rather than

Counsel, by applying her verbal acumen and felicitous propensity for oratory, accomplished a feat of legerdemain regarding this conceptual proposition.

Unusual words, even if the reader does know what they mean, force the reader to stop and think. Busy legal readers usually will not stop mid-thought to ponder the nuances of an individual word, and so your meaning may be lost. For more information, see FLOWERY LAN-GUAGE.

4. Use consistent wording.

Use the same term for the same concept throughout the document; do not change it just for VARIETY.

The defendant *proposes* that his repair of the water heater was adequate. This *proposal*, however, ...

rather than

The defendant *proposes* that his repair of the water heater was adequate. This *suggestion*, however, ...

Using consistent terms aids readability by helping the reader know immediately that you mean the same thing. For more on this point, see REPETITION.

5. Keep the subject and verb undivided and focused on your point.

Keep the subject within seven words of the verb and make sure the subject and verb state the main point of the sentence.

If this case were retried, the *result would be* different because of the combination of the numerous defects in the proceedings below and the newly discovered evidence.

rather than

The total *effect* of the numerous defects in the proceedings below, which in combination with the newly discovered evidence referred to above creates a miscarriage of justice, *would* if this case were to be retried under optimum circumstances *produce* a different result.

In the second example, the subject (**effect**) is divided from the verb (**would produce**) by twenty-four words, and the two words of the verb (**would** and **produce**) are divided by ten words. By the time the reader finally finds the verb, the subject will be forgotten and the reader will have to re-read the sentence several times to find it. For more ways to restructure sentences, see SENTENCE STRUCTURE.

Additionally, PRECISION is lost when the subject and verb do not clearly state the writer's point. In the previous example, **effect would produce** does not state the reader's main point. Moving the subject and verb together would have exposed this problem to the writer, who could then revise it to **the result would be different**. For more on this see SUBJECT–VERB COMBINATIONS. For related problems, see AGREEMENT, SUBJECTS AND VERBS.

6. Use precise transitions.

Use transitions that convey exact connections. For example, use **nevertheless** only when **nevertheless** is the logical connection between the two thoughts.

The litigation may cost more than the amount our client could recover if she wins the suit. Nevertheless, she has chosen to pursue her claim.

rather than

The litigation may cost more than the amount our client could recover if she wins the suit, although she has chosen to pursue her claim.

In the second example, using the wrong transition confuses the reader. For more on this and for a list of transitions, see TRANSITIONS.

7. Use consistent word signals.

If you use **second**, make sure that you used **first** earlier. Similarly, if you used **not only**, use **but also** later. Without these parallel signals, the skilled reader is left frustrated, like the waiting listener who hears one shoe drop but never hears the second. For related information, see CONJUNCTIONS and CONNECTIONS, MAKING THEM.

8. Accurate and adequate punctuation.

PUNCTUATION marks are the road signs of legal writing, and inaccurate punctuation can lead to wrong turns. Revise once just for accurate punctuation. For more information on punctuation needed but often omitted, see COMMAS and SEMICOLONS. For ways to spot these problems, see REVISING.

READER
See AUDIENCE.

READING OPINIONS
See OPINIONS.

REALLY
Really means **in reality** or **indeed**. It is overused, so avoid it unless it accurately conveys your meaning. Because **really** is used frequently and loosely in informal speech, it is probably best to replace the word with **in reality** in formal legal writing.

REASONING
Reasoning refers to the process by which a court or lawyer analyzing the law moves from a general proposition of law to a specific conclusion. This process is called deductive reasoning and is usually

based on a syllogism. The legal reader is particularly interested in each step of the reasoning process, so consider the following when presenting your reasoning.

1. Make the presentation of the general RULES thorough and precise. For example, if the entire statute is necessary for analysis, include the entire statute at the beginning of the reasoning process; if several cases must be synthesized to pull together one rule, synthesize them at the beginning of the analysis.

2. Explain any relevant exceptions to the rule.

3. Provide examples of previous applications of the rule.

4. Explain the LEGALLY SIGNIFICANT FACTS in the case being analyzed and show how those facts fit under the rules and the exceptions. Explain how this case compares to the examples.

5. Explain how this application results in the conclusion.

Remember to consider this list but not to follow it mechanically, because legal reasoning is a complex process, unique to each problem. For related information, see SYLLOGISMS, DISCUSSION SECTION; and ARGUMENT SECTION. For more suggestions on how to build reasoning, see P. Schlag and D. Skover, *Tactics of Legal Reasoning* (Carolina Academic Press 1986).

RECOMMENDATIONS

Recommendations are appropriate in the Conclusion of a memo when the memo's purpose is to analyze the law and to predict the outcome in the context of pretrial discovery. Often the reader, another person in the same office, has assigned the writer the job of analyzing the law so that the reader can make a decision about a particular pretrial activity. For example, a partner might assign an associate to write a memo on whether or not the partner should move for summary judgment in a case. The associate should make the recommendation as specific as possible, after explaining the reasons in the DISCUSSION SECTION.

Similarly, an attorney might recommend certain action in an opinion letter. This recommendation should be within the realm of professional, not personal, advice. See MEMOS, OPINION LETTERS, and OPINION OR ADVICE?

RECORD, CITING TO IT

Cite to the record in the STATEMENT OF THE CASE in pretrial, trial, or appellate BRIEFS. Be scrupulous about using PINPOINT CITES in the references so the reader can quickly locate exact passages. For the reader's convenience, also refer to the record in the ARGU-MENT SECTION if the reader might need to check sources.

Check your jurisdiction for the appropriate format for these cita-tions to the record. Some prefer parentheses, (Tr 38), some use none, CP

19, and others use periods, **R. 76**. For related information, see CITA-
TIONS, and CITATIONS, PARALLEL.

RECUR OR REOCCUR?

The difference in meaning between these two words is slight, but in some contexts it is important. **Recur** implies that the event happens repeatedly; **reoccur** implies that the event is repeated only once.

REDUNDANCY

See CONCISENESS. For related information, see REPETITION.

REFERENCES

See CITATIONS; FOOTNOTES; and RECORD, CITING TO IT.

REFERENTS

See ANTECEDENTS.

REGARDLESS OR IRREGARDLESS?

Regardless, always.

REJECTION LETTERS

See BAD NEWS, SOFTENING IT and BAD NEWS, GIVING IT, subsection 1.

REOCCUR OR RECUR?

See RECUR OR REOCCUR?

REPETITION

Repetition by careful design works in legal writing. Rather than avoiding repetition absolutely, avoid it only when it does not have one of the following uses.

1. Use repetition when it is needed for ACCURACY.

If you mean **contract**, do not shift to **document** or **agreement**. Changing terms confuses legal readers, who will think that you must mean something else if you changed terms.

2. Use repetition when it is needed for READABILITY.

For example, repeating the same first word at the beginning of each item in a list can be very helpful to the reader when each item in the list is long. See LISTS, STRUCTURE OF.

Any proposed method for reducing marital status discrimination *must* reflect the statutory complexity creating discrimination, *must* avoid reproducing the undesirable effects of the current taxation structure, and *must* show awareness that compromising one or more important policy goals is necessary in any tax scenario.

3. Use repetition as a transition to logically dovetail two sentences or paragraphs.

Repeating a key word from a previous sentence or paragraph shows how the idea that word represents fits in with the idea of the new sentence of paragraph.

Environmental Impact Studies could be handled similarly without *delaying* the hearing.

Even if there were some *delay*, ...

4. Use repetition when it is needed for EMPHASIS.

Sometimes the very fact that a repeated word gains attention can be an advantage. For example, you may repeat a word or structure that states a dramatic or important point.

The defendant stated this intention to his girlfriend. He stated it to his coworkers. He stated it to the cabdriver who took him to the airport.

For related techniques, see ALLITERATION.

REPETITION OF SOUNDS
See ALLITERATION.

REQUESTS FOR PAYMENT
There are four do's here. First, do consciously decide what you want. If you want money, focus on that and set aside your moral outrage at the way you have been treated. In contrast, if you really want to express your moral outrage, do so in temperate language. Realize, however, that this expression may not do much to help you get your money.

Second, do consider the possible motivations your reader may have and try to employ those motivations to get what you want. Choose not what persuades you, but what will persuade your reader. For example, if you are trying to persuade a party to settle out of court, do not use threats when you think the party would view that threat as a challenge and submission as a weakness. In that situation, you might instead explain that the cost of litigation would exceed the cost of settlement. Similarly, if you think that the reader is someone motivated by certain values, try to explain how the action you recommend is consistent with those values. For example, you might argue that paying a bill is essentially the same as keeping a promise. In short, try to explain how the action you recommend is consistent with some goal the reader has. Try to help the reader feel good, or at least not defeated, about taking the action you recommend.

Third, do consciously decide what TONE you want to create. For example, do you want to be nice, giving the reader the benefit of the doubt, or do you want to be tough? If you want to be nice, you may use kind opening and closing paragraphs. For more on this, see BAD NEWS, SOFTENING IT. If you want to be tough, you may use shorter sentences and impersonal language. For more on this, see TOUGH, SOUNDING THAT WAY. For related information, see TONE IN LETTERS.

Finally, do make sure what you say is literally correct. Satiric comments or broad hints can be misread easily and can lead to further delays in getting the results you want. Do not resort to diatribe, even if your anger is completely justifiable. Lay out in objective language the facts, the options, and the results. Similarly, do not make empty threats; if your reader knows or finds out that one threat is empty, he or she may assume that later ones are empty too. See EMOTIONAL LANGUAGE.

RESEARCH STRATEGY CHART

The following ten-step Research Strategy Chart is designed to maximize your efficiency in the process of finding all the sources necessary to complete your research task. The first five steps take place before you leave your desk. Fight the temptation to run to the library without having completed this portion of the strategy. The preliminary issue statement is particularly important because it helps you focus your research from the very beginning. It is essential to do this before you leave for the library, so you can decide what books you should go to first, second, third, and so on. This saves the time spent wandering from one book to another.

For further elaboration on each step, see the specific pages cited to in C. Wren & J. Wren, *The Legal Research Manual: A Game Plan for Legal Research and Analysis* (A–R Editions 2d ed. 1986). These cites are noted by *LRM*, followed by the specific page number.

RESEARCH STRATEGY CHART

At your desk

Step 1. Collect the facts.

Just as a journalist does, make sure you know the who, what, when, where, why and how of the facts. *LRM* 30.

Step 2. Analyze the facts.

Using whatever system you prefer or have, such as West's or Lawyers' Co-op, group the facts into their general categories. For West, use Parties, Objects, Basis, Defense, and Remedy. For Lawyers' Co-op, use Things, Acts, Persons, and Places. Give each category a page or column. Transfer your facts from Step 1 to these columns. Then brainstorm synonyms and antonyms for the facts in each column. These terms become your search words.

Step 3. Formulate a preliminary issue statement.

A. This can be done before you know the law by following a format that goes from general to specific, using the key words **Under, did,** and **when,** as follows:

Under Missouri assault law, [general law—indicate as specific a category as you can without doing any research]

did Fred assault Harvey [legal question]

when he waved an unloaded gun in Harvey's face

[legally significant facts]?

The first part of the question tells you what books to look under, such as the Missouri Statutes Annotated index. The second part tells you what topic to look under in the book, such as **assault.** The third part tells you how to filter through the summaries of the cases found in the annotated statutes. For example, you would look for **cases involving a loaded gun or an unloaded gun waved in the vicinity of someone or in someone's face.** You can eliminate those cases whose summaries do not indicate a similarity to these legally significant facts.

B. Organize the issues logically. For example, put threshold issues such as **standing** first. *LRM* 37.

Step 4. Verify jurisdiction.

Make sure you know whose law applies. If not, make a note to find this out first when you go to the library.

Step 5. Make a research plan.

Map out where you will go first, second, and so on. It is crucial to think this through before you start researching to avoid wasting time wandering from shelf to shelf or from database to database at the computer. For example, after you look through the annotated statutes, you might plan to go to the Missouri Digest, then to the Missouri Patterned Jury Instructions, and then to SHEPARD'S.

At the library

Step 6. Find the law.

The purpose of this step is to make sure you find all relevant primary sources, provisions, statutes, regulations, and cases. If you were given a statute or case name, for example, you might start with A. If you were not given a known authority, you might start with B. And if you are completely unfamiliar with the area of law, you might start with C.

A. Known authority.

(1) Statute or regulation. *LRM* 51.

(a) Go to the statutes or regulations annotated for that jurisdiction.

(b) Shepardize in the appropriate volume.

(c) Check looseleafs if researching administrative regulations.

(d) Do a computer search if available.

(e) Check pocket parts and supplements.

(2) Case. *LRM* 53.

(a) Find the volume containing the case and review the headnotes.

(b) Choose the headnotes that are pertinent and note the topic title and key or section number.

(c) Retrieve the digest volume containing that topic and turn to the topic and section number; you now have all the published cases about that topic.

(d) Check the pocket parts.

B. Descriptive word or fact word.

(1) Statute or regulation: *LRM* 46.

(a) Take the list developed in Step 2 and look up those words in the index to statutes or regulations to see if there is a statute or regulation on that subject.

(b) If so, follow steps listed in A(1) above.

(2) Case. *LRM* 49.

(a) Find the appropriate digest for that jurisdiction.

(b) Take the list developed in Step 2 and look up those words in the index to the digest.

(c) Move from the index to those topics in the digest.

(d) Check pocket parts.

(e) Use the words from your list to write a query and search the computer database.

C. Encyclopedias, treatises, and other sources useful for your own background. *LRM* 65.

(1) Check the *A.L.R.* Quick Index. Use descriptive words; you may find a gold mine here if there is an annotation on your topic.

(2) Check the *Index to Legal Periodicals* and the *Current Resources Index* for law review articles. Also check *C.J.S.*, *Am.Jur.*, and the *Restatements*.

Step 7. Read the law (before you copy it).

A. Evaluate internally. *LRM* 79.

(1) Statute.

(a) Evaluate the language of the statute itself.

(b) Is there a general factual similarity to this case?

(c) Is there ambiguity in the legislative intent that favors this case?

(d) Does the statute's context give it a focus applicable to this case?

(e) Does the statute's legislative history illuminate its meaning?

(f) How do the canons of construction augment the statute's meaning? *LRM* 88.

(2) Case.

(a) Is there a factual similarity to this case?

(b) Is there a general similarity that is useful if the facts are recharacterized?

(c) Does the POLICY provide a useful basis for argument?

B. Evaluate externally. (See Step 8 below.) *LRM* 89.

(1) Current status.

(a) Has the statute been invalidated, repealed, or amended?

(b) Are these subsequent interpretations of cases useful to this case?

(2) Extend the law.

(a) Can a new rule or innovative twist be formulated?

(b) Is the statute a codification or a departure from previous rules?

(c) Has a novel policy or doctrine emerged?

Step 8.   Update the law.

A. Shepardize. *LRM* 95.

(1) Find the right set of Shepard's.

(2) Collect all the necessary volumes (see box in front cover of each volume).

(3) Find the correct tables for your statute or case.

(4) Find the volume and page number, or statute number.

(5) Examine entry. For more detailed assistance, see SHEPARD'S.

B. Check the pocket parts and supplements.

C. Check the looseleaf reporter services.

D. Do a computer search. See COMPUTERS. *LRM* 133.

E. Check other possible sources, such as newspapers, for recent opinions or references to the source.

Step 9. Take effective notes.

A. Have a system and write out the plan. See NOTES. *LRM* 123.

B. Reread your preliminary issues periodically to maintain your focus.

C. Record full CITATIONS in proper form.

Step 10. Ask or call.

This can be inserted wherever necessary when conventional tools provide insurmountable stumbling blocks.

RESTRICTIVE PHRASES

See THAT OR WHICH?

REVISING

Revising occurs after REWRITING in the WRITING PROCESS. Revising concentrates on small-scale organization, SENTENCE STRUCTURE, TRANSITIONS, PARAGRAPHING, GRAMMAR, and PUNCTUATION. For related information, see ORGANIZATION, SMALL–SCALE.

There are two things to remember about revising. First, do not revise while you write; this slows down both the writing and the revising processes. When you are writing, concentrate solely on your ideas, no matter how unpolished your writing may seem. Revise later. Second, when you revise, do it in stages. It is exhausting and inefficient to try to revise on every level at once. As the following list illustrates, you can subdivide the time available for revising into categories that move from general writing problems to more specific ones.

1. ACCURACY.

No amount of readability will replace accuracy, so make sure you check first for the content of each legal point. Ask yourself the following questions.

(a) Is the content accurately stated? Could any points be misinterpreted because of ambiguity? See AMBIGUITY, WAYS TO AVOID.

(b) Are irrelevant facts or other irrelevant information excluded?

(c) Are TERMS OF ART used correctly?

(d) Are KEY TERMS used correctly? See SUBJECT–VERB COMBINATIONS.

(e) Are paraphrases accurate? See PARAPHRASE.

(f) Are names of parties and their status correct?

(g) Are the CITATIONS accurate? Are PINPOINT CITES used for specific propositions, rules, holdings, quotes? Are case names spelled accurately? Are page numbers and years accurate?

2. Small-scale organization.

(a) Are PARAGRAPHS internally logical?

(b) Are there TOPIC SENTENCES that give the overall message of each of the paragraphs, usually at the beginning of the paragraphs?

(c) Are there clear and precise TRANSITIONS between paragraphs?

(d) Are there strong transitions between sentences?

3. READABILITY.

(a) Are subjects and verbs close together?

(b) Is there more ACTIVE VOICE than PASSIVE VOICE?

(c) Are sentences free of NOMINALIZATIONS?

(d) Are unnecessary MODIFIERS eliminated, such as **clearly** and **obviously**?

(e) Are sentences not overly long? See SENTENCE LENGTH.

(f) Are lists clearly structured? See LISTS, STRUCTURE OF.

(g) Are unnecessary prepositional phrases eliminated? See PREPOSITIONS and CONCISENESS.

(h) Is the text generally concise? See CONCISENESS.

4. STYLE.

(a) Is style consistently objective or persuasive, depending upon the purpose of the text? See OBJECTIVE WRITING and PERSUASIVE WRITING.

(b) Is the TONE and level of formality appropriate and consistent?

Try to give each of these categories your full attention for the specific amount of time you have parcelled for the task. Then take a break between categories, even if it is to walk around the room or get a drink of water. Trying to do all tasks at once is overwhelming; by separating them and doing each in a short period of time, you will also actually save time. Then, when you have finished revising, you can move on to POLISHING.

REVISING THE WRITING OF OTHERS
See EDITING OTHER PEOPLE'S WRITING.

REWRITING
Rewriting follows the writing stage in the WRITING PROCESS, and it addresses large-scale organization and logic. This is the stage where criticism takes over from creativity and starts moving the text from the writer-oriented first draft toward a reader-oriented final draft.

Rewriting should be done separately from PREWRITING, WRIT-ING, REVISING, and POLISHING. The most common mistake most writers make, one that costs them hours and hours, is to rewrite and write simultaneously. This forces the id of creative thought to work simultaneously with the super-ego of correction, an impossible and insufferable pairing.

Separate the two by first writing all at once and then stopping. Let the draft sit, even if it is for a few hours, or even if parts of it are sitting while other parts are getting rewritten.

Then, in the rewriting stage, set aside a substantial amount of time to make sure that all possible ideas appear in the draft and that the content is accurate and thorough. You may find at this stage that you add to your first draft to cover all the possible ideas.

Rewrite by concentrating on content, ideas, information, and OR-GANIZATION. Make sure all the large parts of the analysis are present and in a logical order.

The following checklist can guide your revision in BRIEFS, MEMOS, and OPINION LETTERS. For other kinds of documents, see GENERAL CORRESPONDENCE LETTERS; CASE BRIEFS; CON-TRACTS, DRAFTING; and other specific entries.

1. Content and ideas.

   (a) Is the law right?

   (b) Have I included all the relevant constitutional provisions, stat-utes, or cases?

   (c) Have I considered the strengths and weaknesses of both sides' arguments?

   (d) Have I balanced those strengths and weaknesses against each other?

   (e) Have I included all the steps in my REASONING?

   (f) Have I included all the LEGALLY SIGNIFICANT FACTS?

   (g) Have I included the essential BACKGROUND FACTS?

   (h) Have I included the significant EMOTIONAL FACTS?

   (i) Have I considered all the possible issues?

   (j) Have I reached a prediction or asked for a specific result?

2. Large-scale organization. (See ORGANIZATION, LARGE–SCALE.)

   (a) Do I have a logical organization?

   (b) Have I put threshold issues first?

   (c) Have I given the answer first and then the explanation?

   (d) If writing persuasively, have I organized the issues in the most persuasive order, putting the strongest first, the second strongest last, and the weakest in the middle, unless logical organization precludes doing this?

   (e) Can any legal reader follow my logic?

(f) Have I used POSITIONS OF EMPHASIS well?

Use this stage to make sure that all the parts of your analysis are present, that no major steps are missing, and that your arguments are built from the ground up. When you are satisfied that everything needed is present and in an overall logical order, move on to REVISING.

RHETORICAL QUESTIONS

Rhetorical questions, which have either an obvious answer or no answer, usually irritate legal readers and invite them to question your point. Therefore, avoid them. Ask questions only in your ISSUE STATEMENTS or QUESTION PRESENTED; give the answers to those questions in your ARGUMENT SECTION or DISCUSSION SECTION. To make a rhetorical point, state it in declarative sentence form.

RHYMES

Avoid them in legal writing unless you intend to be humorous and the humor is appropriate to the content. You may, however, use ALLITERATION if you use it with discretion.

ROUGH DRAFTS

See WRITING and WRITING PROCESS.

RULES

Legal rules are statements of law that provide the structure for legal analysis. As such, they follow a hierarchy of authority. Thus, if a constitutional provision is involved in your issues, it should be discussed first. If a statute is involved, it should come next, or first if no constitutional provision is involved. Case law comes last. If there is no constitutional provision or statute, then case law provides the rules. Consider the following in presenting the rules.

1. Place rules at the beginning of your DISCUSSION SECTION, ARGUMENT SECTION, or explanation in OPINION LETTERS.

Because legal rules provide the structure for your analysis or argument, the legal reader needs to know those rules right away. Similarly, the reader needs to know the rule's source, so cite accurately and thoroughly.

All citizens are protected from unreasonable searches not only in their homes, but wherever they have a right to be. Wash. Const. art. I, § 7.

The Plaintiff's recovery is barred when the plaintiff's negligence exceeds the defendant's negligence. Or. Rev. Stat. § 18.470 (1994).

Jury misconduct occurs when a juror supplies information to other jurors that is outside the recorded evidence of the trial and not subject to the protections and limitations of court proceedings. Salverson v. Anderson, 99 Wash. 2d 746, 752, 913 P.2d 827, 830 (1993).

2. Decide how case law presents a rule.

For example, a case may explicitly state the definitive rule; if so, you may cite the case singly as the source of that rule. Or several cases may be synthesized to form the rule; if so, you must cite those cases separately, each standing for a proposition that contributes to the rule. Finally, several cases may provide a rule plus exceptions; if so, you should cite the case giving the rule first, with the cases giving exceptions after.

3. In constructing your rule from cases, synthesize when needed.

Synthesizing a rule means pulling pieces from several cases together. Courts do not always state these rules because they rule on specific factual situations and thus do not need to pull the larger rule together. As a result, you must try to do the synthesizing yourself when the courts have not done it. To do this, step back from the pieces and try to see the larger picture. Then characterize that picture in your own words as a topic sentence. (See TOPIC SENTENCES.) Follow this sentence with the sections of the cases that create this picture, and give appropriate citations.

4. When constructing a rule from cases, include exceptions.

Remember that any rule may have exceptions so, after making sure that the rule and its source are clear to the reader, follow with the exceptions.

5. Check for ACCURACY and LOGICAL LINKS.

Your presentation of the law outlines the structure of your entire analysis, argument, or explanation, so make sure the rules are accurately presented. Check for logical links between subparts, so that the reader knows exactly how the rule works when applied. Then you are ready to follow this logic in applying the rules to the facts of your analysis.

SALUTATIONS

The salutation is the line beginning with **Dear** that traditionally introduces the text of a letter. There are three common questions about salutations: (1) whether to include them, (2) how to write them when you do not know the sex of the reader, and (3) whether to punctuate them with commas or semicolons.

1. Including or omitting the salutation.

In general, include the salutation. Some writers omit the salutation in business letters, substituting instead a subject line, and this is not technically wrong. Omitting the salutation, however, makes the letter seem rather abrupt and impersonal, which is not the tone you usually want in a letter. For more on this generally, see TONE IN LETTERS.

2. Writing non-sexist openings.

If you do not know the sex of the person to whom you are writing, substitute the name without a title of **Mr.** or **Ms.**

Dear D. A. Young:

Dear Terry Holmes:

If you do not know the name, use the person's title or some appropriate generic term.

Dear Administrator:

Dear Client:

If you cannot come up with a generic term, you may use the following.

Dear Sir or Madam:

Use **Dear Sir** only when you are sure the reader is male.

3. Choosing commas or colons.

Use colons in business writing. If you are writing something that is a social courtesy, such as a thank you note or an expression of congratulations, you may use a comma. A colon would also be appropriate, except in a note that is much more personal than businesslike in tone.

SARCASM

Do not use sarcasm in legal writing; it is too easy for the reader to take it literally. Even if the reader catches your sarcastic TONE, that tone is usually inappropriate in legal writing. In general, sarcasm is only effective when writing to readers who already whole-heartedly agree with your position.

SCARCELY

Scarcely is an adverb that means **barely** or **assuredly not**. As such it has a negative meaning and should not follow another negative.

The defendant could scarcely deny the charges.

rather than

The defendant couldn't scarcely deny the charges.

Place **scarcely** just before the word or group of words that it modifies.

The defendant heard the pronouncement of sentence with scarcely a change in demeanor.

rather than

The defendant heard the pronouncement of sentence scarcely with a change in demeanor.

SECTION

Section should always be spelled out in text and when it begins a sentence. For further reference, see Blue Book rule (6.2(b)). If you have the symbol § on your typewriter or word processor, use that symbol in footnotes and cites. Use **s.** or **sec.** only if your jurisdiction permits.

SELF– OR SELF?

Use **self-** when adding it as a prefix to another noun: **self-interest, self-serving,** and **self-sufficient** Use **self** as the first syllable in words such as **selflessness, selfish,** and **selfsame.** For related information, see HYPHENS.

SEMICOLONS

Semicolons have two uses.

1. You may use a semicolon instead of a period between two sentences if those sentences are closely related logically but could each stand as complete sentences.

The Plaintiff did not intend to destroy another's property; he broke the window only because he saw flames inside the house.

Avoid, however, allowing yourself to use semicolons without clarifying the logical relationship of your points.

This action violated Tremont's rights to both freedom of speech and due process.

rather than

This case involves not only freedom of speech, but also due process; each of these issues indicates that Tremont's rights were violated.

Do not use a comma between two independent clauses unless a conjunction such as **and** follows the comma. This error occurs frequently when **however** connects the clauses.

Cutts denied being at the scene of the crime; however, he admitted having been there two hours earlier.

rather than

Cutts denied being at the scene of the crime, however, he admitted having been there two hours earlier.

2. You must use a semicolon, instead of a comma, at the end of each element in a list if a comma occurs within any one element in the list.

The Company warrants for one year that its compressors (1) are free from defects in material and workmanship; (2) have the capacities and rating set forth in the Company's catalogs, provided that no warranty is made against corrosion, erosion, or deterioration; and (3) meet all relevant federal safety standards.

The Company is not liable for any delay in performance due to any of the following:

(1) any act of God, including but not limited to floods, epidemics, fires, storms, or earthquakes;

(2) any acts of others beyond the reasonable control of the Company, including but not limited to strikes or other labor disturbances, riots, wars, acts of civil or military authority, or acts of the Customer; and

(3) any cause beyond its reasonable control, including but not limited to delays in transportation, inability to obtain necessary materials or components, or labor shortages.

The semicolon helps the reader see where each item on the list begins and ends.

Do not use a semicolon at the end of each element in a list solely because the list is tabulated rather than run in text. Commas are still sufficient if there are no commas within any of the items listed.

"Remanufacturing equipment" included the following processes:

(1) disassembly to a predetermined standard established by the Manufacturer for each model,

(2) cleaning,

(3) refinishing,

(4) inspecting and testing to new machine test standards,

(5) installation of all retrofits, and

(6) operational testing.

For related information, see CLARITY; TRANSITIONS; HOWEVER; and LISTS, STRUCTURE OF.

SENTENCE LENGTH

In general, avoid making sentences longer than three lines of text. The one exception to this is sentences containing lists, which are easier to read because of their more obvious structure.

A doctor may forego disclosure to his patient if any of the following situations occur: (1) if the patient is unconscious, incompetent, or otherwise incapable of understanding the information; (2) if the patient is a minor; (3) if in the doctor's opinion the information would have a disproportionately adverse reaction on the patient's ability to make a rational decision; or (4) if an emergency exists which allows no time to safely consult with the patient.

One handy way to check sentence length is to scan several pages of your text and mark slashes after each period, which you can do without actually reading the text. Then look at the slashes. If you see several sentences in a row that run more than four lines, try to shorten at least one.

Similarly, if you see several sentences in a row that are one line long, try to combine two of them or make some other changes. This will help avoid a choppy tone. Occasionally, however, you may want this choppy effect.

The major purpose of the trial court's established procedure is to give the litigants a fair opportunity to address their claims and have them resolved by a court of law. *That purpose was met here.* *The litigants had eight*

190

years of opportunity. In this context, their arguments on appeal are particularly specious. . . .

For related information, see SENTENCE STRUCTURE; SHORT SENTENCES; and TOUGH, SOUNDING THAT WAY.

SENTENCE, PARTS OF

Knowing the parts of a sentence can help you understand SENTENCE STRUCTURE, which in turn can help you write sentences that convey your meaning clearly and emphasize your points effectively. If you have trouble understanding other entries because you have trouble identifying such things as verbs or indirect objects, this quick overview may help. If you want more detailed explanations, see a grammar handbook, such as W. Ebbitt & D. Ebbitt, *Writer's Quick Index to English* (Scott, Foresman 7th ed. 1982).

1. Verb.

Each sentence has at least one verb. The verb expresses either an action, such as **hit** or **received**, or a state of being, such as **is** or **seemed**. The verb may be one word, such as **signed** or **appeared**, or more than one word, such as **must complete** or **will have been signed**. When the verb contains more than one word, it is called a **verb phrase**.

The following verbs express an action.

Faulkner *signed* a waiver of rights form.

All nonresidents living in Illinois for more than three months of a calendar year *must complete* the following section.

The defendant *agreed*.

The contract *will have been signed* by that date.

The trial court *determined* that the defendant's statements were voluntary and *admitted* them at trial.

The following verbs express a state of being.

The settlement *seems* reasonable in light of the facts.

The plaintiff *is* a former employee of Stills, International.

The defendant's statements *were* voluntary.

For more information see VERB TENSES; VERBS, AUXILIARY; VERBS, IRREGULAR; VERBS, LINKING; VERBS, MOODS; or VERBS, PARTICIPLES.

2. Subject.

Each sentence has at least one subject. The complete subject is the person, thing, or idea about which the verb speaks, and may be one word or many.

Faulkner signed a waiver of rights form.

All nonresidents living in Illinois for more than three months of a calendar year must complete the following section.

The defendant agreed.

The contract will have been signed by that date.

The trial court determined that the defendant's statements were voluntary and admitted them at trial.

The settlement seems reasonable in light of the facts.

The plaintiff is a former employee of Stills, International.

The defendant's statements were voluntary.

The simple subject is the main word in the complete subject.

3. Predicate.

Each sentence has a predicate. The predicate is the part of the sentence that says something about the subject.

All nonresidents living in Illinois for more than three months of a calendar year *must complete the following section.*

The defendant *agreed.*

The trial court *determined that the defendant's statements were voluntary and admitted them at trial.*

The contract *will have been signed by that date.*

The settlement *seems reasonable in light of the facts.*

The plaintiff *is a former employee of Stills, International.*

The defendant's statements *were voluntary.*

Every predicate includes at least one verb, and it may include any or all of the following: direct objects, indirect objects, prepositional phrases, and participial phrases.

4. Direct Object.

A direct object is the person, object, or idea receiving the action of the verb.

The plaintiff built *the house* with his own hands.

Faulkner signed *a waiver* of rights form.

The defendant's action destroyed *that right.*

All sentences have a subject and predicate, but not all have a direct object.

5. Indirect Object.

An indirect object receives the direct object, rather than the action of the verb.

The plaintiff gave *the defendant* the house when she agreed to cohabit.

Here, **the defendant** received the house, and thus is the indirect object. **The house** is the direct object, because it was the object of the verb, **gave.** Not all sentences have an indirect object.

6. Prepositional Phrase.

A prepositional phrase is a group of words that work together to show the relationship of a noun or pronoun to the rest of the sentence.

This noun or pronoun is called the object of the preposition. A preposition, which is always the first word in a prepositional phrase, shows how the rest of that phrase is logically related to the sentence. Examples of prepositions are **of, to, on, off, between, through, in, at, without, over,** and **under.** The following examples of prepositional phrases illustrate the variety of information they can convey.

He built the house *with his own hands.*

All nonresidents living *in Illinois for more than three months of a calendar year* must complete the following section.

The contract will have been signed *by that date.*

The settlement seems reasonable *in light of the facts.*

7. Participial Phrase.

A participial phrase is a group of words that work together to show the relationship of some action to the rest of the sentence. A participle, which is always the first word in a participial phrase, is either the **-ed** or **-ing** form of a regular verb, (**followed, following, covered, covering**) or the past tense or **-ing** form of an irregular verb (**held, holding**). The following examples illustrate how participial phrases can be used in a sentence.

The boat, *built by Mr. Tremat,* should not be considered community property.

The attorney focused her argument on this issue, *building carefully on these facts.*

Covered by snow, the edge of the ditch was not visible.

The statute *covering this issue* is unambiguous.

This right, *held inviolate since the founding of our country,* must not now be extinguished.

Any court *holding on this issue* must address the elements of the statute.

8. Clause.

A clause is a group of words that includes both a subject and a predicate.

subject   predicate
The trial court determined this issue.

In contrast, a phrase does not include both a subject and a predicate.

a case of first impression

determining this issue

There are two kinds of clauses: independent (or main) and dependent. An independent clause can be set off as a sentence by itself.

The defendant knew or should have known this.

The company gave a free water heater to residential customers.

Every sentence must include at least one independent clause.

A dependent clause cannot by itself form a sentence because it begins with a subordinating conjunction and thus is logically dependent on an independent clause.

that the plaintiff would not be aware of the stock market usage of the phrase "passed its dividends"

who installed electric space heating

Therefore, make sure all dependent clauses are part of a larger sentence including an independent clause.

The defendant knew or should have known that the plaintiff would not be aware of the stock market usage of the phrase "passed its dividends."

rather than

The defendant knew or should have known. That the plaintiff would not be aware of the stock market usage of the phrase "passed its dividends."

The company gave a free water heater to residential customers who installed electric space heating.

rather than

The company gave a free water heater to residential customers. Who installed electric space heating.

For related information, see SENTENCE STRUCTURE.

SENTENCE STRUCTURE

Mastering the basics of sentence structure provides a valuable tool for effective writing. After you learn how to change the structure of a sentence, you can use that skill to emphasize or de-emphasize points, to increase READABILITY, to change the TONE of your text, and to clarify TRANSITIONS between paragraphs and sentences. For help identifying the grammatical parts of a sentence, see SENTENCE, PARTS OF.

What follows are explanations of four basic sentence structures (subsections 1–4) and examples and explanations of ways you can exploit those basics to create sentences that are both readable and effective (subsections 5–7). For more detail about sentence structure, consult a grammar handbook, such as J. Hodges & M. Whitten, *Harbrace College Handbook* (Harcourt Brace Jovanovich 9th ed. 1982).

1. Simple Sentence.
Grammatically, this sentence includes only one set of SUBJECTS and VERBS, although it may have many modifying phrases.

     S   V
This case involves three issues.

     S   S   V
Mr. Smith and his attorney will confer on the matter tomorrow.

```
         S          S      V            V
```
The defendant and his wife ransacked the house and took items worth $3,000.

Strategically, use a simple sentence that has only a few words, usually fewer than ten, if you want the dramatic impact that a simple sentence can have.

The Court of Appeals refused to consider this argument because it "was not properly . . . presented to the trial court." *The court did not elaborate.*

2. Compound Sentence.

This structure includes two or more independent clauses joined by a conjunction, semicolon, or colon. An independent clause could be set off as a sentence by itself.

```
S    V                        conjunction        S   V
```
There can be no negligence without duty, and in this case there is no duty.

```
S    V                        semicolon          S    V
```
There can be no negligence without duty; in this case, no duty exists.

```
              S                   V  colon S  V
```
In this case, one element of negligence is missing: there is no duty.

This structure can create a one-two punch. This effect will be stronger if second of the joined sentences is short. For related information, see CONJUNCTIONS, SEMICOLONS, and COLONS.

3. Complex Sentence.

In a complex sentence, one or more DEPENDENT CLAUSES are inserted into another sentence, which is the independent clause.

dependent clause

Because more married women entered the labor market as second earners,

independent clause

more married couples were subject to the tax penalty.

The independent clause includes the main subject, verb, and object of the sentence. Because this is the structural heart of the sentence, you want to put your main information here.

More married couples were subject to the tax penalty.

Often you will want to use dependent clauses to add some background information, elaboration, or other less important points to the sentence. A dependent clause cannot by itself form a sentence because it begins with a subordinating word and thus is logically dependent on an independent clause.

because more married women entered the labor market as second earners

The complex sentence is useful because it allows the writer to show the logical interrelationship of two or more points while giving more emphasis to one point. As a result, the complex sentence is common in legal writing. To use it effectively, however, you must keep the complex sentence readable and logically structured.

This court interpreted this statute broadly in previous cases, when it applied the statute to parents of minor children, trustees of the estates of handicapped adults, and foster parents.

rather than

This court, when it in previous cases applied the statute to parents of minor children, trustees of the estates of handicapped adults, and foster parents, interpreted this statute broadly.

Avoid using complex sentences exclusively; also exploit the strengths of simple and compound sentences. Too many complex sentences make the text less interesting, because VARIETY is lacking. If all your sentences are complex, try restructuring some important points into simple sentences.

Also avoid overdoing the complexity of the sentence. In general, do not insert more than two dependent clauses in one sentence; doing so gives the reader a bite too big to chew. If you decide you must show the logical interrelationship of more actions, try putting those actions in separate sentences and using a connecting word or phrase that explains that logical interrelationship.

Waivers of constitutional rights not only must be voluntary; they must also be knowing, intelligent acts done with sufficient awareness of the relevant circumstances and likely consequences. Breckenridge v. United States, 900 U.S. 321, 323 (1992). Furthermore, waiver of the right to counsel cannot be presumed from a silent record. Kelstad v. Karney, 969 U.S. 506, 516 (1992).

For more on the use of the complex sentence, see subsection 7. For help connecting two sentences, see TRANSITIONS and CONNECTIONS, MAKING THEM.

4. Inverted sentence.
One final structure you can use occasionally is the inverted sentence. In this structure, some part of the predicate, such as the object of the verb, comes before the subject.

Imprudent it was, but not illegal.

rather than

It was imprudent, but not illegal.

In the inverted version of this sentence, the predicate adjective, **imprudent** is placed before the subject, **it**, rather than after the linking verb **was**. The inverted sentence is dramatic precisely because the parts of the sentence are out of their usual order. It is so dramatic, however, that it is hard to find an occasion to use it in legal writing without sounding self-conscious, as would be the case if someone said, **While coming to work today, an old friend I saw.**

5. Using subjects and verbs effectively.

   Put your main point in the main subject and verb in your sentence. Conversely, de-emphasize points by putting them in DEPENDENT CLAUSES. For example, the following sentence emphasizes **he had slowed and was not accelerating** by making that the main subject and verb.

   Although the defendant had not come to a full stop at the official stop sign, he had slowed to less than five miles per hour and was not accelerating at the time of the accident.

6. Choosing the best sentence structure.

   In general, vary your sentence structure. This VARIETY should come naturally, however, out of the logical structures needed by your content. Never use a sentence structure that goes against the logical structure of your content. To do so is tantamount to signalling that you plan to move to the right lane on a freeway and then moving to the left lane instead. Even if the reader manages to keep up with you, that reader will be distrustful and unhappy. For more help in determining what structure fits your content, see subsection 7.

7. Inserting information in a sentence.

   Although the unmodified, simple sentence is strong and effective, you will usually need to add more to the sentence because you need to add more information. There are three places where these extra phrases can be inserted.

   (a) Insert extra phrases after the independent clause.

   This inflationary effect was especially marked for two-earner married couples, *whose income is aggregated for tax purposes.*

   Triavil offered no treatment or cure for tension headaches, *as testified by Dr. Paul Wyles* (R. 1159).

   The minority arrived at the same conclusion, *although for different reasons.*

   This structure is the mainstay of communication because it is the easiest for the reader to follow. For example, in the following sentence you understand the point immediately because you get the independent clause right away, before getting the elaboration.

   I saw an old friend while coming to work today.

   As such, this structure is useful for presenting routine information that needs no special emphasis.

   This inequity affected more people in the early 80's when more married women entered the labor market.

   It is also useful for presenting information that is complex and thus must be presented in a simple form.

Unmarried individuals paid substantially greater taxes than married individuals between 1948 and 1969, in some cases more than 40% in excess of a married individual's tax on an identical income.

(b) Insert extra phrases before the independent clause.

Until recently, others have supported inserting legislative veto provisions in statutes covering most agency rulemaking.

Despite the difficulty of this test, the gravity of the situation required that it be done.

This structure, a mainstay of storytellers, is useful when you want to create a touch of suspense. For example, after reading the following sentence, you expect more after hearing the introductory phrase.

While coming to work today, I saw an old friend.

The change in structure alone tells the reader that this is the beginning of a story. You might use this touch of suspense to present either facts or an argument.

Pointing the gun at the teller, the defendant ordered her to fill the bag with cash.

Because there was no timely notice, this opportunity for hearing provided no opportunity at all.

Additionally, placing information before the independent clause is a useful way to provide a transition at the beginning of a paragraph. In the following example, the information placed at the beginning of the paragraph both reminds the reader of the topic of the previous paragraph and shows the reader how that topic relates to this paragraph.

Environmental Impact Studies could be handled similarly, without delaying the hearing.

Even if there were some delay, that delay would present no procedural difficulties.

Finally, placing information in a dependent clause before the independent clause can signal to the reader that the added information is less important than the independent clause.

Although there are three kinds of marital status discrimination, this comment focuses only on the marriage penalty.

This structure can be useful when you need to include an unfavorable fact and you want to make that fact seem as unimportant as possible.

Although Mr. Allerton was in the room during the signing of the will, he was there only because it was his habit to sit in the living room while reading the evening paper.

(c) Insert extra information in the middle of the independent clause.

Anorexics, *by failing to eat*, passively expose themselves to harm.

This structure, a tool of orators, creates a very formal tone. For example, the following sentence sounds rather stuffy.

I, while coming to work today, saw an old friend.

This structure is harder to read because to understand the main point the reader must remember the first part of the sentence, read the interrupting clause, and then reunite the last part of the sentence with the first in his or her memory. Therefore, avoid using the structure in sentence after sentence; give the reader breathing space between these difficult sentences. Also, avoid allowing the interruption to exceed seven words. After that long an interruption, the reader would have to reread the sentence to get the point.

The burden is on the defendant to show, not just that the tax is excessive, but also that the defendant was taxed for more than its fair share.

These issues, controversial but crucial, must be resolved by this court.

Dr. Barnard, who attended the plaintiff immediately after the accident, has testified that her internal injuries were caused by the faulty seatbelts.

For information in problems associated with long interruptions, see AGREEMENT, SUBJECTS AND VERBS.

SENTENCES, MAIN
See TOPIC SENTENCES.

SENTENCES WITH "AND"
See SENTENCE STRUCTURE, subsection 2 on compound sentences; LISTS, STRUCTURE OF; and COMMAS.

SETTLEMENT LETTERS
A settlement letter is a letter written to encourage a party to settle a case. It is usually written by one client's attorney and directed to the other client's attorney. A settlement letter is designed to inform the reader of the writer's argument and to persuade the reader to accept that argument. Consider the following in writing a settlement letter.

1. Choose the approach you think is most likely to influence the other attorney. For example, if you think the attorney can be persuaded gently, you might want to begin with a friendly opening, show you have considered the other side, and then build your argument, leading to the settlement offer. If you think this attorney would be more convinced by a stronger opening, start with the offer of settlement. For related information, see PERSUASIVE WRITING and AUDIENCE.

2. Make sure the attorney knows that you understand the other client's position. For example, if the client and attorney have already

offered a settlement, remind them that you are aware of that offer, of how much it was, and that you are grateful for the offer.

3. Choose a TONE appropriate to the method of persuasion, such as tough if you expect unreasonable opposition, or friendly if you want them to be convinced that your offer is fair. For more information, see TONE IN LETTERS.

4. Follow a format that includes the following, adjusting the order and content to suit your purpose, tone, and audience:

(a) a heading,

(b) a salutation,

(c) an introduction that identifies the settlement purpose of the letter,

(d) your terms for settlement and the reasoning behind them,

(e) a course of action on the settlement matter,

(f) a specific directive to the attorney to call you or answer your offer of settlement,

(g) a closing. For help here, see CLOSINGS FOR LETTERS.

See also GENERAL CORRESPONDENCE LETTERS, PERSUA-SIVE WRITING, OPINION LETTERS, and TONE IN LETTERS.

SEXIST LANGUAGE, WAYS TO AVOID

The first thing to remember when avoiding sexist language is that it is legitimate and even desirable to use **he** or **she** when you are talking about a specific person, as you usually are in BRIEFS or MEMOS. Sexist language here would be to use **he** when referring to a woman or **she** when referring to a man.

Sometimes, however, you will be discussing general principles that apply to all persons. When a singular pronoun is needed in that situation, use **he or she**, or **she or he** if you prefer. If you find yourself awash in **he or she's**, you can use any of three techniques to avoid the pronoun problem.

1. Reword the phrase to omit the pronoun.

Anyone desiring a position with this firm should submit a resumé at the interview.

rather than

Anyone desiring a position with this firm should submit his or her resumé at the time of his or her interview.

2. Substitute **one** throughout the text.

One cannot apply for a loan if one does not have collateral.

rather than

A person cannot apply for a loan if he or she does not have collateral.

This technique, however, is hard to use gracefully. It often creates phrasing as awkward as the original **he or she**.

3. In general discussions, such as in law review articles, refer to people in the plural so that you can substitute **they** for **he or she.**

All attorneys must adjust their trial strategies in response to this ruling.

rather than

Each attorney must adjust his or her trial strategies in response to this ruling.

Do not, however, resort to using a plural pronoun to refer to a singular noun.

Anyone desiring a position should submit a resumé.

rather than

Anyone desiring a position should submit their resumé.

This use of the plural pronoun is not only grammatically incorrect, but also dangerously ambiguous. For example, **each party should get their share** could result in either a **he** or **she** claiming someone else's share.

Do not resort to using S/HE. It is convenient for the writer but not for the reader, who will stumble slightly over the term, substituting **he or she** to read the sentence. Always write with the reader's convenience in mind, rather than your own.

If you find that nothing you try sounds graceful, choose the accurate **he or she** rather than the inaccurate **he.** In legal writing, a conflict between accuracy and elegance should always be resolved in favor of accuracy. For avoiding sexist language when beginning a business letter, see SALUTATIONS. For related information, see ACCURACY.

SHALL

In all legal writing except LEGISLATION, use **must** instead of **shall** to state that something must be done; use **may** when stating something that may be done. Legislation traditionally treats **shall** as establishing a requirement, and therefore **shall** is not ambiguous in that context. The general public, however, does not necessarily give **shall** this more specific reason. To them, **shall** is often an archaic or fancy version of **will.** They also may read **shall** as meaning either **must** or **may,** and thus it can be ambiguous.

S/HE

Resist the temptation. Use **he or she,** or **she or he** if you prefer. **S/he,** besides looking funny, is hard to read aloud, and anything that is hard to read aloud is hard to read silently. Write for the reader's convenience; the reader will be grateful. If **he or she** seems cumbersome to you, see SEXIST LANGUAGE, WAYS TO AVOID for other tactics.

SHEPARD'S

Shepard's Citations is indispensible for updating the law. *Shepard's* is the main resource book you can use to determine whether the source you are using has been overturned, distinguished, endorsed, or modified in any way. In other words, this lets you know if your source is still usable law. When using *Shepard's,* follow these steps.

1. Find the proper set of *Shepard's* in the library. For example, if you are updating a Third Circuit Decision, you should have *Shepard's Federal Citations.*

2. Make sure you have all the volumes; check the box in the lower right hand corner of the most recent volumes, which will tell you what volumes you need.

3. Find the correct tables, including the table for the parallel citation. For example, if you are using the *Minnesota Reporter* and shepardizing a Minnesota case, make sure you also shepardize its parallel citation in the *Northwest Reporter*; the tables are not identical.

4. Find the volume number of the statute, case, or law review article that you are using.

5. Find the beginning page or section number of that text.

6. Review the signals and the raised numbers. The signals, which are described in the beginning of each *Shepard's* volume, let you know if the case was subsequently overturned, if it has been distinguished from other cases, if there is a dissenting opinion, and so forth. The raised numbers refer to the specific HEADNOTES in the published case.

7. Note that there are differences in *Shepard's* for the type of law you might be sheparizing. For example, cases, statutes, regulations, law review articles, ordinances, court rules, city charters, and constitutions are all shepardized differently. Inspect the set you are using for specific guidelines.

See also RESEARCH STRATEGY, step 8; and UPDATING THE LAW. For more extensive detail in Shepardizing, see C. Wren & J. Wren, *The Legal Research Manual: A Game Plan for Legal Research and Analysis* (A–R Editions 2d ed. 1986).

SHORT SENTENCES

Short sentences provide one of the most effective ways to emphasize a point.

This was an error.

He failed to do so.

The Court of Appeals refused to consider this argument because it "was not properly . . . presented to the trial court." *The Court did not elaborate.*

Several short sentences in a row also create a clipped, no-nonsense tone.

My client, Ms. Ambrose, does not intend to pay this bill. She has no reason to pay this bill. She did not receive any software from your company. She did not order any software from your company. Until receiving your bill, she did not know your company existed.

Avoid using short sentences for unimportant points or using several short sentences in a row when you do not want a clipped or exasperated tone. This will help you avoid creating any unintended EMPHASIS.

For related information, see SENTENCE STRUCTURE and TOUGH, SOUNDING THAT WAY.

SHOULD

Should can be ambiguous when used to express a requirement. If you mean to state a requirement, use **must**. In LEGISLATION, you may use **shall**, although **must** would still be clear.

Should generally means that something should have been done and was not.

The police should have read him his Miranda rights before searching his car.

Should can also mean that something should happen in the future, but that the writer or speaker is not sure it will happen.

The contract should be ready by next Thursday.

To increase readability, avoid using **should** at the first of a sentence when you really mean **if**. While **if** is precise because it can only mean that what follows is an **if** . . . **then** situation, **should** is less precise because it can introduce either a question or an **if** . . . **then** situation.

For related information, see VERB TENSES.

SIC

This is a Latin word that means **thus** or **so**. It is used in quotations to indicate that a surprising or unintelligible word or phrase is not in fact a transcription error, but appeared in the original version. **Sic** is surrounded by brackets.

The police read defendant his Mirenda [sic] rights.

For related information, see PUNCTUATING QUOTES.

SIGNALS

Signals are used before CITATIONS as shorthand to indicate their exact use. As such, signals replace unnecessary text, such as **the court held that or another court also agreed that**.

The BLUE BOOK separates signals into four categories:

(1) signals that indicate support,

(2) signals that suggest a profitable comparison,

(3) signals that indicate contradiction, and

(4) signals that indicate background material.

Keep these four categories in mind and use the signals accordingly. For further reference, see Blue Book rule 2.2.

1. Signals that show supporting authority.

(a) [No signal] indicates that a cited authority states the proposition, is the source of a quotation, or is the authority referred to in text. This is the cite used most often to indicate the direct support for the authority used in legal analysis.

(b) **See** indicates that the cited authority directly supports the proposition but does not say it explicitly. Use **see** when the proposition in the text is not stated by the cited authority but follows from it.

(c) **E.g.,** indicates that the cited authority states the proposition and that other authorities also state the proposition, but citing them would not be helpful. This signal can also be used in combination with other signals, such as **see, e.g.,** or **but see, e.g.**

(d) **See also** indicates that the cited authority adds source material that supports the proposition. Use this signal when you have already cited an authority that supports your proposition and you want to add other cites. It is often good to use PARENTHETI-CALS after these additional cites.

(e) **Cf.** means that the authority supports a proposition different from the main proposition you have stated, but sufficiently like that authority to lend support. Because this comparison needs explanation, use a parenthetical here as well.

(f) **Accord** indicates that the cited authority directly supports the proposition, but in a way slightly different from that of the authority cited first. Use **accord** when you have two or more cases that are on point but you refer to only one specifically in the text. Introduce the others by **Accord**. For related information, see CITA-TIONS, STRING.

2. Signals that show a comparison favorable to your point.

Compare . . . [and] . . . **with** . . . [and] . . . indicates a comparison that will support or illustrate the proposition stated in text. Again, this needs explanation, so use parentheticals.

3. Signals that show contradicting authority.

(a) **Contra** indicates that the cited authority states the opposite of the proposition. Use this where you would have used [no signal] for support, that is, if this authority is exactly opposite to the proposition.

(b) **But see** indicates that this authority directly contradicts the proposition. This would be used where **See** would have been used for support.

For related information, see CITATIONS; CITATIONS, PARALLEL; and CITATIONS, STRING.

SIMPLE SENTENCE

A simple sentence includes only one set of SUBJECTS and VERBS, although it may have many modifying phrases.

```
     S      V
```
This case involves three issues.

```
     S              S     V
```
Mr. Smith and his attorney will confer on the matter tomorrow.

```
     S              S     V                 V
```
The defendant and his wife ransacked the house and took items worth $3,000.

Strategically, however, use a simple sentence that has only a few words, usually fewer than ten, if you want the dramatic impact that a simple sentence can have.

The Court of Appeals refused to consider this argument because it "was not properly . . . presented to the trial court." *The court did not elaborate.*

For related information, see SENTENCE STRUCTURE and SHORT SENTENCES.

SIMPLICITY

Simplicity has gained status in legal writing over the years, mostly because of the universal overload under which lawyers and judges operate; most legal readers want to finish the job and go home. Confine your presentation to the information essential to your case, nothing more and nothing less. Achieving the delicate balance between thoroughness and simplicity in your writing will win you respect and credibility.

To achieve simplicity, concentrate on (1) using TERMS OF ART and other KEY TERMS in subjects and verbs, (2) focusing issues specifically, (3) using clear and logical organization, (4) REVISING for CONCISENESS, and (5) using PLAIN ENGLISH, rather than LEGALESE or FLOWERY LANGUAGE. For specific suggestions, see REPETITION; PARAGRAPHS; WORD CHOICE; ORGANIZATION, SMALL–SCALE; ISSUE STATEMENTS; and SENTENCE STRUCTURE.

SINCE OR BECAUSE?

See BECAUSE OR SINCE?

SINGLE QUOTATION MARKS

Although writers in some other countries conventionally use single quotes ('___') instead of double quotes ("___"), the United States currently uses double quotes. Single quotes are used only for A QUOTE WITHIN A QUOTE.

For related information, see PUNCTUATING QUOTES.

SLANTED LANGUAGE
See EMOTIONAL LANGUAGE.

SLANG
Avoid using slang in legal writing because it is too informal and often too imprecise.

SLASH
The only time you should use a slash (/) in legal writing is when you are writing a form in which the person signing is to mark out the inappropriate word, as in **Mr./Ms./Mrs./Miss**. For related information, see AND/OR and SEXIST LANGUAGE, WAYS TO AVOID.

SMOOTHNESS
See COHERENCE, EMPHASIS, and CLARITY.

SO
So has several different meanings and thus must be used carefully to avoid potential ambiguity. For example, when used as a conjunction, **so** can introduce a clause stating a consequence of the point stated before **so**.

The defendant was in the hospital at the time, so he could not have been at the meeting.

When **so** introduces a clause stating a consequence, substitute **and as a result** if **so** could be ambiguous.

The defendant was in the hospital at the time, and as a result he could not have been at the meeting.

So can also introduce a clause stating the purpose of the point stated before **so**.

Mrs. Williamson asked for the check to be mailed to her mother's home so her husband could not intercept it.

To avoid ambiguity, substitute **so that** when you are introducing a clause stating a purpose.

Mrs. Williamson asked for the check to be mailed to her mother's home so that her husband could not intercept it.

So may also intensify an adjective or adverb.

So serious was the oversight that, had it not been caught by Ms. Abrahams, it would have cost the company millions of dollars.

The car moved so slowly that it created a traffic hazard.

SOMEBODY

Use **someone** instead in formal legal writing because **somebody** sounds informal. Like **someone, somebody** is singular and takes a singular verb.

Somebody claims to have seen defendant elsewhere that night.

SOMEDAY OR SOME DAY?

Someday means at some future time; some day means a day in the past or the future.

SOMEONE

Someone is singular and uses a singular verb and a singular pronoun.

If someone needs to contact me, he or she should call this number.

SPECIFICITY

See PRECISION.

SPELLING PROBLEMS

See MISSPELLINGS, HOW TO AVOID.

SPLIT INFINITIVES

An infinitive consists of **to** plus the verb. The standard wisdom has been that one should always avoid splitting infinitives.

to move afterwards

rather than

to afterwards move

Because many of your readers will be of that opinion, avoid splitting infinitives when possible.

On rare occasions, however, a split infinitive will avoid ambiguities.

The mayor agreed to only suggest the alternative if the matter came up in committee meeting.

In this case, putting **only** before **to** would communicate that this was the only thing to which the mayor agreed.

The mayor agreed only . . . .

Putting **only** after **suggest** would communicate that this is the only alternative the mayor would suggest.

suggest only this alternative . . . .

When forced to make a choice like this, choose the clarity of the split infinitive over the elegance of the ambiguous unsplit version.

You may often find, however, that you can avoid the problem by restructuring the sentence altogether.

The mayor agreed that she would only suggest the alternative if the matter came up in the committee meeting. She would refrain from requesting it.

This is the safest route; your revised version will offend no one and still avoid ambiguity. For related information, see PRECISION; ACCURACY; and AMBIGUITY, WAYS TO AVOID.

STANDARD OF REVIEW

The standard of review is the standard by which appellate courts measure errors made by trial courts on specific legal issues. The standard of review differs with each legal issue and must therefore be discovered by researching that specific subject matter.

For example, an appellate court in one state might reverse a trial court in child custody matters if the trial court **abuses its discretion** by failing to make specific findings of fact under that state's statute. Derive the specific definition of the standard of review for your issues by examining the facts of each case in that subject area and determining the exact circumstances under which the court was willing to reverse the trial court. Those circumstances define what constitutes **abuse of discretion**.

In a similar case in another state, however, the appellate court might reverse the trial court only if the trial court has **manifestly abused** its discretion. Worse, your state may have two standards. This is because the term **standard of review** is relatively new and has only recently been singled out as a specific entity of analysis. If you find contradictory standards, inform the reader of the contradiction or choose that standard most recently used by the highest court in your state.

In writing an APPELLATE BRIEF, make sure you state for the court the standard of review for the issue you are appealing. Place the discussion of the standard of review at the beginning of each main section right after the point heading.

STATEMENT OF FACTS

This is one section in an objective memo. It may be placed either after the caption or after the QUESTION PRESENTED and Brief Answer. It contains both LEGALLY SIGNIFICANT FACTS and any BACKGROUND FACTS or EMOTIONAL FACTS needed to orient the reader to the information being analyzed in the memo. The writer may choose a chronological or topical organization, depending on the amount and kind of information to be presented. This section should be concise, giving only necessary information. For ways to do this, see CONCISENESS. For related information, see MEMOS, CAPTIONS, BRIEF ANSWERS, CHRONOLOGICAL ORGANIZATION, and TOPICAL ORGANIZATION.

STATEMENT OF THE CASE

The Statement of the Case section is used in persuasive legal writing, such as Memoranda of Points and Authorities, PRETRIAL BRIEFS, TRIAL BRIEFS, APPELLATE BRIEFS, or SETTLEMENT LETTERS. It is written in persuasive style and contains LEGALLY SIGNIFICANT FACTS, BACKGROUND FACTS, and EMOTIONAL FACTS. Often this section is divided into **Procedural History**, which outlines the procedural details of the case, and **Statement of Facts**, which gives the chronological or topical organization of the events leading to the motion, trial, settlement, or appeal. For related information, see PERSUASIVE WRITING, CHRONOLOGICAL ORGANIZATION, and TOPICAL ORGANIZATION.

STATUTE DRAFTING

See LEGISLATION.

STRING CITES

See CITATIONS, STRING.

STRUCTURE

See SENTENCE STRUCTURE or ORGANIZATION, LARGE-SCALE.

STUFFY LANGUAGE

See PLAIN ENGLISH, FLOWERY LANGUAGE, and TONE.

STYLE

In legal writing, style refers primarily to objective or persuasive style. The first appears in MEMOS and OPINION LETTERS, the second in BRIEFS and SETTLEMENT LETTERS.

Style is also used to refer to grammar rules, which have to be followed, such as rules regarding usage, PUNCTUATION, VERB TENSES, and SUBJECT–VERB AGREEMENT. See BENDING THE RULES.

Finally, style may refer to a writer's personal method of presentation, which has developed throughout his or her writing experience. As clothes reflect your personal tastes, so your written product reflects your personal level of formality, your choice of TONE, and your patterns of ORGANIZATION. For a discussion of aspects of writing that influence your style, see OBJECTIVE WRITING, PERSUASIVE WRITING, WORD CHOICE, POSITIONS OF EMPHASIS, SENTENCE STRUCTURE, TONE, and TONE IN LETTERS.

Focus on these aspects one at a time to become comfortable and versatile with each. Begin with the basics: sentence structure and word choice. As versatility develops with these basics, keep adding other skills to develop your objective, persuasive, and scholarly styles. Gradually, these skills will merge into a pattern that is your own style.

Do not, however, become preoccupied with the problem of developing or losing your personal style. Instead, focus on mastering the various aspects of good writing. From this seed of individual mastery, your personal style will blossom naturally and inevitably.

SUBHEADINGS
See POINT HEADINGS and HEADINGS.

SUBJECT
See SENTENCE, PARTS OF, subsection 2.

SUBJECT–VERB AGREEMENT
Sometimes, when the subject and verb are far apart in a sentence, the writer accidentally uses a plural verb with a singular subject, or a singular verb with a plural subject.

In the interviews, *each* of the many therapists currently finding their practice restricted by these recent holdings *is* [not *are*] less likely to be willing to treat these patients.

One good way to avoid having this happen is to avoid putting more than seven words between your subject and verb. This will not only help you avoid agreement problems, but will make your writing more readable. See READABILITY.

SUBJECT–VERB COMBINATIONS
Subject-verb combinations help move the legal reader along when they are specific and concrete; they halt and reverse the reader when they are vague and abstract. Because the subject and verb are the main part of the sentence, try to place important information in your subjects and verbs; concentrate especially on using TERMS OF ART and KEY TERMS. Do not waste subjects and verbs on information that is unimportant to the reader.

The *show-up I.D. negated* the effect of capturing the defendant one block from the crime.

rather than

The *court stated* that the show-up I.D. negated the effect of capturing the defendant one block from the crime.

In this example, the legal point is more important than the narration that the court stated it. Use a citation to give that information.

Also avoid abstract combinations like **it is, there is, there were**. Use nouns instead of those pronouns, specific verbs instead of those verbs of being.

False imprisonment occurs when a person is restrained without his or her consent.

rather than

There is false imprisonment when a person is restrained without his or her consent.

For related information, see CONCRETE NOUN, TERMS OF ART, and CONCISENESS.

SUBJUNCTIVE TENSES
See moods, subsection 2.

SUBORDINATING CONJUNCTIONS
See CONJUNCTIONS; EMPHASIS; SUBORDINATION; and BAD NEWS, SOFTENING IT.

SUBORDINATION
You are subordinating when you make one point in a sentence depend structurally on another point.

Although our client did not look both ways immediately before stepping into the street, this fact alone is not enough to constitute contributory negligence.

The writer here subordinates a fact that works against his case by placing it in a dependent clause beginning with **although**. Similarly, the following sentence downplays an unfavorable fact by putting it in a dependent clause beginning with **even though**.

Even though he had not come to a full stop at the stop sign, the defendant had slowed to less than five miles per hour and was not accelerating at the time of the accident.

See also SENTENCE, PARTS OF; BAD NEWS, SOFTENING IT; and EMPHASIS.

SUBSTANTIVE OR PROCEDURAL?
See PROCEDURAL OR SUBSTANTIVE?

SUMMARY OF THE ARGUMENT
The Summary of the Argument is a section used in long briefs to state the gist of the writer's arguments without making any references to authority. The purpose of this section is to pull together the writer's arguments without stopping the flow with references to details of authority. Thus at one glance the reader can understand the writer's argument.

A general rule for writing summaries is to use one paragraph per issue. Make sure you state the Summary of the Argument in your own words, as if you were making an oral presentation, rather than solely quoting cases.

Writing a Summary of the Argument can be a good way of GETTING STARTED. Even if this summary is not included in the final product, it can help you focus issues, answers, and explanations. For related information, see ISSUE STATEMENTS, BRIEFS, and APPELLATE BRIEFS.

SYLLOGISMS
A syllogism is a form of deductive reasoning that consists of a major premise, a minor premise, and a conclusion. It moves from general to specific.

Major premise: All dogs have four legs.

Minor premise: Spot is a dog.

Conclusion: Therefore Spot has four legs.

Syllogisms are similar to the logical structure used most often in legal writing. The major premise is created by the law itself, which is the rule or rules governing the specific situation. The minor premise is created by the application of RULES to the specific facts of the case being analyzed. The conclusion is the result, whether it be a prediction, as in a memo; a holding, as in opinion; or a request for relief, as in the ARGUMENT SECTION of a brief.

Major Premise: False imprisonment occurs when there are words or acts intended to confine, there is actual confinement, and there is awareness by the plaintiff that he or she is confined.

Minor Premise: Martin told Knight he intended to keep him in the car, he did keep Knight in the car for seven hours, and Knight knew he could not get out of the car.

Conclusion: Martin falsely imprisoned Knight.

When reading cases, make sure that you yourself understand the connection among all three parts. If the connections are faulty, these holes in the reasoning may allow you to distinguish the case from the case that you are advocating; you can then fill the holes according to your own reasoning and perhaps reach a different result.

When writing, make sure your reader understands the connections among these three parts. For more suggestions on how to build reasoning, see P. Schlag & D. Skover, *Tactics of Legal Reasoning* (Carolina Academic Press 1986). For writing techniques that help show the connections, see CONNECTIONS, MAKING THEM.

TACT
See BAD NEWS, GIVING IT; BAD NEWS, SOFTENING IT; TONE; and TONE IN LETTERS.

TAKING NOTES
See NOTES.

TENSES
See VERB TENSES.

TERMS OF ADDRESS FOR COURTS
See JUDGES, HOW TO ADDRESS.

TERMS OF ART
Terms of art are those terms used specifically in the law to describe legal theories, RULES, or doctrines. They are the words that carry the most weight in legal writing and the words on which the legal reader focuses. Because of their importance to the legal reader, terms of art should be used as subjects and verbs.

The Parol Evidence Rule prevents admission of this evidence.

Terms of art should also be used at POSITIONS OF EMPHASIS, such as the beginnings or ends of sentences.

Plaintiff brought an action under the theory of *res ipsa loquitur*.

The police escaped the strict requirements of the search and seizure rule by claiming that they were operating under *exigent circumstances*.

Washington is one of a minority of states to use the *Family Car Doctrine*.

Terms of art should always be used in the legal questions of QUESTIONS PRESENTED or ISSUE STATEMENTS. Make sure they are used precisely as intended under the authority specific to them.

Under the *exigent circumstances exception* to the Fourth Amendment, were police in "*hot pursuit*" when defendant had sold drugs to an undercover officer four hours before the search and had not left the premises?

Under Washington *tort* law, can a five-year-old commit an *intentional tort* when he pulls a chair away from an elderly lady who is in the process of sitting down?

Use Latin terms when they are terms of art, such as **res ipsa loquitur.** Do not, however, use them when they can be replaced by plain English. For example, use **before** rather than **a priori.** Similarly, terms such as **hereinafter** or **aforesaid**, are LEGALESE, not terms of art.

"THAT" NEEDED?
Omit **that** only if doing so will not confuse the reader.

Mr. Salovar agreed he would pay the overtime costs.

or

Mr. Salovar agreed that he would pay the overtime costs.

but

The court decided that the ruling was an abuse of discretion.

rather than

The court decided the ruling was an abuse of discretion.

213

If you have difficulty determining when the omission of that would confuse the reader, try the following test. First write the sentence without that.

The prosecution found the key here was the defendant's own admission.

Then put your finger over everything that comes after the first noun or pronoun following the verb. If the uncovered portion would not make sense by itself, you may omit that, as in the following example.

The defendant believed his safety procedures were adequate.

Here, **the defendant believed his safety procedures** would not make sense by itself, so that is not required.

If, however, the uncovered portion could make sense by itself to the reader but is incorrect, as in this example, you need to add that to avoid confusion.

The prosecution found that the key here was the defendant's own admission.

For related concerns, see THAT OR WHICH?

THAT OR WHICH?

Grammatically, there is a distinction between that and which, and that distinction can be crucial in legal writing. Confusion arises here because that is a restrictive pronoun, which introduces a phrase restricting the term that precedes it, but which can technically be either a restrictive or nonrestrictive pronoun. Using which as a restrictive pronoun thus causes ambiguity because the reader must guess which role the writer has chosen for which. To make your meaning absolutely clear, use that to restrict, which not to restrict.

1. Use that when you are introducing information that limits the definition of the word before that. This limiting information is a restrictive phrase.

All cars that remain in the lot after 10 p.m. will be towed.

Remain in the lot after 10 p.m. limits the definition of **cars** by saying exactly which ones will be towed. Do not put commas before or after a that phrase.

2. Use which when you are introducing information that is extra, not limiting. This extra information is a nonrestrictive phrase.

Your car, which was still in the lot at midnight, was towed.

The which phrase does not limit the definition of car. Your car, no one else's, was towed. Put commas both before and after a which phrase. The commas work like parentheses, showing that the phrase could be lifted from the sentence without changing the essential meaning. In summary, if a comma, which; if not a comma, that.

3. For ACCURACY, use both commas and which to distinguish nonlimiting phrases from limiting ones. If you do not, your sentences may suffer from AMBIGUITY.

The taxes, which have been paid, should not appear on this statement.

or

The taxes that have been paid should not appear on this statement.

rather than

The taxes which have been paid should not appear on this statement.

In the first version, all the taxes have been paid. In the second, some of the taxes have been paid. In the last version, however, you are not sure if all or part of the taxes have been paid.

Similarly, the last version of the following sentence could be ambiguous if two contracts existed.

The contract, which was signed on January 5, governs this transaction.

or

The contract that was signed on January 5 governs this transaction.

rather than

The contract which was signed on January 5 governs this transaction.

4. **Which** can be substituted for **that** when two **that's** appear in a row.

That which is good is not always pleasant; that which is pleasant is not always good.

rather than

That that is good is not always pleasant; that that is pleasant is not always good.

When possible, however, revise to avoid **that which**, which is rather awkward to read.

THE

Do not omit **the, a,** or **an** solely to gain conciseness.

The owner of the car gave the keys to Hendricks, who was supposed to move the car to a legal parking spot.

rather than

Owner of car gave keys to Hendricks, who was supposed to move car to legal parking spot.

Omitting these articles will give the text an abrupt tone, like a telegram, and will decrease the text's READABILITY.

THEIRS OR THEIR'S?

Theirs, always.

THERE IS . . . THAT

Omitting this phrase when you can do so creates a more concise sentence.

No cases address this issue directly.

rather than

There are no cases that address this issue directly.

Similarly, revise to omit it is . . . that and there are . . . that. For related information, see CONCISENESS.

THIS

This frequently creates ambiguity because it can refer to any idea or object and because it often starts a sentence.

You must ultimately make a judgment about the weight of the evidence. This judgment will help you decide what the verdict should be.

rather than

You must ultimately make a judgment about the weight of the evidence. This will help you decide what the verdict should be.

For related information, see AMBIGUITY, WAYS TO AVOID, subsection 2.

THOUGH OR ALTHOUGH?

See ALTHOUGH OR THOUGH?

TITLES OF JUDGES

See JUDGES, HOW TO ADDRESS.

TO ALL INTENTS AND PURPOSES

Find a shorter way to say this idea or omit the phrase. If the sentence needs something more, try to find one word that makes your point.

Therefore my client is innocent.

rather than

To all intents and purposes, my client is innocent.

TONE

Tone communicates the writer's point of view, or attitude toward the reader and the subject matter. Choose a tone appropriate for the medium, such as objective for office memos, persuasive for briefs, friendly for informative client letters, or stern for tough settlement letters. Then choose words and sentence structures to convey that tone. For more specific information, see also TONE IN LETTERS.

Tone is established and conveyed through attention to many details. As the following subsections explain, you can convey tone through (1) WORD CHOICE by choosing the appropriate subjects, verbs, and MODIFIERS; by choosing appropriate TERMS OF ADDRESS; and by choosing words that have the appropriate emotional overtone and level of formality. You can also convey tone through (2) SENTENCE STRUCTURE by making effective use of active and PASSIVE VOICE and POSITIONS OF EMPHASIS, and by choosing appropriate SENTENCE LENGTH, SUBJECT–VERB COMBINATIONS, and various kinds of SENTENCE STRUCTURE.

1. Conveying tone through word choice.

    (a) Choose appropriate subjects, verbs, and MODIFIERS. For example, in MEMOS, when you want to convey an objective and businesslike tone, use TERMS OF ART as subjects and verbs to keep the text focused on the issue being analyzed.

    The *Family Car Doctrine holds* parents liable for their child's negligence.

    Keep modifiers to a minimum, and then use only factual, specific information.

    Jamison grasped Hendricks by the arm and led him to the door.

    rather than

    Jamison rudely grasped the unfortunate Hendricks by the left arm and inexorably led him slowly to the battered wooden door.

    In BRIEFS, when you want to convey a persuasive and more assertive tone, retain terms of art as subjects and verbs to help the reader focus on your point. But also use stronger subjects and verbs when stating favorable facts, that is, subjects and verbs that give the reader a vivid picture of those facts.

    Jamison grasped Hendricks left arm and pulled him slowly toward the door.

    When stating unfavorable facts, use weaker, more abstract subjects and verbs.

    The defendant then took Hendricks by the arm and moved to the door.

    Also use modifiers with subtle emotional connotations that favor your position.

    Muttering threats, Jamison grasped Hendrick's bruised left arm and pulled him slowly toward the door.

    But do not overdo, or you may hamper your credibility.

    (b) Choose the appropriate terms of address.

    In a memo or brief, you want to avoid terms of address that refer to yourself or the reader because the focus should be on the legal issues and the parties rather than on the attorneys or judges.

    Granting a summary judgment is not justifiable in this case.

    rather than

    You must not grant a summary judgment because these facts preclude it.

    In a letter to a client, however, you will often want to refer to yourself and the reader because you are indeed speaking as one person to another.

    At our meeting on Tuesday, April 11, you asked me to give you a legal opinion on whether . . . .

    rather than

In response to the request made on Tuesday, April 11, for an opinion on whether . . . .

If you avoid all personal references in letters, you create a distant, cold tone. You may want to use this cold tone occasionally, as in a tough SETTLEMENT LETTER, but it is not wise to use it with your current clients. For related information, see TOUGH, SOUNDING THAT WAY.

(c) Choose the appropriate level of formality.

In general, use more formal language in official documents, such as BRIEFS or OPINION LETTERS, because you want to sound respectful and serious. Use less formal language in other writing, such as MEMOS or GENERAL CORRESPONDENCE LETTERS, where you want to be readable and avoid being stuffy. For example, you might say the following in a conference with another attorney.

Helen Thomas bought her computer at the local Apex store.

But you might write it this way in a brief.

Ms. Thomas purchased her computer at Apex Computers, located at 417 Cherry Street.

Avoid creating a stuffy tone by using overly formal language, especially when describing everyday concepts.

the trash truck

rather than

the refuse management vehicle

2. Conveying tone through SENTENCE LENGTH and structure.

(a) For a clipped, no-nonsense tone, use shorter sentences.

My client, Ms. Ambrose, does not intend to pay this bill. She has no reason to pay this bill. She did not receive any software from your company. She did not order any software from your company. Until receiving your bill, she did not know your company existed.

(b) For a more conversational tone, use longer sentences with the subject and verb near the beginning of the sentence.

You asked me to research the possibility of recovering part or all of your down payment on a stereo you later decided not to purchase.

rather than

In our phone conversation, you stated that, after some consideration, you wanted to recover . . . .

or

You asked me to research a question for you. Specifically, you want to know if you can recover part or all of a down payment. The down payment was made for . . . .

(c) For a more formal tone, use some interrupting phrases in your sentence structure.

Anorexics, *by failing to eat,* passively expose themselves to harm.

This sentence structure is harder to read because to understand the main point the reader must remember the first part of the sentence, read the interrupting clause, and then reunite the last part of the sentence with the first in his or her memory. Therefore avoid using it in sentence after sentence; give the reader breathing space between these difficult sentences. Finally, never allow the interruption to exceed seven words. After that long an interruption, the reader would have to reread the sentence to understand the point.

For information on problems associated with long interruptions, see AGREEMENT, SUBJECTS AND VERBS. For related general information, see SENTENCE STRUCTURE. For related information, see TONE IN LETTERS; TOUGH, SOUNDING THAT WAY; BAD NEWS, SOFTENING IT; OBJECTIVE WRITING; PERSUASIVE WRITING; ARGUMENTATIVE WRITING; EMOTIONAL LANGUAGE; and STYLE.

TONE IN LETTERS

Tone is especially important in letters. As the tone of your voice creates an impression in the mind of the listener, so the tone of your letter creates an impression in the mind of the reader. Thus, although your tone in various letters may range from friendly to tough, it should always be within the limits of temperate, businesslike communication. A chatty tone will seem slightly unprofessional in all but purely personal letters. A tirade will also seem unprofessional, even in the toughest collection letter.

Within these limits, however, you must make your own choices, based on what is appropriate to the situation and what suits your personal communicating style.

Using tone effectively in letters involves three tasks: (1) choosing the appropriate tone, (2) creating that tone through word choice and sentence structure, and (3) keeping the tone consistent.

1. Choosing the appropriate tone.

Before you begin writing the letter, consider first what your relationship is to the reader. For example, if your reader is a judge or your supervisor at work, you will probably want to use a tone that is both businesslike and respectful. This means that you will state your points as concisely as possible but will not omit appropriate opening and closing sentences, such as the following closing to a letter requesting a favor.

Thank you for your help in this matter.

If your reader is a client or colleague, you may choose to be polite and businesslike or, if appropriate, you may choose a friendly tone.

Please call if you have any further questions.

or

I am looking forward to our next tennis match.

If your reader is your client's opponent or a client who has not paid you for three months, you may sometimes choose a tough, businesslike tone.

Please pay this bill promptly.

or

I trust this settles the matter.

2.   Creating the appropriate tone through word choice and sentence structure.

Choosing your words carefully is one effective way to establish your tone. For example, if you want to create an informal and friendly tone, use less formal words, such as **talk** and **meeting**. If you want to create a more formal tone, use more formal words, such as **confer** and **discussion**.

Avoid, however, using formal words to the point that your letter becomes hard to read or stuffy.

Regarding this question, I have conferred with Ms. Jamison's attorney, who explained that .   .   .   .

rather than

In pursuit of this query, I have held consultations with counsel for Ms. Jamison, who elucidated the point by stating that .   .   .   .

Another way to avoid a stuffy tone is to avoid inappropriately using the third person, such as **this attorney**, when the first person, **I**, is accurate. In general, letters are addressed from one person to another, and so the use of **I** is appropriate, or **we** if you are speaking officially for a group of people, such as a whole law firm.

You may also establish your tone by using appropriate SENTENCE STRUCTURE. For example, if you want to create a friendly, informal tone, use longer sentences rather than terse ones.

Thank you for your kind invitation to speak at your annual banquet honoring outstanding alumni from the law school.

rather than

Thank you for the invitation to speak at the law school alumni banquet.

·Conversely, if you want to create a tough, no-nonsense tone, use short, rather choppy sentences.

My client, Ms. Ambrose, does not intend to pay this bill. She has no reason to pay you. She did not receive any software from your company. She did not order any software from your company. Until receiving your bill, she did not know your company existed.

rather than

My client, Ms. Ambrose, does not intend to pay this bill because she has no reason to do so. She did not receive or order any software from your company, and in fact did not know your company existed until receiving your bill.

3. Keeping the tone consistent.

Inconsistent tone occurs most often when a letter includes words that are noticeably more formal or informal than the rest of a letter. For example, a writer may use a formal phrase, such as **please be advised that**, in an otherwise informal letter. Or a writer may use a colloquialism, such as **ripped off**, in an otherwise businesslike letter.

Uneven tone also sometimes occurs when sentence structure changes markedly. For example, a reader might be taken aback by a series of three SHORT SENTENCES near the end of an otherwise friendly letter. Similarly, a reader might be put off by a long, complex sentence in an otherwise informal letter. Therefore reread your letters just for consistent tone.

For more help in choosing the appropriate tone, see the following more specific entries: GENERAL CORRESPONDENCE LETTERS; REQUESTS FOR PAYMENT; or TOUGH, SOUNDING THAT WAY. For more help in keeping the tone consistent, see WORD CHOICE and SENTENCE STRUCTURE.

TOPIC SENTENCES

Topic sentences, or main sentences, deserve particular attention in legal writing because they convey the main points of PARAGRAPHS. Topic sentences are therefore most effective at POSITIONS OF EMPHASIS. For example, use a topic sentence at the beginning of a paragraph to state the conclusion the paragraph supports. Alternatively, use it to create a question in the reader's mind and then explain the answer in the body of the paragraph. Thus the topic sentence sets up an expectation that the body of the paragraph fulfills.

Although the 1969 Act eased the singles penalty, it did so at the expense of married couples.

The questioning legal reader will ask, "Okay, so how exactly did the Act disadvantage married couples?" If this is the point the paragraph explains, the topic sentence has prepared the reader for the paragraph's content. Or use a topic sentence at the end of a paragraph to summarize or conclude; remember, however, that busy legal readers may skip the end or get impatient about any suspense created by waiting for the point.

For related information, see ORGANIZATION, SMALL–SCALE; POSITIONS OF EMPHASIS; PARAGRAPHS; and TRANSITIONS.

TOPICAL ORGANIZATION

Topical organization refers to organizing the facts or the analysis by legal topic. In a memo, topical organization can be used in the STATEMENT OF FACTS, the DISCUSSION SECTION, or both. In a brief, it can be used in the STATEMENT OF THE CASE, the ARGUMENT SECTION or both. For example, when an appellate brief contains both procedural and substantive issues, under topical organization the procedural and substantive facts would be presented separately. The Argument section would then follow the same large-scale organization.

Use topical organization when the chronology of events is not as important as the legal character of the events themselves. For example, when a memo discusses two issues, such as one on **the Family Car Doctrine** and another on the **definition of a minor child under the wrongful death statute**, following the chronology of events would not be as important as organizing the events into two groups: those to which the Family Car Doctrine applies and those to which the wrongful death statute applies. To make this topical organization clear to the reader, try separating the topics by paragraphs or, if each covers several paragraphs, by subheadings.

In contrast, see CHRONOLOGICAL ORGANIZATION. For related information, see MEMOS; BRIEFS; APPELLATE BRIEFS; ORGANIZATION, LARGE–SCALE; and REWRITING.

TOTALLY
See COMPLETELY.

TOUGH, SOUNDING THAT WAY
Try the following techniques to sound tough.

1. Use shorter sentences, perhaps several in a row. This creates a clipped, no-nonsense tone.

My client, Ms. Ambrose, does not intend to pay this bill. She has no reason to pay you. She did not receive any software from your company. She did not order any software from your company. Until receiving your bill, she did not know your company existed.

2. Use objective language. If you use emotional words (**unabashedly, horrendous, outrageous**), you will sound angry, but not tough. Tough people stay in control. Think of Joe Friday saying, "Just the facts, Ma'am, just the facts." Instead, persuade with careful use of POSITIONS OF EMPHASIS and SENTENCE STRUCTURE. See OBJECTIVE WRITING and PERSUASIVE LETTERS.

3. If appropriate, explain the options the reader has and the results of those options. This puts the responsibility clearly in the reader's lap. If the reader is at all inclined to feel guilty, this explanation makes that reader squirm. If the reader has no sense of guilt, the explanation will still make your position clear, so you have lost nothing.

4. Never threaten idly. The people with whom you most likely need to get tough are often those people who have heard many threats in their lives and have learned to ignore them. They may be experienced enough, however, to recognize a genuine threat that is well-presented.

For related information, see LETTERS; GENERAL CORRESPON-
DENCE LETTERS; SETTLEMENT LETTERS; BAD NEWS, GIVING
IT; TONE IN LETTERS; and TONE.

TRANSITIONS

One way to communicate the logical connection between two points
is to use a transition word. Transition words signal the logical connection between the content of one sentence or paragraph and the next.
To make these connections clear, choose an accurate, exact transition
that reveals the nature of the connection.

You may find that you use only one or two transition words most of
the time, perhaps repeating one word three or four times on a page.
This overuse can signal several problems. Sometimes, overuse of one
transition signals ORGANIZATION problems. For example, if you use
however frequently, check to see if you are combining points that could
better be presented in separate paragraphs. Other times, overuse of
one transition may mean that you are using the word out of habit
rather than out of conscious choice. If so, some other word will
probably be more precise. For example, **similarly** may be more precise
for a comparison than **additionally**. To help you choose the most
accurate transition quickly, consult the following list of transitions
grouped by their logical functions.

1. Signalling similarity: **similarly, analogously, as.**

2. Signalling contrast: **not . . . but; but; conversely; however; in contrast;
nevertheless; on the contrary; while; yet.**

3. Introducing conditions: **although, even if, if, only if, provided that, unless,
when, whenever, whereas, while.**

4. Introducing results: **if . . . , then; when . . . , then; accordingly; as
a result; consequently; hence; so; so that; therefore; thus.**

5. Introducing reasons for a result: **because, if, since.**

6. Introducing examples or explanations: **as if, as though, for example,
namely, specifically.**

7. Signalling a list: **first, second, third, etc.; both . . . and; either . . . or;
neither . . . nor; additionally; also; and; furthermore; last; nor; or.**

8. Showing time relationships: **after, afterward, as, as long as, before, before
this, during, earlier, later, meanwhile, now, once, since, simultaneously, then,
until, when, whenever, while.**

9. Showing relationship of place: **where, wherever.**

10. Summarizing: **finally, in conclusion, in summary.**

For other ways to make transitions, see CONNECTIONS, MAKING
THEM.

TRIAL BRIEFS

Trial briefs are filed with the court before the trial begins. They inform the trial court of counsel's theory of the case by presenting the applicable rules and the arguments constructed from the rules as they are applied to the facts. A trial brief should indicate what is to be proven, how it is to be proven, and what the outcome of the case should be.

Each side files a trial brief so that the court has an idea of the structure of the trial before it begins. Except under extraordinary circumstances, both sides exchange trial briefs.

Check your jurisdiction for the specific requirements for format of a trial brief; in particular, consider your AUDIENCE; if possible, check with someone who knows that judge. For the usual FORMAT for a trial brief, see BRIEFS.

For related information, see PERSUASIVE WRITING, POINT HEADINGS, ISSUE STATEMENTS, and STATEMENT OF THE CASE.

UNCLEAR MEANING

See MODIFIERS, DANGLING; PRECISION; AMBIGUITY, WAYS TO AVOID; or READABILITY.

UNDERLINING

Underlining has five specific uses in legal writing. To avoid confusion, underlining should not be used solely to recreate the emphasis a word would be given in speech.

1. Underline to add emphasis to important terms in quotes, such as in a rule or holding. When you underline part of a quote, add **(emphasis added)** after the citation following the quote.

As this court itself has stated, "[T]he court must intervene because the issue of mutuality, not to mention that of duress, requires that the court examine the parol evidence surrounding the signing of the contract." Durant v. Colt, 945 F. Supp. 641 (D.D.C. 1994) (emphasis added).

2. Underline to add emphasis to the key phrase in QUOTATIONS long enough to be indented and single-spaced in the text. Underlining may encourage the legal reader to read the quote by making the single spacing more palatable. Again, when you underline add **(emphasis added)** after the citation on the first line of text following the indented quote, not within the indented quote itself. The phrase **(emphasis added)** within a quote would signal that that phrase was present in the original quote.

The court in this case addressed the issue of mutuality.

> Despite the defendant's emotional plea regarding the central-
> ity of upholding contracts to the free working of a democracy, we
> cannot ignore the plaintiff's complaint. In this case, the court must
> intervene because the issue of mutuality, not to mention that of

duress, <u>requires that the court examine both the contract's wording and the parol evidence</u> surrounding the signing of that contract.

<u>Holmes v. Cardozo</u>, 945 F. Supp. 498 (D.D.C. 1994) (emphasis added).

3. Underline cases in citations in text.

<u>Peabody v. Hart</u>, 958 F.2d 391 (7th Cir. 1989).

4. Underline references to the record, if your jurisdiction so requires.

Defendant failed to use his turn signal. <u>Tr. 17</u>.

5. Underline phrases from other languages if they are not commonly incorporated into English. Often, however, the phrase you use will have been incorporated, such as Latin phrases that are TERMS OF ART.

The court appointed a guardian ad litem.

6. Do not use underlining to replace the emphasis you would give a word when speaking. This use of underlining is acceptable in casual writing, such as in a letter to a friend or an informal memo to a coworker, but it is less effective in briefs or research memos for several reasons. First, the use of underlining can be confusing. Often the legal reader's first reaction to underlining is to assume you are highlighting a quote or indicating one of the other four specific uses of underlining in legal writing. Second, legal readers may think you are resorting to the obvious, which can make you seem less in control of the text. To avoid this problem, use POSITIONS OF EMPHASIS and SENTENCE STRUCTURE techniques instead of underlining. For ways to do this, see EMPHASIS. For related information, see PUNCTUATING QUOTES and CITATIONS.

UNDERSTANDABILITY

See CLARITY and READABILITY.

UNDOUBTEDLY

Avoid the term. The point is probably not undoubted by all legal readers. If it is, you do not need to tell the reader this. If you must use **undoubtedly**, do not spell it **undoubtably**.

UNINTERESTED OR DISINTERESTED?

See DISINTERESTED OR UNINTERESTED?

UNIQUE

Unique means that the item or idea referred to is the only one of its kind, or without an equivalent. **Unique** is not preceded by qualifying adverbs. For example, do not say **the most unique** or **rather unique** or **somewhat unique**. If it is unique, it is **unique**.

UNITY

See COHERENCE.

UNLESS

Use **unless** with care because it is easily misread. **Unless** is actually a negative, like **not** or **no**, but often readers do not realize this. As a result, readers may miss the negative and think the **unless** phrase means the opposite of what the writer intended. To avoid this ambiguity, substitute another word for **unless** when possible.

Come to the hearings only if you are subpoenaed.

rather than

Do not come to the hearings unless you are subpoenaed.

Signatures on absentee ballots must be notarized. The only exception to this is absentee ballots signed by members of the military.

rather than

All signatures on all absentee ballots must be notarized unless the absentee voter is a member of the military.

UNOBTRUSIVE DEFINITIONS

Unobtrusive definitions are short, conveniently placed explanations of technical terms that may not be completely familiar to the reader. These definitions are helpful to include when you are not sure whether or not you should include a definition. The reader who understands the term can skip over the definition easily, because the definition is structurally identifiable as a definition. The reader who needs the definition, however, will read it and thus understand your point. There are three ways to include unobtrusive definitions.

1. Include an appositive, or a few words in a phrase inserted right after the term being defined.

The tortfeasor, the person committing the tort, ...

For related information, see APPOSITIVES.

2. When a longer definition is needed, insert an explanatory sentence right after the sentence using the phrase.

At least 80% of the net tax should be paid during the tax year. Net tax is the tax remaining after all deductions have been included.

Sometimes these definitions are placed in parentheses. But be careful to avoid overusing PARENTHESES because they can become a visual distraction to the reader.

3. If you need to insert many definitions, you can include an alphabetical list of those definitions in a separate section, such as the definition sections in statutes, contracts, or trusts.

Sometimes writers are afraid they will offend sophisticated readers if they define legal terms, and occasionally readers are indeed irritated by excessive definitions. More often, however, readers are frustrated by undefined terms. For example, a judge may be frustrated by **exercise of purchase option** because the judge has to stop a minute and remember exactly what that contract term means. Similarly, a client may be frustrated by **tortfeasor** because the client is not sure exactly what the word means. When in doubt, give your AUDIENCE the definitions for any KEY TERMS or TERMS OF ART that may be unfamiliar. For related information, see READABILITY, LEGALESE, JARGON, and PRECISION.

UNTIL SUCH TIME AS

Substitute **until**; you will gain CONCISENESS with no loss in PRECISION.

UNTO

Just use **to**. **Unto** means **to**; it does not mean **onto**.

UPDATING THE LAW

There are four major ways of updating the law, all indispensible to thorough research.

1. Use *Shepard's Citations*.

This set of books provides specific updating service for all cases, statutes, rules, and constitutional provisions. For specific directions in using *Shepard's*, see SHEPARD'S.

2. Use pocket parts and supplements.

Pocket parts and supplements update volumes in the law, such as case digests, annotated statutes, treatises, legal encyclopedias, and the words and phrases book. Those volumes using pocket parts have them enclosed in a pocket within either the front or back cover. Those using supplements have the supplements stacked separately after the volumes on the library shelf. Whichever your volume uses, make sure to check both the main volume and the pocket part or supplement for the most current developments in that topic.

3. Use looseleaf reporters.

Looseleaf reporters cover specific areas of the law. These are useful for updating the law because they sometimes get cases and information on a specific area of law before that information appears in the reporter system, and sometimes before it appears in the computer. Each looseleaf has its own system for use, so check the how-to-use section in each looseleaf you use.

4. Use a computer system.

Each computer system has its own supplementary method of updating the law in addition to *Shepard's*, so use both *Shepard's* and the computer. For help here, see COMPUTERS.

For related information, see RESEARCH STRATEGY CHART.

UTTERLY

Omit this word; in legal writing, it almost always strikes the reader as an overstatement that weakens the statement rather than strengthening it. To emphasize a point, try using a short, direct statement rather than adding **utterly**.

The plaintiff's statement is false.

rather than

The statement made by the plaintiff is utterly false.

For related information, see EMPHASIS, ACCURACY, and LITERAL MEANING.

VAGUE WORDS

See AMBIGUITY, WAYS TO AVOID; PRECISION; and WORD CHOICE.

VARIETY

The word **variety** is sometimes used as a noun meaning a **collection of various things**. As such, it is too general to be useful in legal writing. If there is a variety, that variety will usually have to be explained.

In legal writing, avoid varying NOUNS or VERBS solely for the sake of variety. Legal readers look for consistency, particularly in TERMS OF ART and KEY TERMS. For more on this, see REPETITION.

Do vary SENTENCE LENGTH and SENTENCE STRUCTURE, but let this variety arise naturally from the logical relations of your content. For ways to achieve this, see SENTENCE STRUCTURE and EMPHASIS. Also vary your choice of transition words by using those that reflect the precise relationship of ideas. For help with this, see TRANSITIONS. For related information, see CONNECTIONS, MAKING THEM.

VERB TENSES

Verb tenses must be used accurately to clarify the chronological relationship between events, but they can also be used to add shades of meaning. The following list shows you the various tenses available in English and suggests ways to use them to your advantage in legal writing. For more detail about the grammar of verbs, consult a grammar handbook, such as J. Hodges & M. Whitten, *Harbrace College Handbook* (Harcourt Brace Jovanovich 9th ed. 1982). For related information, see VERBS, AUXILIARY.

1. Present Tense.

Use the present tense for a current or habitual action.

I *handle* all the estate planning in the firm.

Its main use in legal writing is for referring to statutes or other rules still in effect.

False imprisonment *occurs* when . . . .

This statute *requires* all nonresidents to . . . .

Do not use the present tense in situations where you do not want to imply that this is a habitual action. Instead, use the present progressive tense.

Our client *is complaining* that the Jones Corporation . . . .

rather than

Our client *complains* that the Jones Corporation . . . .

2. Present Progressive.

Use the present progressive tense for actions currently in progress.

The client *is suing* the Jones Corporation.

This tense is formed by **am, are,** or **is** and the **-ing** participle.

Also use the present progressive tense for actions going on during or in the context of some present action.

Even as we *are debating* the issue here, the courts face the same issue in Colson v. Perry.

3. Present Perfect.

Use the present perfect tense for actions now completed but related to a current action.

After the testator *has executed* the will, the will becomes valid.

The present perfect tense is formed by **have** or **has** plus the past participle. When used in context with another action, that action is usually stated in the present tense, as in the previous example.

The present perfect tense is useful for showing that a current action is logically subsequent to a previous recent action.

Once the offeree *has relied* to his detriment upon the offer, the contract is enforceable.

4. Past.

Use the past tense for actions completed before the current writing.

The court *decided* to review the case.

The past tense is useful for suggesting an action is finished and cannot be changed.

The Supreme Court *resolved* this issue in . . . .

5. Past Progressive.

Use the past progressive for actions completed before the current writing but going on over a period of time in relation to some other past action.

Mr. Jones *was changing* a flat tire when Mr. Smith's car struck him.

The past progressive tense is formed by **was** or **were** and the present participle, or the **-ing** form of the verb. When used with another action, that action is usually stated in the past tense, as in the previous example.

So bad was Julia's health that, even though he *was battling* cancer at the time, Colonel Hart insisted that Julia never be left alone.

6. Past Perfect.

Use the past perfect tense for actions completed before some other past action took place.

Because Anderson *had accepted* the original offer, the contract was legally valid.

The past perfect is formed by **have, had,** or **has** and the past participle. When used in context of another action, that action is usually stated in the past tense, as in the previous example.

The past perfect is useful for expressing a previous past action that logically led to a subsequent past action.

Since the tenant *had given* the landlord permission to enter the apartment to repair the faucet in the kitchen, the landlord assumed he could also repair the broken latch on the bedroom closet door.

7. Future.

Use the future tense for actions not yet done.

We *will send* you a draft of your new will so that you can review it before our next conference.

The future tense is formed by **will** and the same form of the verb that would go after **to** in the infinitive verb, such as **send, finish,** or **be.**

The future tense suggests that the action will in fact happen, even though it has not yet happened. It is useful for suggesting a result is certain.

Judge Roland Hausler *will win* the election.

8. Future Progressive.

Use the future progressive tense for actions that will be going on over a period of time in the future.

This action *will be pending* for many years before the court reaches a decision.

The future progressive is formed by **will be** plus the present participle, or **-ing** form of the verb. When used in the context of another action, that action is usually stated in the present tense, as in the previous example.

9. Future Perfect.

Use the future perfect tense for actions that are not yet completed but will have been completed before some other action.

The company *will have bound* itself legally to the contract when it accepts the offer.

The future perfect tense is formed by **will have** and the **-ed** form of the verb. When used in the context of another action, that other action is usually stated in the present tense, as in the previous example.

This tense is useful for showing the logical consequence of future possible actions.

If the court accepts the plaintiff's reasoning, then it *will have opened* the door to unharmed plaintiffs seeking to recover damages.

10. Emphatic.

You may use the emphatic tense to underscore a positive or negative response.

He *does plan* to pursue the matter.

She *does* not *consider* this offer acceptable.

The emphatic tense is formed by adding **do** to the verb.

11. Past Future.

Use the past future tense for actions that may happen, depending on some other future action. The past future tense is formed by adding **would** to the verb.

He *would settle* if the conditions were right.

12. Past Future Perfect.

Use the past future perfect for actions that would have happened, but did not because of some other past action. The past future perfect is formed by adding **would have** to the verb.

He *would have settled* if his attorney had advised him fully of the difficulties of the case.

13. Infinitive Verbs.

Although the infinitive is not technically a tense, it can be used to clarify sequence and meaning, like a tense. The infinitive form is not tied to any person or time. It consists of **to** plus the verb.

To appeal may be too expensive.

It is useful when you want to suggest that the point you are making is always true, rather than focusing particularly on the present instance.

To say that one idea cannot be expressed in print is *to say* that all ideas are subject to potential censorship.

VERBAL OR ORAL?

See ORAL OR VERBAL?

VERBOSITY

See CONCISENESS.

VERBS

Verbs, which are words expressing an action or a state of being, focus the legal reader more than any other part of speech. Legal readers want to know what was done, what can be done, what will be done. The following five guidelines can help you use verbs effectively.

1. Use active voice.

Active voice describes an action done by the subject.

The court decided that freedom of association was not an issue.

rather than

It was decided that freedom of association was not an issue.

Active voice is easier to read and more concise. It also adds PRECISION because it makes clear who did what. Therefore, use active voice unless the writing requires passive voice for effect. For more help here, see ACTIVE VOICE, PASSIVE VOICE, and CONCISENESS.

2. Use specific verbs.

Verbs move legal writing when they are specific, halt it when they are vague. Try to state important action in the verb, rather than wasting this part of the sentence on information less important to the reader.

The show-up I.D. *negated* the effect of capturing the defendant one block from the crime.

rather than

The court *stated* that the show-up I.D. negated the effect of capturing the defendant one block from the crime.

In this example, the legal point is more important than the fact that the court stated it. Use a cite to give that information.

Avoid abstract combinations like it is, there is, or there were. Use nouns instead of those pronouns, specific verbs instead of those verbs of being.

False imprisonment *occurs* when a person is restrained without his or her consent.

rather than

There *is* false imprisonment when a person is restrained without his or her consent.

For related information, see CONCISENESS and THERE IS . . . THAT.

3. Use the auxiliary verb that best expresses your shade of meaning.

Careful use of auxiliary verbs can clarify the exact meaning of your verb. For example, if you wanted to communicate that the defendant had the capacity to do something but did not, use **could**.

The defendant could have set the emergency brake.

Conversely, if you want to communicate that the defendant had good reason for not setting the brake, use **would have**.

The defendant would have set the emergency brake had he not been rushing to assist the people in the other car.

For specific information about this use of verbs, see VERBS, AUXILIARY.

4. Split infinitives only if it is necessary for ACCURACY. For a definition of infinitives, see VERB TENSES.

The standard wisdom here has been to avoid splitting infinitives at all times.

to move afterwards

rather than

to afterwards move

Because many of your readers will be of that school, you should avoid splitting infinitives when possible.

On rare occasions, however, a split infinitive will avoid ambiguities.

The mayor agreed to only suggest the alternative if the matter came up in committee meeting.

In this case, putting **only** before **to** would communicate that this was the only thing to which the mayor agreed.

The mayor agreed only . . . .

Putting **only** after **suggest** would communicate that this is the only alternative the mayor would suggest.

The mayor agreed to suggest only this alternative . . . .

When forced to make a choice like this, choose the clarity of the split infinitive over the elegance of the ambiguous unsplit version. You may find, however, that you can avoid the problem by restructuring the sentence altogether.

The mayor agreed that she would only suggest the alternative if the matter came up in the committee meeting. She would refrain from requesting it.

This is the safest route; your revised version will offend no one and still avoid ambiguity. For related information see PRECISION; ONLY, WHERE TO PLACE; and MODIFIERS.

5. Make sure subjects and verbs agree.

Sometimes when the subject and verb are far apart in a sentence, the writer accidentally uses a plural verb with a singular subject, or a singular verb with a plural subject. One good way to avoid having this happen is to avoid putting more than seven words between your subject and verb. This will not only help you avoid agreement problems, but will also make your writing more readable.

Each of the therapists interviewed had become less willing to treat these patients after finding their practice restricted by these recent holdings.

rather than

In the interviews, *each* of the many therapists currently finding their practice restricted by these recent holdings *were* less willing to treat these patients.

For related information, see READABILITY.

For more detailed information about specific kinds of verbs, see SPLIT INFINITIVES; VERBS, LINKING; VERBS, PARTICIPLES; VERBS, IRREGULAR; VERBS, AUXILIARY; VERBS, MOODS; VERBS, PARTICIPLES; and VERB TENSES.

VERBS, AUXILIARY

Auxiliary verbs, or **helping verbs**, are added to the basic verb to change VERB TENSES and to add specific shades of meaning. Choosing the correct auxiliary verbs, therefore, can help you be more precise and persuasive. The following list explains how to use specific auxiliary verbs.

1. **Should.**

Should implies that some action was preferable, but was not in fact taken. For example, it can be useful for suggesting a breach of duty.

The defendant should have set the emergency brake.

2. **Could.**

Could implies the capacity to do something, but suggests that the action will not or has not been done.

The defendant could have set the emergency brake.

3. **Would.**

Would implies that an action would have been taken had conditions been different.

The defendant would have set the emergency brake had he not been rushing to assist the people in the other car.

4. **Can.**

Can implies capacity to do something, although the action has not yet been taken.

When weighing the evidence, the jury can take into account the witness's apparent intelligence and the clarity of the witness's memory of the event.

5. **Might.**

Might implies possibility.

The district attorney might prosecute.

Often **might suggests if facts were otherwise.**

6. **May.**

May implies permission to do something.

If the Seller fails to comply with the nondiscrimination clauses of this contract, the Seller may be declared ineligible for further government contracts . . .

May also implies the possibility of something happening.

The grand jury may subpoena you.

Because it has two possible meanings, watch for potential ambiguities when using **may** in drafting. Sometimes, but not always, the meaning of **may** will be clear in context. When ambiguity is possible, use **might** for possibility and add some phrase like **if he or she chooses** for permission.

7. **Must.**

Must implies a requirement to do something or to refrain from doing something.

The Seller must not in any manner advertise the fact that the Seller has contracted to furnish goods to the Buyer without first obtaining the Buyer's written consent.

8. **Shall.**

Shall can imply a requirement, and is used to mean this in LEGISLATION.

All Petitioners shall file . . . .

But in general writing **shall** also implies the future tense.

The Williams opera shall premiere in December, if all goes as planned.

Therefore **shall** can be ambiguous to nonlegal readers. Whenever ambiguity is possible, use **must** for requirements and **will** for future tenses. For related information, see SHALL.

9. **Do.**

Do adds emphasis. It often indicates a positive answer when a negative one is expected.

On the contrary, I do plan to attend the hearings.

10. **Do not.**

Do not denies an action.

My client does not know of any such plans.

11. **Am, are, is, was, were, had, have,** and **been.**

These auxiliaries combine with the main verb to form other tenses.

I *am meeting* with the client today.

We *are considering* the matter.

The defendant *is planning* to testify.

We *were considering* the matter, but decided it was not worth further pursuit.

The defendant *was planning* to testify before this evidence came to light.

Ms. Wiley *had considered* settling out of court.

Both attorneys *have filed* pretrial motions.

They *have been planning* this banquet for months.

For more details, see VERB TENSES.

VERBS, IRREGULAR

Irregular verbs are verbs that do not form their past participles in quite the same way that regular verbs do.

Present

Regular verb: I finish, you finish, it finishes.

Past

Regular verb: I finished, you finished, it finished.

Present

Irregular verb: I am, you are, it is.

Past

Irregular verb: I was, you were, it was.

Common irregular verbs are **to be, to go,** and **to have.** For more information, see VERBS, PARTICIPLES and VERB TENSES.

VERBS, LINKING

Linking verbs, such as **to be** or **to seem,** link a subject and a predicate but show no action. They are roughly equivalent to equal signs. Avoid overusing linking verbs, because they are not as emphatic, interesting, or precise as active verbs.

The court *reasoned* that . . . .

rather than

The court's reasoning *was* that . . . .

VERBS, MOODS

Mood refers to changes made in the form of the verb to indicate whether or not the action described by the verb happened in fact. These changes in the form of the verb are called inflections, and create three moods. These moods are important conveyors of meaning in legal writing.

1. Indicative.

The indicative mood refers to actions that have in fact happened, are happening, or will in fact happen. This mood is used most often in legal writing, and can be used with any tense.

The defendant *filed* a motion for failure to state a claim.

The buyer *is agreeing* to assume this responsibility.

The legislature *will consider* the matter in the next session.

236

2. Subjunctive.

The subjunctive mood refers to actions that will not necessarily happen, but are being discussed hypothetically.

If I *were* you, I would file a claim.

The subjunctive mood can be used with any verb tense, as the following list illustrates.

(a) Past Subjunctive.

If the legislature *intended* for the law to exempt owner-operated bars, it should have stated so in the law itself.

(b) Past Progressive Subjunctive.

If the legislature *had been planning* to exempt owner-operated bars, documentation of that plan would surely have appeared somewhere in the legislative history of the law.

(c) Past Perfect Subjunctive.

If the legislature *had intended* for the law to exempt owner-operated bars, it surely would have stated so in the law itself.

(d) Future Subjunctive.

If the legislature *were to exempt* owner-operated bars, it would create a suspect classification.

(e) Future Progressive Subjunctive.

If the legislature *were planning* to exempt owner-operated bars, local bar owners' associations would surely be made aware of that plan.

(f) Future Perfect Subjunctive.

If the legislature *were to have exempted* owner-operated bars, they certainly were not aware of that intention when they drafted the law.

For related information, see VERB TENSES.

3. Imperative.

The imperative mood states commands. It is used only with the present tense.

Return the bottom portion.

Please *sign* and date the attached lease agreement.

It is particularly useful when explaining how to do something.

VERBS, PARTICIPLES

Participles are the forms of verbs that combine with auxiliary verbs to form different VERB TENSES. This entry provides an overview of participles. For more detail, consult a grammar handbook, such as W. Ebbitt's & D. Ebbitt's *Writer's Guide and Index to English* (Scott, Foresman 7th ed. 1982).

The present participle ends in -ing, such as **deciding, continuing, being, losing,** and **going.** It is used to form progressive tenses.

The trial is *continuing* to draw much attention from the media.

The children were *playing* near the pool when the accident happened.

The Court will be *deciding* this issue next month.

The past participle of regular verbs ends in **-ed**, such as **decided** and **continued**. The past participles of irregular verbs such as **been, lost**, and **gone**, do not end in **-ed**. Past participles are used to form past and perfect tenses.

The attorneys had already *decided* how to proceed when the settlement offer came.

The defendant has *lost* on appeal, but is going to pursue other possible actions.

Participles are also used to introduce phrases.

Discouraged by this lack of response, Allen decided to leave the organization.

The defendant tried to put out the flames with a blanket but was forced back, *coughing* and *gasping* for air.

VERY

Avoid overusing **very**. Often it adds little meaning, and often it detracts from the word it modifies, rather than emphasizing it.

This issue is crucial.

rather than

This issue is very important.

For related information, see MODIFIERS, EMPHASIS, and CONCISE-NESS.

VIRGULE

See SLASH.

VIRTUALLY

Virtually means **essential to all purposes** or **in effect**.

It contrasts with LITERALLY.

The exceptions have virtually swallowed the rule.

VIZ.

Viz., or **videlicet**, is unnecessary because there are clear English equivalents. Use **namely, that is**, or **that is to say** instead.

For related information, see LEGALESE and JARGON.

VOICE, ACTIVE OR PASSIVE?

Voice is a verb form that indicates the relation between the subject and the action expressed by the verb. In ACTIVE VOICE the subject does the action; in PASSIVE VOICE the subject receives the action.

The boy hit the ball. [Active voice]

The ball was hit. [Passive voice]

The defendant assaulted the victim. [Active voice]

The victim was assaulted. [Passive voice]

The court held the identification evidence admissible. [Active voice]

The identification evidence was held admissible. [Passive voice]

Using active voice instead of passive voice usually eliminates extra words. Using active voice also eliminates the ambiguity that might be caused by abstract verbs, such as **consists of** or **concerns** or **involves**.

Passive voice is useful, however, in four specific situations. In legal writing, use it consciously and for these reasons only; otherwise eliminate it.

1. Passive voice is useful for de-emphasizing unfavorable facts or law. For example, the attorney for the defense might want to write the following.

The plaintiff was assaulted by the defendant.

The attorney for the prosecution, however, might write the following.

The defendant assaulted the plaintiff.

2. Passive voice is useful for hiding the identity of the actor.

A decision was made to cut your salary.

Here, passive voice avoids telling who made the decision.

It can be argued that the defendant assumed the risk.

3. Passive voice is also useful when the subject is very long. In this situation, using passive voice creates a more readable sentence because the active voice would put the subject and verb so far apart that the sentence would be too hard to read.

This action is required by statutory law, by the common law principle of due care, and by a general sense of justice.

rather than

Statutory law, the common law principle of due care, and a general sense of justice require this action.

4. Finally, passive voice is useful when the subject is much less important than the object.

Freedom of speech cannot be encumbered by concerns of propriety.

rather than

Concerns of propriety cannot encumber freedom of speech.

WE

Use **we** as a plural subject. Be careful to use it precisely, so that you include only those people who should be included in **we**.

We [the members of the firm] **suggest you try to settle the case.**

rather than

We [I, but I don't want to admit it] think the merits of the case are too weak.

or

We [who?] now move on to the next issue.

For more on problems with we, see AMBIGUITY, WAYS TO AVOID, subsection 2.

We can also be used in constructions where a verb is implied. For example, as well as we implies as well as we are, and such as we implies such as we are.

I am sorry to inform you that the defendant's firm is unwilling to discuss a settlement with lawyers such as we.

WELL OR GOOD?
See GOOD OR WELL?

WHEN
Use when to refer to a relationship of time; use if to refer to a logical relationship. See also WHEN OR WHERE?

WHEN AM I DONE?
See WHEN TO STOP.

WHEN OR WHERE?
When indicates a point in time; where indicates a physical place. In Questions Presented and ISSUE STATEMENTS, use when because it is more precise, describing events in time. Use if, however, when referring to a logical relationship rather than a relationship of the occurrence of events in time.

WHEN TO STOP
The purpose of this section is to help you overcome any tendencies you may have to fiddle with a document forever, miss your deadlines, frustrate your coworkers and typists, or drive yourself crazy with uncertainty about your writing. Ideally, each document you produce would be perfect. Realistically, that is not possible. It is seldom possible to get even one document perfect, let alone all that you write. You therefore have to make some decisions about which documents are worth pushing closer to perfection and which must be turned in sooner.

The following guidelines can help you make these difficult decisions at each stage of the WRITING PROCESS. But also use your COMMON SENSE and revise the list as needed to suit your circumstances. For related information, see WRITING BLOCK.

1. When to stop researching.

Stop when you keep finding the same sources. Save time by following the RESEARCH STRATEGY CHART and by completing all updating. Do not waste time looking for the fictitious smoking gun, or the case exactly like yours; concentrate instead on the sources that turn up repeatedly.

2. When to stop PREWRITING.

If you tend to linger at this stage so long that you have inadequate time for the later stages of the WRITING PROCESS, stop when you have completed enough of an outline to give shape to your general ideas and when you have listed specific points under each general idea. In general, however, allow plenty of time for this stage; it will prevent time-consuming errors at later stages.

3. When to stop WRITING.

The critical factor here is to stop REWRITING during this first draft. Let your ideas flow, unedited. If you sense holes in your reasoning, let them pass for now; fill them in later in the rewriting stage. If you sense awkward phrases, let them pass also; you can revise them later.

4. When to stop REWRITING.

Stop when you have the large-scale ideas in place, the PARAGRAPHS in a logical order, the TOPIC SENTENCES in place, and all needed content and explanation in the text. Make sure the organization is clear enough to be followed by any legal reader. Also make sure any unneeded information is omitted. Then move on to revising.

5. When to stop REVISING.

The key here is to do first things first. Ask yourself the following critical questions before you move on to those concerns that are desirable but not critical.

(a) Does each topic sentence state the point clearly and unambiguously? For help here, see TOPIC SENTENCES.

(b) Is every supporting sentence accurate and logically connected to the paragraph in which it is included? For help here, see ACCURACY and ORGANIZATION, SMALL–SCALE.

(c) Is all unneeded information omitted?

(d) Is the POINT OF VIEW consistent and appropriate?

Then, as you have time, revise the text further, asking yourself each of the following questions.

(e) Are the sentences readable? For help here, see READABILITY.

(f) Are POSITIONS OF EMPHASIS used effectively?

(g) Are EMPHASIS techniques used effectively?

(h) Is TONE consistent and appropriate?

6. When to stop POLISHING.

When polishing, first ask yourself the following questions.

(a) Are all CITATIONS complete and written in accurate form?

(b) Does the document meet all FORMAT requirements?

(c) Are all quotes letter perfect? See PUNCTUATING QUOTES.

(d) Are all numbers correct, including such details as numbers in citations and dollar amounts?

(e) Are all names spelled properly?

Then proofread the text for typographical, grammatical, and punctuation errors. Make sure to incorporate your own frequent errors.

When this is done, if you have time left, you may go back and check any other concerns that you wish. If you have no time left, at least you can take comfort in the fact that you have avoided major writing errors.

WHERE OR WHEN?
See WHEN OR WHERE?

WHETHER
Whether is a subordinating conjunction that introduces a dependent clause.

Whether the court will address this question is unknown.

Therefore a **whether** clause by itself cannot be a complete sentence.

whether the court will address this issue

In legal writing, however, **whether** is often used to introduce questions presented and ISSUE STATEMENTS.

To avoid writing your issue or QUESTION PRESENTED as an incomplete sentence, you may simply reformulate it as a question, leaving out **whether**.

Did the trial court err in awarding custody of both children to the mother when . . . ?

rather than

Whether the trial court erred in awarding custody of both children to the mother when . . . .

If you use the **whether** form of a Question Presented or Issue Statement, end it with a period, not a question mark.

WHICH OR THAT?
See THAT OR WHICH?

WHO OR WHOM?
Use **who** as a subject, **whom** as an object. Thus, use **whom** whenever it is the object of a preposition.

For related information, see READABILITY and EMPHASIS.

6. Use the most specific term possible. For example, do not say **vehicle** when you mean **school bus**. Use more general terms only when you need to be ambiguous for some reason, or the context requires them.

For related information, see REPETITION and AMBIGUITY, WAYS TO AVOID. For a discussion of situations where you may need to be vague or ambiguous, see EMPHASIS, subsection 2.

7. Make sure all PRONOUNS are unambiguous. For example, if two or more women are mentioned in a text, then **she** is likely to be ambiguous. Therefore, check each pronoun.

Ms. Jones did not ask Ms. Wilson to double-check the amount because Ms. Wilson routinely checked all the amounts listed.

rather than

Ms. Jones did not ask Ms. Wilson to double-check the amount because she routinely checked all the amounts listed.

Also make sure each **this** is unambiguous. **This** is the pronoun most likely to cause inaccuracies. **This** can refer to an idea or a thing, one word or a whole sentence; as a result, you must make sure that the reader always knows what **this** means. If there is any question, add the appropriate noun after **this**.

The court reasoned that the difference in the age of the fetuses was not the factor determining this issue. This reasoning . . . .

For more examples, see THIS and AMBIGUITY, WAYS TO AVOID.

WORDINESS
See CONCISENESS, READABILITY, and MODIFIERS.

WORDY PHRASES
For general information, see CONCISENESS. For a discussion of specific phrases, see AS A MATTER OF FACT; AT THIS POINT IN TIME; AT THE TIME THAT; CLEARLY; FACT THAT, THE; FACT OF THE MATTER, THE; FOR THE PERIOD OF; IN ABSENCE OF ; IN QUESTION; IT IS SAID THAT; IT IS . . . THAT; OBVIOUSLY; OF COURSE; POSSIBILITY THAT; PRIOR TO; REALLY; THERE ARE . . . THAT; TO ALL INTENTS AND PURPOSES; UNDOUBT-EDLY; UNTIL SUCH TIME AS; UTTERLY; and VERY.

WOULD
Would implies that something should have been done but was not in fact done.

The defendant would have set the emergency brake had he not been rushing to assist the people in the other car.

Therefore, do not use **would** if you mean to imply that something will be done or if you do not want to imply that it should have been done. For related information, see VERBS, AUXILIARY.

WRITER'S BLOCK
See WRITING BLOCK.

WRITING
Writing is a creative act, not a critical one. It is translating your ideas into a first draft. When you reach this stage of the WRITING PROCESS, try to write the whole paper without stopping to correct anything: don't get it right, get it written. At this stage, your ideas need to be translated unencumbered by revision concerns. The critical voice will have time to correct and revise later, in the REWRITING and REVISING stages.

One way to do this is to keep your words flowing onto the page. If you get stuck on a point because you are suffering from WRITING BLOCK, either skip that part or break it down into smaller pieces, but try not to stop. If necessary, even write nonsensical phrases to keep you writing. Keep the creative energy moving throughout the entire writing process. When you finish, leave the draft, even if only for a few minutes. Let it breathe before you begin rewriting. Then, after you finish this first draft, remember that rough drafts, although necessary, are not final drafts. Go on to rewriting and revising.

Other ways to keep writing creative, rather than critical, include changing the medium you use to write, writing before you outline rather than after, and writing a middle section first rather than starting at the beginning. For example, you might try dictating rather than typing the first draft. You might write a draft as a means of brainstorming before you outline. Or you might begin by writing about the point most familiar to you.

There is no one right method to use; the right method is the one that helps you get the job done.

WRITING BLOCK
Writers may suffer from writing blocks at any stage of the WRITING PROCESS, but usually the cause is that the writer (1) feels overwhelmed by the task, (2) believes the written product must be perfect, (3) feels he or she is inadequate to the task, or (4) experiences all of the above. Almost all writers suffer from writing blocks occasionally; some endure them on almost every project.

Fortunately, writing blocks can usually be overcome by using any or all of the following techniques.

1. Divide and conquer.

Break the writing task into littler steps, and keep breaking it down until you see a step that does not look overwhelming. Never mind if the list of steps is pages long; each of those steps may go rather quickly. These small tasks may be boring, but they will not be overwhelming. Then order the steps and start doing them. To gain a sense of progress, check each one off as you finish. For example, if the whole project seems overwhelming, start by listing all the tasks involved, such as **research, outline, write, rewrite,** and **revise.** Then break each one of those down. You might break **outlining** into **list all possible points, group those points somehow, summarize each group,** and **decide which group goes first , second , etc.** If this is still overwhelming, you can break **list all possible points** into **list all points that make sense to me, list all points mentioned in any analogous cases,** and **identify all points that occur on both lists.**

2. Start somewhere else.

If you are stuck on a particular writing task, set it aside and work on something else. For example, if you cannot decide how to organize the facts section of a memo, leave it and begin writing the issues. If you cannot write the issue, try writing the conclusion. You need to complete many tasks in any writing project, but you need not complete them in any particular order.

3. Separate the essential from the desirable.

You do not have time as a legal writer to make everything perfect; you must focus on quality and adequacy, but not on perfection. For example, when REVISING, focus on essentials, such as ACCURACY and clear ORGANIZATION, before you tackle desirables, such as EMPHASIS and TONE. For help doing this, see WHEN TO STOP and WRITING PROCESS.

If you are finding it hard to get started, see GETTING STARTED. If you are having trouble finishing, see WHEN TO STOP. For related information, see WRITING PROCESS and PERFECTIONISM.

WRITING PROCESS

The writing process is the entire creative, analytical, and critical experience that begins with an idea or assignment and ends with a finished document. The process incorporates five stages: PREWRITING, WRITING, REWRITING, REVISING, and POLISHING. You can save a great deal of time and become much more effective throughout the process by understanding each of these stages. The key to success in streamlining your writing process is breaking it into pieces and fixing one piece at a time. Over a period of time, your techniques will work themselves into a smooth process that is strictly yours. The following suggestions can help you make your writing process both more efficient and more effective.

1. Identify at which point in the process you are most comfortable. You might like research but hate revising, or you might feel comfortable correcting mechanics and citations but very uncomfortable in writ-

ing. You are probably fastest at that point where you feel most comfortable, so you can allocate the least amount of time for that step when you establish your schedule.

2. Identify where you are least comfortable. For example, you may dislike revising because you are not sure of grammatical structures and how to fix them, so you get bogged down in miscellaneous questions. Or you may dislike writing because you feel each sentence has to be perfect before you go on to the next one. Separate the creative from the critical and decide if you are trying to do too many things at once. Then allocate the greater amount of time for those least comfortable.

3. Start with your deadline and work backwards toward the starting point, setting interim deadlines for each stage of the process. By allocating the most time for the place that is the least comfortable and the least time for the place that is the most comfortable, you can set a more realistic schedule that you will be more likely to meet.

4. Break each writing task into subtasks and give your full attention to each subtask. For example, if you dislike revising, try not to revise all of every sentence all at once. Instead, revise the whole text once just for SENTENCE STRUCTURE. Then revise it again just for TRANSITIONS. Revise a third time for accurate WORD CHOICE. These small read-throughs can be done in between other tasks during the day. Additionally, by giving them your full concentration, you can complete them effectively in a minimal amount of time.

5. Concentrate on breaking bad habits by conquering one bad habit in each major writing assignment that you have. For example, if you are weak on TRANSITIONS, concentrate primarily on transitions in the revision process on one paper. Keep working on transitions on subsequent assignments until you feel comfortable with them; then move on to another bad habit. For example, you might concentrate next on better SENTENCE STRUCTURE.

The following example shows one way you might organize your writing process and interim deadlines for an appellate brief.

Notice of appeal filed	April 16
Read Record For Error	April 18
Preliminary Issues	April 22
Research Strategy for Each	April 22
Research	April 22–May 2
Select Arguments	May 5
Complete research	
OUTLINING	May 6
Draft POINT HEADINGS	
Fill in holes by more research	
WRITING (Dictating) First Draft	May 8–9
Issue I to sec'y	May 12

YET

Yet, a conjunction, can be used in legal writing to indicate **nevertheless** or **despite this**. Like **but**, **yet** can be an effective transition to show contrast and opposing ideas.

Plaintiff still claims my client is guilty, yet he has failed to meet his burden to prove that guilt.

Most commentators rely on this reasoning. Yet none has provided adequate authority on which to base that reasoning.

For related information, see CONJUNCTIONS; TRANSITIONS; and CONNECTIONS, MAKING THEM.

YOU

Use the second person, **you**, to address the audience directly, when appropriate. For example, you may use **you** in GENERAL CORRESPONDENCE LETTERS where you want to sound like you are talking to a person face to face.

You asked that I write to you about the legal consequences of your automobile accident.

You may also use **you** in consumer contracts or other situations when you need to tell someone clearly what he or she can or cannot do.

If you choose to change attorneys, you must notify . . . .

Do not, however, use **you** in BRIEFS to the court or in other situations when you are not addressing a person directly. In those situations you are focusing on the argument itself, rather than on a one-to-one conversation.

Equity requires consideration of this issue.

rather than

You must consider this issue.

†

To whom did you present the question about the gun?

Use **whom** as the object of a verb.

Whom did you see on the night of the incident?

Or use **whom** as the subject of a complementary infinitive.

Defendant is the person whom the plaintiff saw on the night of the crime.

Use **who** as a subject of a sentence.

Who took my shoes?

Also use **who** as the subject of a clause.

You are the person who called me yesterday.

WILLS, DRAFTING

The principles for writing wills are much the same as those for writing CONTRACTS. You might also want to use forms to help you get started. For help here, see FORMS, USE OF. In addition to the principles listed under CONTRACTS, DRAFTING, keep these general principles in mind when drafting wills.

1. Check your jurisdiction for the legal requirements for wills.

Generally, wills include at least the following parts: (a) an introductory clause naming the testator, (b) appointments of executors, (c) general and specific bequests, (d) what to do with anything left over (the residuary clause), (e) a place for the testator's signature (the testimonium), and (f) a place for witnesses to sign, saying that the will was properly executed. Some wills also include trust arrangements, instructions to pay burial expenses, and other special clauses. But check your jurisdiction, rather than relying on this list.

2. Make sure that the will accomplishes your client's wishes.

To accomplish these wishes, anticipate general problems, such as potential challenges to the will, and specific ones, such as potential ambiguities of a particular clause. Consider also the abilities of the executor and make sure that the will is written so that he or she can understand it well enough to use it. Avoid JARGON and LEGALESE, and never include even a word that you do not understand, because it may cause legal consequences you did not anticipate. After writing, revise the will for CLARITY and READABILITY.

3. Use FLOWERY LANGUAGE only if your client prefers this because of the seriousness of the situation. Never substitute flowery language for PRECISION.

4. Revise painstakingly for grammatical accuracy and correct PUNCTUATION. Mistakes in these areas can translate into thousands of dollars, as the following phrases show.

my daughter's share of the estate

or

my daughters' share of the estate

divided equally among my nephew, my son, my daughter and my son-in-law

or

divided equally among my nephew, my son, my daughter, and my son-in-law

WOMAN, LADY, OR FEMALE?

Use woman.

WORD CHOICE

Choose words carefully because every word counts in legal writing. The following list provides an overview of the major concerns involved in effective word choice.

1. Use concrete nouns and specific verbs rather than ABSTRACT NOUNS and general verbs. This will help focus the reader on your main points.

The defendant moves to dismiss the case under Fed. R. Civ. P. 12(b)(6).

rather than

This concerns the defendant's motion to dismiss.

For related information, see PERSUASIVE WRITING and EMPHASIS.

2. Use TERMS OF ART or KEY TERMS, but avoid unneeded verbiage, such as LEGALESE.

For related information, see PRECISION and READABILITY.

3. Avoid unneeded MODIFIERS; use only modifiers that give the reader essential information.

An *alcoholic* father cannot serve the *best* interests of *his* children.

rather than

A *habitually* alcoholic father *clearly* cannot serve the best interests of his *unfortunate* children.

For related information, see CONCISENESS and EMPHASIS.

4. Use accurate TRANSITIONS to convey the precise LOGICAL LINKS between ideas.

The litigation may cost more than the amount our client could recover if she wins the suit. *Nevertheless,* she has chosen to pursue her claim.

rather than

The litigation may cost more than the amount our client could recover if she wins the suit, *and* she has chosen to pursue her claim.

5. Use consistent wording. Use the same term for the same concept throughout the document; do not change it just for VARIETY.

The defendant *proposes* that his repair of the water heater was adequate. This *proposal*, however, ...

rather than

The defendant *proposes* that his repair of the water heater was adequate. This *suggestion*, however, ...